I Own You

By Dawn McConnell

with Katy Weitz

D0111645

PAN BOOKS

First published 2017 by Pan Books
an imprint of Pan Macmillan
20 New Wharf Road, London N1 9RR
Associated companies throughout the world
www.panmacmillan.com

ISBN 978–1–5098–3088–6

1 3 5 7 9 8 6 4 2

A CIP catalogue record for this book is available from the British Library.

Typeset in Adobe Caslon Pro 11.25/14 pt by
Palimpsest Book Production Limited, Falkirk, Stirlingshire

Printed and bound by CPI Group (UK) Ltd, Croydon, CR0 4YY

Visit www.panmacmillan.com to read more about all our books
and to buy them. You will also find features, author interviews and
news of any author events, and you can sign up for e-newsletters
so that you're always first to hear about our new releases.

I Own You

Nemo me impune lacessit

'Never crossed with impunity'

*Latin motto of the Order of the Thistle and
the Royal Regiment of Scotland known as
'Black Watch', the Scots Guard and
Royal Scots Dragoon Guards*

Contents

PART III – GROWING UP

PART IV – ESCAPE

PART V – THE WARRIOR

Prologue

Sitting on the cold, hard terracotta tiles, I drew my legs to my chest and wrapped my bare arms around my knees. *How on earth had I got myself into this mess?*

Inside the villa – *my* villa, my beautiful Portuguese villa – I watched my husband Stuart as he poured himself another glass of red wine. Through the glass doors on the balcony I examined the back of his head as he sat on our brand new sofa, adjusting the sound on the TV that played an episode of *The Sopranos*. I couldn't quite believe I was out here, on the freezing tiles in the middle of the night, wearing nothing but a thin white vest and tracksuit bottoms. *What was I to do? Bang on the glass doors? Scream for help? Beg him to let me inside?*

No, after nearly twenty years I knew my husband well enough to know that those tactics would only elicit laughter, mockery, or worse. And it wasn't like we had any neighbours who could come to my rescue. Our villa in the hills could only be reached by a small, red dust track and was surrounded by nothing but orange groves and olive trees. Only the goats made it up this far. I knew there was no way out of this except through him. This was just one of those things I had to endure. And so I sat there, in the cold and dark, watching the stars, wondering how I had got trapped this way . . .

Just a few hours before, I had looked the epitome of a high-achieving businesswoman, speeding across Glasgow from my office to the airport to meet my husband in our newly acquired villa on the hillside overlooking the Algarve. There was so much work to do on the house, Stuart had insisted he come over the week before to hire tradesmen, buy materials and get to work dismantling the ugly dark wood panelling fitted by the previous owners. I was working full time which meant I could only fly out for the weekend, but I was keen to see how much Stuart had accomplished in a week. I called from Faro airport when I arrived, fully expecting he pick me up. But Stuart said he couldn't drive as he'd already had a couple of drinks at lunchtime. My heart sank. This did not bode well.

By the time I got to our villa in the late afternoon, my worst suspicions were confirmed. Pushing my way through empty beer and wine bottles, it was clear Stuart had not even started to dismantle the fittings. Instead he lay slumped on the sofa, suffering from the debilitating aftermath of a massive, all-week bender. I couldn't help myself. I let rip.

'What have you been doing? This place is a tip! I've been working all week and you've been drinking yourself silly. Why? Why can't you just do what you say you're going to do? Just look at you! You're a complete state. Urgh!'

I changed out of my work clothes, put on a vest and track-suit bottoms and got to work cleaning and scrubbing our new house. Three hours later, after I had cleaned up the villa and changed the sheets, I took a bundle of fresh laundry outside on the terrace to hang on the washing line. All that time, Stuart had lain prone on the sofa, sipping from his glass of red wine, occasionally throwing me evil stares. *Let him stare!* I reckoned it would only take another couple of glasses before he fell into unconsciousness. Now it was late as I hung up the laundry. There was a chill in the cool March air. Not a cloud in the sky, I could count every star. I watched my own breath hang in the air as I pegged out the washing, shivering against the cold. Then . . .

Slam!

The verandah door closed with a bang, and I watched as Stuart gave a sinister smile from the other side of the glass, turning the handle anti-clockwise until it was fully locked. Then he resumed his position on the sofa and clicked on the TV. *Ignore him*, I told myself. *He's playing games.* This was his idea of payback for my flying insults earlier. He knew I hated the cold, couldn't stand it. But he'll make me stay out here for twenty minutes, I figured, to punish me. Always to punish me. But twenty minutes came and went and Stuart didn't move from the sofa. With nothing to sit on but the cold terracotta tiles I took my place in the corner of the terrace. There was no wind, no sound but the occasional tinkling of a goat-bell. Everything was silent and still. The damp laundry hung above my head like an imaginary shelter but I had no real protection from the cold, which seeped into my pores and turned my skin white. Through the verandah doors I watched Stuart open another two bottles of red wine. I watched three silent episodes of *The Sopranos* through the glass wall, then observed Stuart as he made himself a steak sandwich, broke out the biscuits and cheese, knocked over a wine glass, and

3

finally, rubbing my aching finger joints together, I saw him pour himself a large brandy. I watched it all. A spectator. My home like a television set that only I could see.

Patiently, I waited as the temperatures reached freezing and then I started to pace to keep warm. Occasionally I jumped up and down but on the whole I just sat there, letting the chill dig into my bones, numbing my fingers and toes until I could barely move them at all. *How had it come to this?* To the outside world I was a successful businesswoman, a woman in charge of her own destiny, and yet here I sat, trapped and frozen cold. At thirty-four years old, I knew I'd had enough. I couldn't go on like this. One day, I resolved to escape. By the time the sun came up from behind the hills in the early hours, I felt the dawn was rising on a new me.

It was 10 a.m. before Stuart woke from his slumber, and by then the warm Portuguese sunshine had thawed me out completely. Kicking over the empty wine bottle, he seemed startled when he looked around to see me outside. In a second, he registered what he had done and started to laugh at his own joke, tickled by his own badness. With a *clunk clink* of the handle, the door opened. I didn't look at him as I walked past. I didn't speak a word. Instead, I dressed in the clothes I had arrived in the previous night and called a taxi to the airport.

These times are sent to test us. There was a reason this had happened. I resolved that night never to forget those hours on the balcony. He couldn't keep me locked up forever. One day I would leave and never look back.

PART I
HOME

Chapter 1

Summer Holidays

'Come on, Dawn!' my mother puffed impatiently as she lugged her large brown leather suitcase into the waiting taxi. 'Keep up. We haven't got all day.'

I scooted along as fast as I could but it wasn't always easy to keep up with the swift pace Mum set. In her smart beige heels, she was a woman on a mission and whatever happened she wasn't going to let the legs of a five-year-old dictate the speed of her movements, especially not when we were at the Gare du Nord in Paris, en route to our usual four-week holiday in Italy. My mother, Penelope McConnell, had spent the previous two weeks packing for my brother, sister and myself: our cases laid out on the dark-green dining-room floor, waiting for freshly washed and ironed clothes to be packed away in a neat order as they became available. Each night over the past fortnight, she'd perched on her haunches, coffee cup at her feet, pen and notepad in hand as she ticked off items on the lists she had compiled of what was needed for each child. At night, I'd fallen asleep to the sound of her checking and rechecking the clothing: 'Two pairs of trousers, one skirt, two dresses, six pairs of knickers, two pairs of shorts . . .'

There were three of us children in my family: I was the youngest at five years old, my sister Susy was ten, and then there was our elder brother John. In that summer of 1974 John was fifteen, a big boy and ten years older than me.

Though we lived in a rough part of Glasgow, Mum liked to think that our family was a cut above the usual types who came to The Drayton Arms, the hotel we owned, and certainly her refined Edinburgh accent distinguished her from the crowd. It was a small hotel with ten rooms that had a bar, a restaurant and a function room that catered for the local community. The dining room was for weddings and funerals mostly. We also provided breakfasts for the residents, with dinner included too if they wished. Mum and Dad worked there day and night, scurrying back and forth between the hotel and our large house, which was next door. It was a relentless way to make a living – but effective. I knew there weren't many children in our suburb who went to private school or enjoyed foreign holidays for weeks at a time.

But such hard work meant those holidays were precious – and impeccably planned. Earlier that morning, Mum had shut the last case tight and stuffed the overnight bag with disprin, toothpaste, toothbrushes, colouring books and spare pants. Once she had checked all the tickets were in order, it had been time to leave.

Only four of us McConnells were squeezed into that Parisian taxi with our luggage. Dad hadn't come this time; not after last year when he had spent most of the holiday complaining loudly. Grumpily, he had paced up and down the beach boulevard, picking out various restaurants where he wanted to take lunch. And yet we never went – because we were on full board at our hotel. It was a source of much friction between my parents.

'It's all budgeted and paid for,' Mum had insisted calmly, while Dad deliberately refilled his wine glass over lunch, staring at her moodily. She always disapproved of his drinking but there was nothing much she could do about it. Especially not this year, when Dad was being left in charge of the hotel while we went on our trip without him.

'He'll be happier there,' Mum had said with a tight smile as he'd waved us off at Glasgow train station. 'He's got his spirit optics to keep him company.'

Now, I almost wished that I was the one keeping him company: the August heat of the train station at the Gare du Nord was unbearable. The black leather seats of the taxi were scorching and sticky on my bare legs.

'Le Bristol, *s'il vous plaît*,' said Mum to the young driver in her best French and at last we sped away from the chaos of the station. This was our overnight stop before Italy – a five-star hotel in the heart of Paris. Mum loved the glamour of the 1920s hotel and never tired of telling us that royalty stayed here, as well as celebrities like Mick Jagger and Sophia Loren.

Once inside, Mum seemed instantly to stand straighter amid the plush corridors, trailing an elegant hand along the gleaming brass handrails. She loved this, I could tell. From the way she smiled at all of us, it was clear this was what my mother wanted more than anything else: the attention and fine living of a luxury holiday. For once, everyone looked after *her* and catered to her every whim, instead of the other way round. For once, she was the guest!

Later, Mum took us out for dinner and we wandered

through the narrow streets of Paris, before taking a table at a small cafe down an alleyway. I breathed in the strangeness of it all – people of all ages and races, classes and colours, chattering away in a variety of exotic languages. Mum ordered a glass of Sancerre and we were allowed a Fanta each. She seemed more relaxed here than I'd ever seen her at our hotel and, without my dad, she seemed happy and at ease.

'This is what I crave,' she sighed, finally. 'This! All this! I should have moved to the continent years ago, I should have stayed in Italy when I had the chance. God knows how I ended up in Glasgow, slaving away in that squalid little hotel day and night . . .'

On and on she went; it was a familiar speech. Meanwhile, Susy and I amused each other by pretending to have a sword fight with the breadsticks. When they both snapped and fell on the ground we looked up guiltily at Mum, fully expecting a telling-off.

But she didn't notice. For once she wasn't watching our every move, checking us over for flaws in our appearance or behaviour. No, tonight she seemed to be staring dreamily into the distance – perhaps into another life she wished she were living.

The next day, we embarked on the last leg of our journey to Tuscany, changing trains in Rome before arriving, late in the day, at the swish seaside resort of Forte Dei Marmi, roughly twenty-five miles from Pisa. We were staying in a stunning hotel, with high-ceilinged rooms decked out in opulent colours and rich fabrics, and the manager himself came over to greet us. I loved Signor Adammo and as soon as I caught sight of him, I ran and jumped into his embrace, wrapping my little arms around his neck.

'I've missed you!' I squealed.

Mum laughed anxiously, embarrassed at my public display of affection. She didn't do kissing or hugging – she was far too regal for all that.

'Come now, Dawn, don't annoy Signor Adammo!' she chided.

'Oh no, *Signora*,' he replied, as he rubbed my head indulgently. 'It's okay. No problem.'

Then he bent down and asked me: '*Ciao*, Dawn, *come stai?*'

'*Siamo molto bene!*' I responded in my best Italian. At last we had arrived and the proper holiday could begin!

Those summer days passed so quickly, swimming by as fast as the fishes that darted and ducked around my little feet as I paddled in the clear-blue sea. By the time we'd been there a week, we were well into our familiar routine.

Each morning, after breakfast, the four of us would head to the beach for a couple of hours. I loved to make sandcastles and frolic in the shallow waters while my brother and sister exhausted themselves playing volleyball or bat and ball on the sand. Frequently, they met other children and played with them, but I was quite content just sitting at my mother's feet, digging moats and arranging seashells on my sandy structures, as she sunbathed in her elegant one-piece.

Lunch was always the same. After leaving the beach, we showered and changed before heading into the dining hall at our hotel. The staff always set up the same table for us, a large circular one against the windows, with views across the sea. It was a grand affair and I think my mother loved the sense of occasion, elevated by the pristine white tablecloth, silver cutlery and crystal wine glasses. Susy and I fought each other for the basket of Grissini breadsticks while my brother poured out the San Pellegrino bubbly water. Waiters in their crisp white uniforms and white gloves glided past, carrying steaming plates of pasta, risotto and broths. I loved spaghetti arrabbiata and was never deprived of a cooling gelato for dessert.

The fun didn't stop in the afternoon. After lunch, we were ordered to our room for an hour-long siesta but after that it was back to the beach for an afternoon of playing and swimming. Every evening, following a bath and a good slathering of aftersun, we returned to the restaurant for our evening meal and then, for me, it was straight to bed, my skin still glowing from the day's sun.

Oh, I loved it! I loved all of it. Every morning that I woke up on that holiday I hugged myself with joy that we had yet another perfect day ahead of us. It was wonderful; such a change from the cold, grey world we had left behind.

I wasn't to know that sunshine doesn't last forever.

I wasn't to know that my innocent childhood was about to come to an abrupt end.

Looking back, years later, I did wonder if Mum ever thought his behaviour strange. I mean, why would a fifteen-year-old boy offer to take his five-year-old sister back to the room for a shower? Was that normal?

I can only suppose that after years of defending John to my dad, of standing up for him and putting herself between that hulking great bear of a man and her trembling young son, she had stopped wondering about what John did or didn't do. Or maybe he could do no wrong in her eyes.

In any case, she never for one moment questioned him or objected when, after a day playing on the beach, he made his casual offer.

'I'll take Dawn back to the room,' John said, flicking the last of the sand from his T-shirt. 'I'm going back early and we can get ready, get bathed and showered before you all come up.'

'That would be very helpful, thank you,' Mum answered from under her wide brimmed hat and sunglasses, before turning to me: 'Now go with your brother and hold his hand crossing that busy road. We will be up shortly.'

I took my brother's hand and stared up into his face, hoping to catch his eye. It felt nice he had chosen to take me back to the hotel – John rarely paid me any attention at all and, in fact, seemed to find me quite annoying at times. He, however, stared directly ahead of him and didn't look down as he led us through the late afternoon beach throng.

His straight, light brown hair was getting blond streaks from the sun, and there were little brown freckles studded along his straight nose. He had blue eyes and a wide mouth like me. Our sister Susy was also fair-skinned, but she had long red hair. Susy was short and sturdy, whereas John and I were long and lean – in that way, we took after our mother. Our dad Duncan, on the other hand, was a great big man in height as well as weight. The difference between dad and son had not gone unnoticed by him.

'Look at him! Reedy as a rake,' my dad would sneer at John.

But I was not a great big man. To my five-year-old eyes, John was a big boy and I looked up to him, in all ways.

I held his hand tightly as we crossed the main road between the beach and the hotel, John's eyes darting from left to right as we zigzagged between the cars and scooters. He steered me through the crowds milling in the lobby and then

13

took me up to the first floor, eventually turning the tasselled key in the door to our suite. The door swung open and I skipped in behind him, already throwing off my beach dress in readiness at getting into a nice, hot, bubbly bath. Only my little swimming cossie remained next my sandy skin.

'Okay, shall we run a bath for you?' John asked me in a singsong way. 'Get all that sand out of your hair?'

Smiling, I nodded enthusiastically.

The large roll-top bath in the marble bathroom filled quickly and after dropping my blue swimming costume on the floor, I was lifted in gently by my big brother. Taking a cup from the sink, John filled it with water and, tipping my forehead back at a slight angle, slowly bathed my head before taking the shampoo and lathering my hair into foam shapes.

'Do the spikes! Do the spikes!' I squealed, as I looked at my funny reflection in the mirror opposite. John, obligingly, molded my hair into two spiky horns at the top of my head.

Then, using the foam from my hair, he washed my back.

'Stand up,' he ordered. 'So I can wash you all over.'

As I stood up, I held my arms in the air and he rubbed my shoulders, my chest, under my arms and my torso. As he reached my bottom he took extra care and attention, slowly working his way through my legs with his hands. He looked at me as he did this, a strange expectant smile on his lips.

'Does this feel good?' he asked.

I just shrugged. It felt fine, I supposed, but why was he taking so long down there? All this foam everywhere, washing me over and over again in the same place. *Down there.*

My mind started to wander. I remembered that tonight there was some entertainment at the hotel. *I will wear my white sailor dress again,* I thought, *the one I love best. Now, is it a disco? Or is it a live band? I don't . . .*

Ow! A pain shot through my private parts. *What was that?* John had put his finger inside me. Just a little bit, but it hurt. I stared at him in surprise and there he was again, watching me, intently.

'This is good,' he said slowly, quietly, still holding my gaze. 'This is what special brothers and sisters do together. But it's our secret. Okay?'

I didn't speak. Spreading my legs further apart with both his arms he carried on working the foam inside me, very softly and slowly.

What is this? Why is he doing it? I don't like this. I don't like this at all. He is touching my private parts and it hurts.

But I didn't know how to tell him to stop. He was my older brother and he knew better than me. This is what special brothers and sisters did together, that's what he'd said.

After a little while, he stopped and for a moment I was relieved, expecting that it was time to shower off and get out of the bath.

But John didn't pick up the shower head. Instead, he stood up and removed his T-shirt and swimming shorts. He climbed into the bath and sat down opposite me, holding onto his *thingy* with one hand between his legs.

'Sit down, Dawn,' he ordered, then he pulled me towards him so that each of my legs went around his waist and I was now sitting on his lap, facing him.

He held his thingy with one hand and, with the other, he moved me onto it.

Oh no. Oh no! Pain shot up inside me.

'Is this hurting?'

15

I nodded, too afraid to talk, confused and scared to do the wrong thing.

His thing was inside me. Placing his hands under each of my arms, he lifted me gently until I was directly on top of him. His eyes now shut, he moved his arms behind the base of my back and with one awful movement, he thrust his pelvis up and pushed me down hard.

I wanted to scream. It felt like my insides were being split in two. I sat motionless as the bath water turned red around us.

'Shhhhh . . .' he whispered, stroking my hair. 'It is always a bit uncomfortable at first but it will get easier the more we do this. As your big brother, I promise.'

I put my arms around his neck as he thrust himself inside me, trusting his words that he would not hurt me. I shook now, my whole body vibrating from the impact and the terrible pain that was growing worse and worse with every single thrust. *If he goes on any longer, I'll surely break apart*, I panicked silently. But I was too scared to cry. I didn't want to upset him and I felt that if I stayed as still as a statue, it wouldn't hurt quite so much.

'Hold onto me tightly,' he instructed and, immediately, I did as I was told. I wrapped my legs snugly round his waist and my arms around his neck. This close, I could smell the sea in my brother's tousled hair and hear the strange deep grunts coming from somewhere in his chest. I fixed my eyes on the gleaming brass taps in the bath as I bounced up and down. His movements were slow and deep and after a few moments, he sighed and pushed with one longer thrust, before exhaling and staying still.

Neither of us moved for what felt like eternity. Then,

slowly, he lifted me off him and stroked my hair, before pulling the plug out of the bath to drain away the pink water.

Finally, he turned on the shower head and washed off all the soap from both of us. I hardly moved a muscle, too afraid even to breathe.

And all the while my brother whispered to me: 'That was very good, Dawn. That was lovely, you made your brother very happy. What a good girl. Are you clean now? All over? Good, come on then, let's get you out.'

Wrapping me in a towel, he carried me through to the bedroom.

'Next time it will be easier,' he said quietly. 'I promise.'

I said nothing in reply. *Next time?*

John crouched down in front of me then and, for once, looked me in the eye. 'Now remember,' he said solemnly. 'This is our special secret. If you tell *anyone* what's just happened, the police will come and take you away. You won't see Mum or Dad again, or any of us. It's okay for me because I'm a big boy, but you're just a little girl so you have to keep quiet. This is *our* secret, so don't tell anyone. Okay? I'm just trying to protect you.'

I lay still, not crying, thinking only of the throbbing pain between my legs – and one other, dark thought.

How will 'next time' be easier?

Chapter 2

This Is Normal

Once John had started, he didn't seem able to stop. Now, after every day on the beach, he took me back to the hotel alone, where he would run a bath for me and put his thing inside me. I hated every single minute of it but I didn't know how to stop him. He was my big brother and I had to do what he said. If I didn't, he would tell Mum and then they would take me 'into care' which meant leaving home forever and never seeing anyone again.

'You're a good girl, Dawn,' he'd whisper in my ear afterwards. 'You're keeping your big brother's secrets safe for him, and you make me very happy.'

I didn't know what this meant but I was pleased at least that this made him happy. So I just carried on as normal and hoped that the problem would go away once we got home.

As the train lumbered into Glasgow station, Dad's huge, oversized frame was easy to spot on the station platform. I was thrilled to see him. I loved my dad so much; he was a big bear to me, the one person in my family who gave me cuddles and love.

'Look at you all!' he laughed as we each hugged him in turn. 'Don't you look tanned! Except you, John. Still white as a sheet, I see. What happened? Did you stay inside the whole time?'

Now back at the hotel, we still had three weeks left of the summer holidays. Not Mum, though. No sooner had she put away her expensive summer clothes in their plastic dry-cleaning covers than she donned her blue apron, all ready to start cooking again. And us children had our chores too. There, up on the kitchen wall, was the rota for our duties in the coming week – walking the dog, taking out the rubbish, setting the table, bringing in the coal, clearing the table – and we were all expected to carry out our domestic duties accordingly.

'It's your turn to take the dog out today,' Mum said to John over breakfast the morning after our return. My brother let out an exaggerated 'Urgh!' and my dad's eyes flashed in anger.

'Come on now, John,' said Mum hurriedly. 'Don't try and get out of it.'

'Fine, fine,' he muttered into his cornflakes. 'Dawn, do you want to come with me?'

The mention of my name made me start in surprise and I looked up guiltily at the faces around the table. He asked me to go with him, right in front of everybody! I didn't know what to say. So I didn't say anything. I just stood up, not wanting to go, but not knowing how to say no. I didn't want to cause a fuss.

Our chocolate Labrador, Misty, bounded up to me the moment I picked up the lead from the side table in the porch, excited to be getting the chance to stretch her legs. John led us both out of the back door and through the great big garden, trudging along one of the many paths which zig-zagged in and out through the trees and sheds at the back.

But instead of going towards the main road, which would take us eventually to a park, he veered off onto a small track, just out of sight of the house.

Keeping tight hold of Misty's lead, I followed John obedi-ently as we picked our way down some stone steps and through a wall of conifers towards the gardener's shed.

What are we doing here? John didn't say a word as he jim-mied open the wooden door before stepping into the dark, smelly shed. I stepped in gingerly behind him, my nostrils in revolt at the putrid, musty stench of the vegetable compost that was rotting in open bags. Beside them sat sacks of crocus and tulip bulbs, ready for potting next year. It was a dank, gloomy place: the sunlight could hardly penetrate the dusty window panes and cobwebs covered every surface, including the one light bulb that hung from the ceiling.

I stood in the corner, squinting into the darkness and stroking Misty's head nervously. She looked up at me, wag-ging her tail slowly, both of us silently waiting for our next instruction. Spiders ran to safety as John busied himself moving garden tools off the dirty wall to make space for him. *Urgh!* I hated spiders. I wanted to run away too at that moment, run back up those stairs and into the safety of the big house.

But I couldn't move. I felt rooted to the spot.

Now John threw the largest hessian bags to the floor by the wall, to create a seat. He turned to me.

'Take off your trousers,' he ordered, as he unzipped his own. I had on my favourite green-and-white striped pedal pushers, the ones I had begged Mum to buy for me while on holiday in Italy. We were each given a 'holiday present' allowance and I was desperate to own these lovely, jolly trousers. They reminded me of peppermint sweets.

Now I felt anxious and scared as they slipped to the filthy floor. *They'll get dirty*, I worried. *I'll get into trouble with Mum and she'll say I can't look after my nice clothes.*

As if sensing my growing panic, John bent down and picked up the trousers, then found a rusty nail to hang them on. Next, he dropped his shorts and there, staring me in the face, was his thing, already big and hard.

'Suck on it.'

I did as I was told, though it didn't taste very nice and I didn't like doing it. I just wanted it to be over as quickly as possible now so that I could get out of there. The shed gave me the creeps. All the while Misty sat patiently in the corner, her big brown eyes watching us the whole time.

Now John positioned himself on one of the closed sacks of bulbs and, with his two hands under my armpits, he pulled me onto his thing. Once I was in place, the thrusting started again; the pain was unbearable. I gritted my teeth as I let him move me up and down, praying it would be over quickly. I did as I was told and kept very still and quiet, frightened of alerting someone's attention and being 'put into care'.

When he had finished and let out his final, shivery grunt, he carefully placed me back on my feet. He then handed me a piece of carefully folded kitchen towel which he took from his back pocket.

Afterwards, I retrieved my jolly trousers from the hook and put them on over my knickers, which were now damp and uncomfortable.

21

'Not yet,' he warned as I stepped out of the shed to go back to the house. 'It hasn't been long enough.' And he nodded at the dog.

Poor Misty had never got her walk and now here we were, standing in a stinking shed, just waiting until enough time had passed to pretend to Mum that we had taken her to the park. I felt sorry for her.

It can't have been more than ten minutes but it felt like hours as we waited in that shed in silence. John had his back to me. He used this time and his sleeve to make a peephole on the cobwebbed covered glass window to make sure the coast was clear.

Eventually, like two captive prisoners, Misty and I were allowed out and the two of us bounded up the stone steps towards the house.

I felt so dirty and horrible as I walked back in that morning. Surely Mum would smell the rotting food on me or see the dirt and grime from the shed? Wasn't there some evidence of what John had just done? I felt guilty as hell, as if the crime was written all over my face.

Frightened, I went straight upstairs to the toilet and peeled off my wet knickers. There were red bloodstains in the gusset so I washed them out in the bidet and stuck them behind my radiator in my bedroom. I didn't want Mum to see what he had done to me. I didn't want her to discover my shameful secret in the wash. I yearned for a bath, but there was no way I could run one myself without attracting attention. Besides, the immersion didn't come on until the early evening, so there was no hot water. Instead, I used my flannel to wipe myself and gave myself a little stand-up wash in the basin.

And so, it carried on. After our holiday in Italy, my brother regularly took me to the potting shed or to a crumbling out-house behind the compost heap in the garden to rape me. That's what it was, even though – at five years old – I didn't know the word. Each time, we stayed at least fifteen minutes, long enough to satisfy Mum that the dog had been walked, which of course she had not. Each time, I was filled with fear that we would get caught, especially when he took me to the compost heap, which was just underneath the kitchen window, where Mum was often stationed at the sink washing dishes.

The smell there was even worse than in the shed. Next to the compost heap, it stank of rotting meat and vegetables, and clouds of insects swarmed the area. At times, the stench was so overpowering I would retch.

Here, we picked our way over piles of bricks and sections of collapsed asbestos roofing until John found a place for me to stand where I could put both feet solidly on the ground. My skirt was hoisted up to my waist and my panties removed. Facing the wall, I would place my hands shoulder width apart for support; the position I was told to adopt when coming here. I'd hear the sound of him unbuckling his belt, then the crumple of his trousers as they fell to the ground. He spread my legs with his knee, then he'd guide himself into me. His hands would move to either side of my small hips and then I'd find myself on the ground, with him fully straddled over me, my body clasped tightly between his thighs. There was nowhere to go. I was trapped.

His thrusts were fast. He panted like an animal, knowing there was no time by the compost heap; it had to be over quickly. Every time he pushed, I could feel myself tearing, his bodily fluid stinging the open wounds. Afterwards, he would wipe me with his sleeve.

I hated it. I cannot tell you how much I hated it. But there was nobody to turn to; nobody who could help. John had told me over and over that this was normal for 'special brothers and sisters', but that I couldn't tell because *I'd* get into trouble.

'It's like if you take an extra chocolate bar from the sweetie tin,' he explained. 'Everybody does it sometimes. It's normal. But you don't tell Mum because she only wants you to have one chocolate bar. Right?'

There was so much of the world I didn't understand, and this was just one of those baffling activities that made no sense. It was normal, said John, but not so normal I could talk about it.

As summer faded and the days got colder, I returned to school. Now, instead of taking me outside, my brother made me do it in his bedroom before lessons. One day in class, I felt a sticky moistness in my knickers. Shyly, I put my hand up, as was usual in our school.

'Just go to the toilet, Dawn, if you need to,' called my primary teacher Miss Vickers over the heads of the other children. I scraped my wooden chair back and hurried out of the door towards the loos. She thought I needed to wee, but it wasn't that. It was him. I rushed into the cubicle and banged the door shut behind me. And there, in my blue-and-white checked summer dress, wearing my white ankle socks and my new black patent Clarks shoes, I wiped away my big brother's semen from my private parts.

Night after night, I lay in bed, curled up in agony, desperate to make it all go away. Why did he have to do this to me? I didn't want it and I didn't like it. My thoughts went round and round in circles, but finally, out of desperation and despair, I came to a decision. *I can't take this anymore*, I thought, *I just want it to stop.* I would do anything – anything – to make that happen.

And so I decided to tell.

Even if it meant I would get into trouble, even if it meant I might be put 'into care', I knew I had to make it stop.

It was one Sunday afternoon in early November that I screwed up all my courage and went to the kitchen to find my mother. If anyone could help me, surely it was her. There she was as usual, pinny tied behind her back, sleeves rolled up and several large pots on the stove, all bubbling away. She had her head bent down and, as I scooted round her, I could see she was carefully laying down the pastry on a lattice tart.

Since it was a Sunday, the bar closed at 2.30 p.m. and re-opened at 5 p.m. Most of the staff did split shifts, which meant there was no point in them going home while the bar was shut, only to have to come straight out again. Consequently, my mother always cooked a big meal for all the staff and the family each Sunday, a large and noisy affair with us five and at least ten other staff members. That was what she was preparing that day as I nervously loitered in the kitchen by her side, watching her amid her hive of industry, waiting patiently for a break in the proceedings so that I could spill the shameful secret that was hurting me so much.

The Sunday lunch menu rarely altered – it was always a home-made broth or lentil soup, followed by a large sirloin roast with all the trimmings. Then it was tart or home-made crumble with double cream, followed by coffee and pots of hot tea for the staff before their next shift. It was a huge job to prepare it all, and Mum never, ever cut corners when it came to food – every dish was made from scratch and from the finest ingredients.

As I watched, steam curled upwards from each large pot on the eight-ringed stove and Mum's hands worked quickly as she threaded the pastry onto her tart, a look of intense concentration furrowing her brow.

I had been very patient, but I couldn't wait any longer. My secret bubbled up inside me like a waterfall that could not be dammed. I *had* to say something.

I took a fistful of her apron and tugged hard.

'Mum! Mum! I have to tell you something, Mum.'

But my mother seemed lost in her own world. She had finished the latticing now and turned her attention back to the stove, where she tasted one of the sauces from the back of a wooden spoon.

'No, no, no,' she tutted to herself. 'More seasoning.'

Then she picked up the large salt cellar and shook it into one of the pots. I gazed up at her, wanting her attention. Mum was 5 foot 4 – she seemed like a giant to me – and wore her green apron that day over a beige Jaeger cashmere sweater and matching woollen skirt.

Nobody ever saw her expensive clothes, though, just the apron over the top. I tugged at it again.

'Mummy, please make him stop. He's really hurting me.'

'Hang on a minute, will you? And stand away from the cooker,' she instructed, still focused on her simmering pans.

'Mum! Mum!' I went on, more determined than ever. I'd come this far and I wasn't going to give up now. I *had* to tell her; had to make it stop. Though I was too young to know what John was doing – I had no words to express the things that gave me such pain – I somehow knew it wasn't good, despite my brother's constant reassurances that it was 'normal'.

Eventually, Mum swiped the back of her forearm over her brow and looked down at me.

'Who?' she asked sternly. '*Who* is hurting you?'

'John.'

'Okay. I'll speak to him. I'll speak to your brother.'

And that was it.

She didn't stop her cooking long enough to ask me what he was doing.

She didn't ask me exactly what was wrong.

She simply said she would speak to him – and then she returned to her cooking, as if that was the end of the conversation. She was on a schedule, you see, and she couldn't break her stride.

I stood there by her side for a second, not quite knowing what to do. And then, because it seemed there was nothing more to say, I walked out and left her to it.

Later that night, after another painful encounter with John, I lay miserably in bed, replaying the scene with my mother in my head, over and over again.

It had meant so much to me to tell her what was going on. I had felt sick with nerves all morning, knowing what I was about to do. After all, John had told me not to tell so many times; he'd said the police would come and take me away if I told anyone; he'd said that I'd never see Mum or Dad again. He'd made me terrified that the world would come crashing down if I confided in a single soul about what he was doing. I'd risked *everything* to tell her.

And, yet, the world hadn't stopped spinning. Mum had

appeared unconcerned, nonchalant. She hadn't even asked me what he was doing or why I was so upset.

Perhaps John's right, I thought to myself. *Perhaps this* was *normal and it was what big brothers did to their little sisters all the time.*

I had told Mum – and it hadn't stopped.

So what now? What do I do now?

Chapter 3
John Jay

'Who is it?' Mum called from the living room one Saturday morning after Dad had picked up the phone in the kitchen.

'It's John Jay,' said Dad, cupping his hand over the receiver. Then, winking at me as I sat hunched over my maths homework at the kitchen table, he whispered conspiratorially: 'It's your mother's boyfriend again!'

I smiled back, as I always did when Dad said this, but it was more out of habit than humour. I was still only six but I had known about John Jay all my life. He was Mum's special friend from Australia. They had met many years before when she worked in Paris.

'Oh, he was very handsome, very handsome indeed,' Mum recalled one evening in 1975 when the conversation turned to John Jay. Dad was at the bar in the hotel as usual so it was just me, Mum and Susy. Mum had the ironing board up and was working her way through a huge pile of washing. She loved talking about John Jay and she told us all about how they first met when she was just a teenager working as an au pair for a rich family. Her eyes now lit up at the memory and a rare smile played on her lips: 'We were very much in love, you know, but he was from this incredibly wealthy family and, well, they had lined up this woman for him, who was the daughter of a famous lawyer. I don't know why they chose her but either way, John didn't have much of a say in it. He certainly didn't *love* her but his dad threatened to cut him off without a penny if he didn't marry her, so he really didn't have a choice, did he?'

She put down the iron then and looked at us both, expectantly, so we both shook our heads, 'no', though I wasn't entirely sure what she meant.

'John was always very ambitious,' she went on thoughtfully, picking up the iron once more and attacking the collar of one of Dad's shirts. '*Fiercely* ambitious and I suppose I admired that about him. I understood, of course I did. The important thing was we stayed friends and he has been a great help to your dad and me over the years, a great help to this family. He got us on our feet with the hotel, for one thing. Gave us a very generous lump sum. Well, he's a generous man, you see. That's his nature.'

Their friendship had survived through the years and once a week without fail, John Jay called from Melbourne to chat to my mother. Dad didn't seem to have much to do with John Jay himself, preferring to tease my mother about their friendship. He called him 'Mummy's boyfriend' or 'Mummy's other man', but Mum never paid any attention to this. She said he was 'childish' and 'silly' for saying such things. Now she raced into the dining room to take the expensive international call while Dad replaced the receiver in its cradle and returned to his job of peeling a stem of root ginger.

Today he was making one of his special curries, treating the kitchen like his own personal laboratory with every work surface covered in onion skins, garlic shells, ginger root, piles of chopped fenugreek and coriander and dozens of little spice pots with strange names like turmeric, cumin, chilli and galangal. This exotic combination had been added to a large pot on the stove, which already contained a whole pig's head. It bubbled away, filling the kitchen with a heady, aromatic scent.

I liked to watch Dad when he was experimenting in the kitchen. It looked like a lot of fun, especially compared to Mum's style of cooking which just seemed arduous. Besides, I had no one to play with today as Susy was out at tennis all day and John was up in his room as usual. Not that he would play with me anyway – well, not in the way I wanted him to.

Suddenly, something occurred to me.

'Daddy,' I said, sucking thoughtfully on the end of my pencil.

'Yes, Dawn?'

'Isn't it funny, Daddy, that Australian John and our John have the same name?'

'Hmmmm. . . ?'

'Isn't it funny, Daddy?'

Dad went on peeling the ginger and a heavy silence filled the room.

'Dad?'

'Yes, Dawn. Very funny.'

But he didn't look in the least bit amused.

Ten minutes later Mum returned, flushed and excitable. She took one look at the kitchen worktops and pushed up her sleeves to her elbows. Now her hands worked at lightning speed, clearing away peelings, stacking up plates and running the tap into burnt, dirty pots.

'I don't know why you can't clear up as you go along,

Duncan,' she snapped at him as she swiped at the worktops with a J-cloth. 'Look at the state of this place! It's a pigsty!'

'Och, quit yer blether, Pip,' Dad muttered.

'No, I won't. I won't quit. It's me who has to clear up all the time and if you weren't so selfish and lazy I wouldn't be constantly stuck in this bloody kitchen, cleaning up non-stop.'

Dad snuck a look at me and rolled his eyes: *here we go again* . . .

'I can't believe the state of this place. If you helped around here a little bit more and drank a little bit less, I wouldn't have to slave away like a kitchen porter all the time. I could be out, shopping in Edinburgh or London, living the life I should be living, enjoying myself instead of this constant, unending *drudgery* all the time. I mean, look at this!'

She held open the lid of one of Dad's discarded pots. We both peered in: the bottom was covered in a weird, sticky black goo.

'What's in here? I mean, what *is* it? Why can't you just clear up as you go along? Hmm? Lazy! That's what you are – a fat, lazy slob. Look at you! Look at the state of you!'

I glanced in Dad's direction – there were fresh brown stains down his shirt from where he had been tasting his new curry, his red bow tie was unfurled at his neck and his trousers were unbuttoned under his giant belly.

'Urgh!' exclaimed Mum, turning away from him. 'I can't stand the sight of you!

Basil and Sybil Fawlty; that's what everyone called my mum and dad; they were the comedy couple from *Fawlty Towers*. The staff were used to the constant rows; the guests found it quietly amusing. She was always shouting at him and he was always ducking behind doors to avoid the pots and pans she threw. The more he laughed, the angrier she got. He goaded her, as if it was a game of cat and mouse, but her disgust when she looked at him was real enough.

My mother had started dating my dad not long after her relationship with John Jay ended. They were both living in France at the time and working for a large department store. She was a shop assistant; he was a buyer. According to my mother, Dad was a tall, handsome Scot, and so charming and good-looking, with his blond hair and sea-green eyes from his Viking heritage, that all the women wanted him.

'But I got him!' she'd tell us with a twinkle of triumph in her eyes.

Fifteen years and three children later, their married life at The Drayton Arms had settled into a familiar, if grinding, routine. Any dreams Mum had once had of a privileged, globetrotting life with the high-class elite were long gone – now this willowy, fair-haired beauty was trapped in a decaying hotel, serving up sausage, egg, mince and tatties seven days a week. It was hardly glamorous. And if she wasn't cooking at the hotel, she was cooking for us at home.

'I'm fed up,' she'd say, ten times a day, hands planted on her hips. 'Fed up of cooking sodding sausages, frying chips, stinking of bloody grease! The same old life. I'm just . . . just *fed up!*'

As a child there was no answer I could give to this, no comfort I could offer. Not that she wanted anything like that from us kids. She wasn't the type of mother who offered cuddles or kisses when she saw us. Her usual greeting was a narrowing of the eyes and a cool, quiet inquisition: 'Have you done your homework today? Have you cleared up your room?

Have you done your chores yet? Did you brush your teeth? *Properly?*'

Mum did her best for us, though; we knew that. She was up at 6 a.m. for the breakfasts in the hotel, worked all day long and then only came back after she had fed the residents in the evening. After a full day's work, she would fall asleep in her favourite chair at 7 p.m., a cup of Horlicks cooling at her feet.

Dad came and went as he pleased, but rarely paid us any attention, not minding about our homework, evening meals or chores. During the week he would pick me up from school in the early afternoon and as soon as we were home, he turned on the TV to watch the news and left me to my own devices. I liked to watch *The Clangers* or *The Flumps* in the playroom until Susy got back, and then she would engage me in a game or a fun activity.

'I know! Let's make pancakes today!' she might announce. Or: 'Let's have a skipping competition.'

Sometimes John was home even earlier than Susy, though, and then Dad returned to the hotel, leaving John in charge of me.

That meant only one thing. As soon as the front door had shut, my brother would wander into the sitting room.

'Come to my bedroom,' he'd order and I'd follow him obediently.

I never said no. I never struggled. Now aged eight, I had come to accept that this was just another part of my life; a part I couldn't change, like homework or bathtime. It was normal and because I didn't like it, I learned to block it out while he did it. I'd stare at the ceiling and examine the tiny cracks in the plaster, imagining myself disappearing down those thin little lines and escaping through the walls. This way, I didn't have to think about what he was doing to me. I could be somewhere else at the time he was doing it, put my mind in a place far away from my body.

I accepted the compliments he offered as if they were sweets. 'You're a good girl,' he'd tell me. 'You're a good sister. You make me feel nice, feel happy.'

In his room, I was always welcome. As long as I let him do those things to me then I was his special sister and I was rewarded with his good feeling.

So those afternoons when John was entrusted to care for me, we would always head on up to his bedroom, with him leading the way quickly. Once inside, I would be hit by the smell of incense – John burned it to disguise the smell of his smoking – and the sounds of Deep Purple playing on his record player. His bed was set tight against one corner of the room, with a bedside table to the left, fitted wardrobes straight in front and a large shelving unit further to the left, housing his collection of toy cars. He had a bureau further down that had a pull-down desk meant for studying, with more cars stationed on top. Inside the bureau, behind his junk, there was a large tub of Vaseline.

The Vaseline was for me.

I would stand and play with the cars; my favourite was the old-fashioned open-top London bus. As I pushed around the red bus on the counter, he'd walk towards me, lifting the tub of Vaseline, and I knew that was the sign for me to take off my pants. He was usually hard already, Vaseline smeared on his penis. Then he would rub Vaseline between my legs before I was placed in the usual position, the one that satisfied him most, where I was on top facing him.

Once he finished, I would leave. I never liked the pain, I never liked what he was doing, but I never stopped him. I simply didn't know how. I had tried telling mum but that hadn't worked so now I just put up with it. Year after year after year.

The rest of the time, John kept himself apart and rarely bothered to make contact with the rest of the family. We were all in our own little worlds. It was only later, when I visited friends at their homes, that I realized how distant we all were from one another. Every evening we sat together at the big wooden table for mealtimes, but then we would retreat back to our own spaces. There were no board games played together as a family, no bonding over favourite TV programmes, no hobbies to be shared. We three siblings were all too far apart in age to have much in common, although Susy was kind and did make time for me. Even so I spent a lot of time in my room, colouring in and drawing. We mostly did our own thing while Mum and Dad worked their long shifts at the hotel. They were there if we needed them, but we weren't encouraged to interrupt them.

Life went on this way, seemingly unendingly: Mum's complaints, Dad's escalating drinking and expanding waistline, John's abuse and my increasing detachment from the world because of what he was doing to me. I had learned to switch off as a defence mechanism. My teachers thought I was daydreaming or not paying attention, when really John's abuse was constantly in my mind, making me seem as if I was in my own little world.

There was no life for us outside of school and the hotel – no friends or family close by. Occasionally we were visited by my mother's younger sister, Aunt Jenny, who put herself at a considerable inconvenience by travelling up to Glasgow by train, all the way from Kent. Or so she said.

Jenny was like Mum in a lot of ways: cool, stand-offish and impeccably well-dressed. Mum always cooed over Jenny's clothes and hairstyles, purchased in the high-end salons and boutiques of Mayfair and Knightsbridge. She complained that up here in Glasgow she was stuck in an 'unfashionable backwater' and Jenny tutted sympathetically, though I suspected she gleaned a secret joy from her elder sister's envy. Jenny had done very well for herself, according to Mum, marrying a banker and carving out a life in London's commuter belt. Though she was 'poor Auntie Jenny' as she had no children of her own; that's how Mum probably made herself feel slightly superior to her sister.

They had both come from 'good stock', she was fond of telling us children, and though Mum refused to say anything more about her family, she hinted that she was educated more highly than most. In her view, there was no one of her intelligence in our working-class suburb of Glasgow. She believed herself to be a cut above her customers: the men generally worked in factories and their wives or girlfriends, who joined them at the weekend for a bevvy and a scampi meal, were also factory workers or cleaners.

'I'm sick of these people,' Mum would gripe when she came home from the hotel, exhausted and bitter from overwork. 'These uneducated women! They know nothing about art or culture – all they want to do is talk about the bloody bingo or what's on offer at Tesco's. Tesco's! I ask you! It's so *common*. I mean, they're nice people, don't get me wrong, but they're so working class. They don't speak any languages, they never travel further than Blackpool and they have nothing to say for themselves. It's depressing. Depressing and very dreary.'

On the rare occasions she took me out shopping, Mum chatted to her neighbours with such a haughty air that those conversations never lasted long.

'Oh the children are doing so well, all of them,' she'd boast. 'Private education, it's so important. Don't you think? I have Susy down for Oxford and John is hoping to get into Cambridge.'

'Och aye.'

'And little Dawn does the most charming drawings at school. She's really quite a talent,' Mum went on, hardly noticing the hostile tone of her companion.

But I heard it. I wondered if Mum never noticed because her prim Edinburgh accent was so different from the broad Glaswegian that everyone else spoke in our neighbourhood.

Where Mum was thin and sour, my dad Duncan was round and soft. He never shouted at me, only laughed. He seemed happy for me to be in his company and I was always an appreciative audience for his incredible stories of travelling in faraway places, peopled by exotic and unusual characters. Ten years older than my mother, my dad had led a wild youth, filled with as much adventure and excitement as the life of Indiana Jones himself. My dad had done all those things in the movies – and more! He had eaten snakes, goat's eyes, cockroaches, alligator and monkey brains, nearly lost his life in numerous crashes and scrapes and found his way into the most fascinating lands in the world. He was a true adventurer and loved to show off the culinary skills he had picked up on his travels. He loved all food, it seemed, as much as he loved his vodka and whisky.

To me, he was always a huge man with a big fat belly, gnawing on bones and sucking marrow from the inside. His glasses perched on his nose, so dirty with grease and finger-prints that it was a wonder he could see through them at all. His teeth were no longer white, but yellow and chipped from crunching on small poultry and shellfish. His hair was thin-ning and dull grey, his once piercing green eyes were now watery and bloodshot from too much drink and lack of sleep, and he stank of stale beer and raw spirits.

It was a far cry from the slim war hero I saw in old black-and-white photos. Dad had been a radio operator flying in Lancaster bombers during the Second World War. It was, by his own words, the making of him.

'The Scots, we're the bravest men in the world,' he'd tell me, thumping his chest proudly. 'You know what they called us: the Ladies from Hell. The Germans thought it was an insult because the Black Watch wear kilts but let me tell you, it's no insult. The Scots are so tough, we can cross-dress and still be shining examples of fighting manhood! Us and the Gurkhas, we're the brave ones, the ones who put our lives on the line.

'Unlike the weak and cowardly English. The snooty-nosed officer class who never left their barracks, or if they did it was only to play a bloody game of cricket! Us Scots, we're war-riors, just like the Gurkhas . . .'

And with that he'd start to well up. Overcome with the emotion of the memory, he'd let big fat tears plop down onto the kitchen counter.

'Because we're working class, you see, we're the peasants. We fought and we died side by side . . . in our thousands. So many brave, heroic men cut down in their prime . . .' and then he would stop, pull out a large, spotted handkerchief and clasp it to his nose, unable to speak about the many friends he had lost in battle. Eventually, when he'd composed himself and blown his nose, he'd look me straight in the eye and say: 'That's your heritage, Dawn. That's the kind of people we are – tough, strong and proud. That's who you are. Never forget it.'

After the war, Dad had a few jobs before he finally ended up in France. He loved working for a Glasgow-based importer best of all.

'They needed a man they could send anywhere, anywhere at all,' he'd say. 'So they chose me. You see, I was happy to rough it, sleep on park benches, in railway stations. I didn't care. I didn't need posh, five-star hotels. No, I was always far happier on the ground, mingling with the locals, being one of them. To me, there is no higher honour than being invited into an Indian's home for a home-cooked dinner, a touch of moonshine or the simple pleasure of eating the flesh of a ripe coconut. That, to me, is the high life!'

This always struck me as quite funny, especially as my mother had such opposite tastes. After all, she was the one who loved the thought of sipping champagne and Bellinis on hotel balconies, dining at the finest restaurants and wearing couture clothes. How the two of them ever found each other I'll never know!

Dad's storytelling was always enhanced by the many accents he could put on and his ability to talk in Urdu or Hindi. He could even take off my mother's Morningside accent and a second later return to broad Glaswegian.

Mum found it baffling.

'Why do you do that?' she asked him one day as he slipped out of Received Pronunciation into an Indian accent and back to broad Scots.

'I'll nae get far if I speak like you,' he joked, 'we'll hae nae customers!'

Dad may have been lazy and, certainly, he paid no mind to us kids for the most part, but he was a keen musician and he often let me sit with him as he knocked out Bing Crosby's 'Swinging on a Star' on the piano in our playroom. He loved listening to old jazz and blues records by Ella Fitzgerald, Sarah Vaughan and Louis Armstrong. We watched all the black-and-white movies from the forties and fifties, sang along to the musicals, especially *The Jungle Book*, and then late at night, when I couldn't sleep, we would watch gory horror films on STV.

Dad was my hero, my idol. But then he was good to me and Susy and he never raised his voice or hands to either of us.

I couldn't say the same for John. In fact, they couldn't be in the same room without a fight breaking out.

One of my earliest memories was of standing in my cot as I watched my mother peel my brother away from my dad, sobbing and crying: 'Leave him alone, Duncan! Just leave him alone!'

'I'll teach that boy!' my dad roared, making a grab for my twelve-year-old brother. 'I'll beat him black and bloody blue!'

'NO, Duncan! NO! Get out!'

It hadn't got any better since then. Why did he hate him so much?

As I grew up, my mind kept turning back to John Jay, the wealthy Australian 'boyfriend' of my mother, and the odd thing I'd pointed out to my dad as he was making curry that day. It really did seem funny, I thought, that Mum's friend had the same name as my brother.

Did it bother my dad, I wondered, that Mum still wore the sapphire ring John Jay had given her in her youth? Did he mind about the regular phone calls ...

Dad didn't seem bothered. He never expressed anything other than quiet tolerance for John Jay.

But as for his son, that was another matter ...

Chapter 4

The Last Time

John seemed very proud of himself as he flashed the large gold watch in my direction.

'Look what Dad gave me!' He grinned, flipping his wrist one way and the other so that the face of the watch reflected harsh sunlight into my eight-year-old eyes.

'What is it?' I asked, unimpressed.

'It's a Rolex,' he said. 'Dad got me a Rolex.'

Later that day, when Mum came in from the hotel to cook tea, I asked her: 'Mum, what's a Rolex?'

'A Rolex, darling, is a very expensive watch you get when you do something good.'

'So what did John do that was good?'

'He got into Cambridge University. He's going to study to be a physicist.'

'Is that good, then?'

'Yes, it's very good. Your dad and I are very proud of your brother.'

It was certainly a happy day for me, too, when, aged eighteen, my brother left home for his first term at Cambridge. It wasn't even in Scotland! John would be hundreds of miles away most of the time, only coming home in the holidays.

Dad, for a change, was very pleased with John and in the run-up to his departure he and Mum lavished money on him to pay for his new books, suits and shoes, not to mention a trunk, ironing board and a host of smaller, essential items he said he needed. Mum looked like she would burst with pride the day he left in his smart blazer and tie, all set for his new life in England.

'You're going to break a few hearts,' she teased him, picking imaginary lint off his jacket lapel. She could hardly keep her hands off him.

'Och, leave the boy alone,' Dad smiled, though I could tell he was equally proud. For the first time I could remember, I saw my dad hugging my brother as they exchanged their goodbyes on the platform of Glasgow train station. And was that a tear in his eye?

John was so puffed up with pride he was unbearably smug. The way he was acting, you'd think he'd won a bloody Nobel Prize! I stood behind Mum, embarrassed by the whole scene.

'Bye John,' I said flatly.

'See ya, Squirt.' He smiled, and then he winked. I could almost hear what he was thinking: *You're not going to tell anyone our little secret while I'm away, are you?*

I met his gaze with a quick shake of my head. The abuse had stopped in the last six months when John got a girlfriend, and I had tried to put it behind me. No, I wouldn't tell a soul. Not now. Not ever. His secret was safe with me.

The fact was, I was embarrassed by what John had done to me and I wanted to forget it had ever happened. So I buried those horrible memories and, thankfully, he stopped doing it after he left home. The rare times I saw him in the holidays he kept to his room, smoking pot and playing loud music.

At this time my parents moved me out of my small box-room and into the old playroom, which was a whole lot bigger. The window looked out onto the main road and I liked to lean out every morning and watch the world go by. A large holly bush partially blocked the view, which meant that I could look out from my window seat but passers-by couldn't peer in.

I felt happy in my new room. I imagined that I had moved into a new world, a new home where the old things of the past never existed and dirty big brothers didn't do horrible things to their scared little sisters.

Home life was certainly easier now that John was away. At school, too, I found a fresh enthusiasm for everything the world had to offer. I threw myself into art and sport. Susy and I cycled down to the public pool every morning, where we took swimming lessons from 5.30 a.m. till 7 a.m. It suited Mum because it meant we were busy while she was cooking up the breakfasts at the hotel. Afterwards, we got ourselves a hot chocolate and sweet yum yum each from the corner cafe, which slightly compensated for going into school with cold, wet hair on my back.

During the summer months we played tennis every weekend and in the winter it was field hockey. I was careful to keep my grades high as Dad constantly complained about 'the money these bloody kids are costing us in school fees'. It was one of my parents' regular rows, the money they had to spend on our private education. For Mum, there was never a question in her mind that it was worth the work and sacrifice. But Dad, well, he was never convinced.

'You two had better knuckle down and work hard,' he'd grumble on the days he dropped us off at school when the polo team had the use of the pool and we had a well-deserved lie-in.

'If I find your grades slipping it'll be straight to the local comp with you both and then your dad will get to enjoy himself a little more and work a little less.'

The prospect terrified me – I had seen the kids from the tough Glasgow estates who hung around the gates of the local secondary school in their tight skirts, smoking, sneering and flicking V-signs at each other. How could I survive in such a place? For there was no doubt about it, even in the small, privileged world of my private school, my friends and I were known as 'the squares'.

Of course, we didn't see ourselves that way; I was just into sport and art and I didn't really know about anything else. Certainly not boys. Besides, our parents were strict with us – we weren't allowed to wear the latest fashions from Topshop or Dolcis, we didn't hang around in town at the weekends and we weren't allowed to go to parties (not that we were invited to many). I didn't have the same kind of freedom I saw other children have, the ones who got to take the bus into town on their own or hang out in the park for hours at a time. No, all my movements had to be accounted for at all times and I obeyed, without a thought, because that was the way I had been raised. If I had any free time between the swimming, tennis and homework, I was set to work helping out in the hotel kitchen or serving the guests. In the holidays I was sent off to hockey camp or tennis camp for weeks at a time and that suited me just fine.

In this way, I grew up, cosseted and shielded from the tough, grimy world on my doorstep. My long blonde hair bounced off my shoulders while my limbs became strong and toned by years of sports and exercise. At twelve years old I was an innocent, oblivious to the girls in my year who flirted and dated boys, obsessed only with tennis and art. And I had almost, almost allowed myself to forget what had happened to me as a child.

If only . . . If only he had just left me alone.

But he didn't. That last time, when I was twelve years old . . . that was the worst time ever.

It had been a hot, clear day that Saturday in July and I had played several hours of tennis, catching the sun enough to leave my skin throbbing with heat. I lay in my bed that night, sweating and struggling to sleep in the still, humid air. Despite the fact that I'd left my bedroom window open, I felt no breeze at all and it took me ages finally to fall asleep.

Next thing, I was woken up by the scrape of an arm against the window frame. In another second, the whole window was wide open and John had flung himself into my room, falling onto the floor and laughing his head off, high as a kite on drugs. This scruffy, long-haired student was a far cry from the smart, blazered boy who had left home four years before.

'Shhhh!' he giggled, putting one finger against his lips.

A wave of revulsion washed over me as he crawled into my bed. I felt my whole body tense up as I lay there, not speaking, not saying a word. Though I was taller now, I still felt small when it came to John. The closeness of his body made me freeze inside and I was unable to do anything to stop him; unable to do anything at all as he lifted my nightie up past my waist and unbuttoned his trousers, pushing them down with one hand.

I knew what was coming but in that moment I could not move. I could not do a thing. I was a helpless five-year-old again, trapped in an unbearable situation from which I saw no escape.

Then something happened which I couldn't explain. It was as if my mind floated up outside of myself, leaving my helpless body behind. From above my bed, I watched it all unfold, as if it was all being done to someone else.

I watched him crawl up the bed so he could enter me.

This time, he was not tender. He gripped my hips and tried to kiss me. His breath was toxic with drink.

My body, no longer that of a small child, was developing in a way that I saw made him more urgent and excited than before. He grabbed at my budding breasts, shoved his rough hands into the thick pubic hair between my legs. Above him and me, I watched.

Somewhere down there, he pulled at my skin, squeezing my nipples. Faster and harder he drove himself into me. He grabbed at my legs, trying to wrap them around him. He held my jaw as he shoved his tongue into my mouth. The body down there was frightened and upset. She tried to push him away, shaking her head, but it made no difference and he held her down with renewed force. I watched it all.

This time it was rape. I knew the word now, but it was also more than that. He *knew* I did not want this but the more I fought, the stronger he became. Fear and shame kept me from shouting out – what if my mother or sister came in now and caught me like this? So I kept silent, my cries locked in my stomach, locked in my throat. They would not come out.

His touch was fierce. His unshaven face scraped across my body. His hands twisted my nipples and pinched them until they were red raw. He did not speak, he did not look at me. On and on it went until with one deep groan he pulled himself out of me and ejaculated over my stomach.

I felt sick but he looked at me and laughed.

'Admit it, you enjoyed this,' he sneered. He smiled cruelly at me as he opened my bedroom door and left.

Finally, my mind floated back down to my body. I curled up in a ball and cried.

Little did he know that that would be the last time he abused me. The following week at school we had a sex education class and I found out that now I was menstruating every month, sex could get me pregnant. It was the first time I had realized sex could lead to a baby.

In the playground after class, my friends and I stood around discussing this earth-shattering news.

'Oh that's disgusting!' said my friend Simone. 'The man pees inside you! That's how you have a baby! Can you imagine?'

'Gross!'

'Revolting!'

'Urgh!'

They stuck their middle fingers into their mouths and made exaggerated 'throwing up' faces and we all agreed this was probably the most despicable thing any of us could imagine. And I played along too: 'I could barf just thinking about it!'

I had to pretend not to know about sex because in that

moment I realized *nobody else knew*. It was as I had suspected for some time but now it was finally confirmed: everything John had told me was a lie. It *wasn't* normal! *Nobody* did this to their little sisters. And, worse, it could get me *pregnant*!

I was terrified that it was already too late. His child could be growing inside me already. What would I do? How would I explain this to my mother? What about school, my life? A baby would ruin everything.

So when John crawled into my bedroom again two weeks later and tried to get into bed with me, I said no. For the first time in my life, I said no.

'No, you cannae do it!' I said firmly. 'I'm going to tell Mum. I'm going to tell Mum if you come near me again!'

The words came out before I could stop myself. I could feel my heart beating through my chest. Faster and faster my heart beat. There was the sheer terror of disobeying, not knowing if he would tell Mum what he had been doing all these years. What would happen then? I would never be able to go to school again. As he slumped off me on to the floor, he looked at me and laughed, then shrugged his shoulders and told me to calm down. Lying on the floor at the side of my bed, he peered under it, as if he had seen something important. Then, pushing my bed-socks to one side, he stretched out his left hand and grabbed the box of tampons that were hidden under my bed.

'Now I get it. My wee sis is all grown up.'

It was over. I was still breathing hard but he didn't even argue; he knew that he could never have sex with me again. For the first time I had said no and it was such a relief. As a child I had never said no to an elder – I was taught to be polite and obedient at all times – but this time I had no choice. I had to protect myself. At the same time I was afraid it was already too late. Every night for the next few weeks I lay in bed, tormented by nightmares of giving birth. I walked around in a daze, deeply scared that inside me was a growing living being, the product of incest and rape.

'Hello, 591522. Penelope McConnell speaking!' my mother trilled in her best 'phone voice'. It was two months later and John was safely back in Cambridge for his final year at university, while I'd finally stopped worrying about being pregnant with his baby. With him away at college, I tried to put my brother out of my mind altogether. Today, I'd been back from school for an hour and was just getting to grips with my French homework at the kitchen table when the big green phone sprang to life.

'Yes, this is John's mother . . .' my mother replied hesitantly to the tinny voice down the line. Silence. And for some reason, I knew that it was bad news.

'Why would he need to hand it back?' My mother sounded confused as she twirled the pearl earring in her left ear.

'Oh.'

Even from where I was sitting, I could hear the sound of her heart breaking.

'Yes,' she replied, sadly. 'Yes, I'll see that he does. Thank you.'

Then she put down the phone and sat staring at the receiver for a long time. I didn't say a word but I noticed that she wiped at her eyes before she went back to the stove, where she was cooking a large casserole.

Later, when Dad came in from serving at the hotel, she told him he had better sit down because she had some 'very bad news' and he wasn't going to like it. Once Dad was seated, she came straight out with it: 'He's flunked his exams. He's dropped out.'

'Who?' asked Dad. 'What are you talking about?'

'John,' Mum replied dully. 'John flunked his exams months ago. The proctor's office called earlier, asking him to return his room key and settle his college bar bill. He hasn't been there for weeks. They can't get hold of him so that's why they called here.'

'What?' Suddenly she had his full attention. Sitting in the dining room, colouring away at my history project, since the hatch between the two rooms was still open after last night's dinner I could hear the confusion and disbelief in his voice. 'He failed his exams? All of them?'

'Yes, all of them. Last April, apparently. He dropped out last term and he owes nearly two hundred pounds to the college bar.'

Dad was now shaking with anger. In a deep growl he spoke to the table in front of him: 'His allowance? HIS COLLEGE RENT? He's been taking money from us this whole time. Thousands of pounds.'

'I know, I know.' Mum shook her head, her mouth set hard in a thin line.

Now Dad rose from the table, his voice getting louder and louder: 'Here we are, scrimping, saving and nearly going bust and that . . . that BASTARD has flunked out!'

'I know . . . I know . . .' Mum sank down into the seat next to her, head hung low, utterly dejected.

Dad was only just getting started: 'THAT NO GOOD, LYING BASTARD! He's really bloody blown it this time. What a waste of money. All of it! Down the sodding drain.

Here's our business slowly dying on its arse and he didn't even have the guts to tell us? We paid for extra tuition for that bloody blockhead. He's nothing but a failure and an embarrassment to us both. Taking us for a ride, all this time, treating us like mugs! That's your precious boy for you. Waste of money. Waste of bloody space!'

Mum just looked down, sad and disappointed. I think she really loved John, more perhaps than any of the rest of us, including my dad. Certainly in later years, when the truth finally came out, she revealed her true colours.

After he dropped out of university, my parents disowned John completely. I overheard one very tense phone call from my dad when John finally found the courage to call home:

'Listen, boy, you're not welcome here anymore. You got it? Your mother and I don't want to see your face. The shame and the financial burden you've put on this family . . . It's bloody disgusting. That's what it is. It's time you woke up because life doesn't come for free. I swear, I shan't be responsible for what I might do if you come round here again so just stay away. We've got enough on our plate now, paying back the loans we took out to finance your bloody college career. So much for that! When you've got a few thousand pounds in your pocket and you can pay us back then I might think, THINK, of letting you back in this house. Until then, you can get lost.'

The fact was, our business was in trouble. It was obvious to everyone, including me, that the hotel was in a kind of terminal decline. The old factory workers who had been our regular customers were now retired or their factories had shut down, and the weekend and summer holidaymakers were not coming in sufficient numbers to keep us afloat. Mum looked ever more harassed and unhappy while Dad drank steadily from mid-morning all the way through till midnight – when he fell asleep on the couch downstairs, too tired even to get himself to bed.

The furnishings in The Drayton Arms had lost their lustre and now the main reception carpet was shabby and stained. Lights broke and weren't replaced, paint peeled off the walls and the furniture in the rooms was scuffed and old-fashioned. And with John having bled my parents dry, they certainly didn't have anything left in their savings to give the hotel a much-needed facelift.

It was during this time that the old schoolhouse opposite the hotel was taken over by a new owner. It was turned into a house of multiple occupancy. At first, it looked like a disaster and my parents were appalled at our new neighbours.

'They're the lowest of the low,' my mother complained. 'All of them on benefits, all of them stealing. You know, last night someone broke into the cellar and took a keg! Your dad's not impressed. He's banned them from the hotel. They've brought the area down and the crime rate around here has soared. I'm telling you, it'll be the end of us all together. We might as well just shut up shop right now.'

My mother was always talking doom and gloom like this; little did she suspect that the new owners of The Schoolhouse were about to change our lives forever. And for me, at least, there would be no going back.

Chapter 5

The Schoolhouse

'Who is this boy you're seeing?' Mum demanded as soon as I walked in the door. It was unusual for her to be at home when I got back from hockey practice so I felt wrong-footed from the word go. I wasn't prepared for this.

'W-what do you mean?' I stumbled.

'Who is the boy you've been seeing? You know exactly what I mean, Dawn. Don't mess me around.'

I knew the game was up but couldn't for the life of me work out how Mum had found out about Dominic. That woman must be psychic or something!

'His name is Dominic, he's just a boy,' I shrugged, peeling off my light summer jacket and putting my book bag down in the hallway, keeping my face hidden from her inquisitive eyes. I wasn't used to lying to my mum. I had this horrible feeling that she always knew everything anyway and it was pointless to try and deceive her.

'Is he your age? Fourteen?'

'No, he's a bit older, I think,' I mumbled.

'How much older?'

'I don't know. Sixteen?'

'I see. And what school does he go to? Is it a fee-paying school?'

'No – he goes to St Andrews.' This was the local comprehensive up the road.

'And what do his parents do?' Mum was on a roll now.

'Urgh! I don't know!' I sighed, exasperated.

'Do you know where he lives? Hmm? I presume this Dominic is working class then, is he?'

'I don't know!'

'Exactly!' exclaimed Mum, triumphantly. 'You don't know anything about him, do you? You don't know where he's from, the area he lives in or what his family are like, do you?'

I just shook my head, angry and resentful now. Why did she have to blow everything up like this? It wasn't like I was doing anything bad. God, she should hear some of the things the girls in my class got up to these days! If she'd known, she probably would have dragged me out of school and enrolled me in a convent by now.

Dominic Farley had been introduced to me by one of my friends from the tennis club; he'd asked me out a few weeks before. I wasn't that into boys, unlike all my friends, who had suddenly taken a terrific interest in the opposite sex. My mates dressed up in sexy, provocative clothes and wore jewellery and make-up when they went out. I wasn't allowed to wear make-up; not that I wanted to anyway. I'd much rather be on the tennis court than anywhere else but, nonetheless, I agreed to go out with Dominic a couple of times, just so that I wouldn't seem like a complete square. I'd already got myself a bit of a reputation as a geek for not being allowed to go to parties like the cool kids, so I thought that if I dated a handsome, older boy like Dominic, I'd stop getting teased.

We'd only met up a handful of times, after school at the local cafe. Our 'dates' were on the days I had hockey practice, so I reckoned Mum and Dad wouldn't notice if I was home a little late, assuming that practice had overrun. Until this afternoon, it had worked out okay – and it had taken some of the pressure off at school too.

'Well, what happened?' Simone had asked excitedly the day after one of my Dominic dates.

'Nothing much, really. We talked, that's all.'

'Did you kiss?'

'Mmm, maybe . . .'

Simone's eyebrows had shot up. 'Maybe?'

'Well, yeah. Just once, though.' Dominic had cornered me in an alleyway on our way to the bus stop and, since he was quite a nice lad, I'd let him give me a French kiss. It was alright, a bit wet, but I certainly didn't feel anything magical.

'Are you going to see him again?' Simone had asked.

'I don't know. Maybe. We'll see,' I'd replied somewhat aloofly, not really that bothered one way or the other.

Mum, it seemed, *was* bothered though. 'Well, you're not seeing him again,' she now announced decisively.

'Why?'

'Because he's not right for you and, frankly, you're too young to be dating boys. Your dad will pick you up from school until the end of term. No more cycling home on your own.'

'You can't stop me!' I objected. 'It's my life and I haven't done anything wrong.'

'Haven't done anything wrong? You lied to me!' Mum retaliated sharply. 'I had to hear it from the hairdresser that you'd been spotted with some . . . some common little runt! Mucky gossip. Can you imagine?'

'You don't even know him!' I was outraged on Dominic's behalf. Mum was such a snob, always passing judgement on others based on nothing more than where they lived, how much they earned or what their parents did. What gave her the right?

'Not. One. More. Word.' Mum's eyes blazed now and she enunciated each word very slowly and clearly, the way she always did when she was really angry. I knew I'd pushed her too far. 'You're grounded! And next week, when you break up from school for the holidays, you're coming to work in the hotel. Find out what real hard work is *for a change*, somewhere I can keep an eye on you!'

My life was over. I wasn't that upset about being banned from seeing Dominic again, though it was humiliating to admit to my friends that I was grounded and couldn't go out. But even being grounded had its perks; square that I was, I actually liked staying home where I could practise my drawing. No, the real punishment was being confined to a quiet, suburban hotel for two months over the summer holidays, serving teas, coffees and sandwiches to a handful of decrepit regulars. After all, it was a place where the highlight of the week was the weekly Saturday funeral.

How on earth am I going to survive this? I wondered, as I surveyed the dismal clientele in the bar one warm, June evening. The Drayton Arms was no longer the busy, vibrant hotel of my childhood. Now the dreary bar was peopled by equally dreary people – tonight there were just two men in their sixties, both standing at the bar, staring into space and nursing half a pint each.

Dad's most loyal bar-person, Jean, was examining her new

manicure, while I shuffled from foot to foot. I was the wait-ress, should anyone order food, or a general mucky-in doing whatever was needed.

'Well, well . . . Who's this, then?' Suddenly, a booming voice woke me from my daydream. A large man in an extraor-dinarily colourful ensemble had walked into the bar, fixing me with an amused smile.

'Hello, sir,' I said politely, as I'd been taught to do.

'Aye, you can get us a drink, a lovely-looking lass like you,' he grinned, flashing a mouthful of gold teeth. 'In fact, you can get me and my friends here a few drinks.'

He gestured towards the group of men walking in behind him.

'We'll have three bottles of Mateus Rosé to kick off. And once they're gone, we'll have three more, darling. And . . .' The man waved a hand heavy with gold rings in the direction of the stunned regulars, who were now openly gawping. 'What-ever these gentlemen are having, of course. It's on us!'

'Yes, of course,' I said quietly, taking in the man's maroon suit, white collar and cuffs and striped pink shirt. Behind him were five other men, all similarly decked out in bold colours, arms and hands dripping with chunky gold jewellery. I'd never seen anyone like them before. Each one wore a heavy camel coat on his shoulders, just like Arthur Daley from *Minder*, and several clutched fat cigars between their teeth.

These must be the men I've heard Mum and Dad whispering about at home, I realized. I'd seen their cars parked outside The Schoolhouse opposite ever since the new owners had moved in, a dazzling and impressive array of Rolls-Royces, Jaguars, Bentleys and BMWs, but I'd never met any of the cars' owners in person. My mother, in her typically snobbish fashion, had referred to them as a 'horde of criminals', using that particular way she had of talking that looked like she was smelling something disgusting as she spoke.

'I would nae complain, woman,' my dad had responded drily from behind the newspaper, his glasses perched on the end of his nose. 'Those men have got money. We'll be lucky to get their custom.'

Now, as Jean rushed around, pulling every single bottle of Mateus Rosé from our bar fridge and gathering wine glasses, the men arranged themselves on a large table at the window. They were loud and jovial and when I delivered their drinks to the table in my black-and-white waitress pinny, they showered me with compliments.

'Here's this beautiful girl again!' said the first man, now talking to his friends, placing his arm around my shoulders.

'Aye, and she's brought the drinks . . .' his pal responded. 'This one can stay, Jim!'

'What's your name, darling?'

'Dawn,' I said shyly.

'Aye, I've been up the crack of Dawn before . . .' one man sniggered.

'Ignore him, Dawn,' said the first man again. 'Peasant! He doesn't know how to behave in the presence of beautiful women! It confuses him, you see.'

He held out his hand: 'Jim Crace at your service! It's an honour!'

I went to shake his hand but as soon as I offered my own, he grabbed it and kissed the back of it. I didn't know where to look or what to do. I could feel the colour rising in my cheeks now. Jim grinned.

'You're a stunner, you ken that?' one of the men called out.

'Look at those long legs! How old are you, gorgeous? Please tell me you're over sixteen.'

'Fourteen,' I replied.

A general groan went up around the table and a couple of the men pretended to swoon.

'Oh darling, you're killing me,' said Jim, pretending to mop sweat from his brow. 'If only I was fourteen again!'

I tried to keep it together but as soon as I turned back to the bar, I grinned to myself. A stunner, he'd called me! They were grown men and they thought I was pretty. Nobody had ever said such nice things to me. And these men, they were so different from anybody I'd ever met before. In our area of Glasgow, it was rare to come across men who so loved to make a point of spending money. 'Flashy', that's what Mum would have called it, but two hours later, when they'd drunk the bar dry of all the rosé and I called up Dad, who was at home with his feet up, he couldn't have been happier.

'Dad, there's no more rosé left. What do I do?'

'There's two old cases in the back,' he said excitedly. 'They're probably no good, but see if they'll have them. Give it to them half price. They'd be doing us a favour; we'd only have to chuck them out otherwise..'

And fortunately, when I offered the men the half-priced wine, they roared appreciatively: 'Course, love! Aye, just keep it coming. And here, take this. It's for you!'

Jim waved a ten-pound note above his head. I took it tentatively: 'Don't look so scared. It's called a tip, love. It's a good thing. Trust me!'

The others laughed and for once I relaxed and enjoyed myself. In the company of these men, I felt special and very flattered. I'd never had so many compliments in all my life.

Later, when Dad came to take over from Jean at the bar, the men were still there, laughing, joking, smoking and drinking like fish.

'You've got a lovely daughter there, Duncan!' Jim said. 'I hope we'll be seeing more of her now.'

'Oh aye.' Dad grinned. 'She's here all summer.'

'Perfect!'

Quite quickly, Mum's attitude shifted from one of disdain towards what she called 'those underworld types' to warmth and hospitality. Money talked and there was no question we could use it. Once the men started spending money and showering her with compliments, they were welcomed into the hotel with open arms.

It turned out that Jim was the new owner of The School-house. That first evening he took my dad aside and assured him that if we had any trouble from his residents, he would personally reimburse us. It was all that Dad needed to hear and from that point on there was no more stealing by Jim's tenants.

Slowly, my mother's appearance started to change. Usually, she was stuck behind the kitchen door in her baggy blue overalls, the kind that button up at the front, unseen and unwilling to be seen by the guests. But now these men were coming into the bar every day, men who showed their appreciation for a good-looking woman, she was more than happy to make an effort. Mum plastered on the make-up, took off her overalls to showcase her best Jaeger suits and wafted round the hotel, smelling of Christian Dior perfume instead of cheese-and-onion pasties.

'Now, can you tell me, Penelope, love, what *on earth* a beautiful, sophisticated woman like you is doing in a place like this?' Jim would ask her.

'Oh, don't!' she'd laugh bashfully, though secretly I could tell she loved it.

'You're a lucky man, Duncan!' the men joshed with my dad.

Dad smiled indulgently at these comments. He never complimented Mum like that, at least not that I ever heard, and I think she yearned for the attention.

Within a few weeks, our drab little hotel had been transformed into a thriving and successful business once again. Jim and his friends brought all their 'associates' to the restaurant and Mum was busier than ever, impressing them with her expert culinary skills and most delicious Italian favourites, like osso bucco (slow-cooked veal shank), chicken cacciatore, bresaola and carpaccio, plus risotto and pasta dishes of every kind. These large men loved Mum's cooking and dubbed her 'the best chef in Glasgow'. I served in the restaurants most nights, marvelling at the number of times a week these men seemed to eat out. *Don't they have homes to go to?* I wondered.

One night, the men brought their wives along and suddenly it all made sense. The women were dressed head to toe in the latest fashions, clacking around in towering heels, plumping up their big hairdos with blood-red fingernails and showing off handfuls of glittering rings. They looked like they would rather be out in swanky restaurants than slaving away in a hot kitchen. 'The nouveau riche ladies,' Mum sneered behind their backs, though to their faces of course she was all smiles.

I didn't care who they were – for the first time in my life, the hotel was an exciting place to be and late at night, after the men had stumbled out of our hotel and gone over the road to The Schoolhouse, I'd sit up at my bedroom window and gaze at the building opposite, wondering what was going on inside. The Schoolhouse was right across the busy main road, midway between the hotel and the house. Whether I was at the hotel or house I had a perfect view of the front door. I'd seen the drunks and teenage prostitutes stumble in and out the whole time and I knew some of those expensive cars stayed all night long, but I couldn't for the life of me imagine the sort of parties they were having in there.

Naturally, I was banned from visiting. Mum insisted that the residents were all the lowest of the low, real deadbeats, and said it was 'no place for a child'. Even Dad agreed with her for a change, describing it as a 'den of vice and thieves'. But like a moth to a flame, I was drawn to this 'other world' and as the weeks passed, my curiosity grew more intense.

One Sunday afternoon in July, I was serving in the restaurant as Jim's group enjoyed a long and booze-fuelled lunch. Mum seemed to practically float around the hotel these days, held up on a sea of compliments.

'Don't just stand there. Clear the plates, Dawn,' she hissed at me as she passed, carrying several more bottles of wine for Jim's table.

I jumped into action, picking up the empty plates that lay in front of the men sat round the table, who were now smoking and clinking glasses of whisky. As I came to the last setting, I recognized one of the men as the dad of a boy in my class. He was holding a twenty-pound note in the air and looking directly at me.

I walked towards the man and, as I did so, he smiled and pointed to his cheek. He wanted a kiss on the cheek for twenty quid. *Well, why not?* He was fairly good-looking with jet-black hair slicked back from his head, and it was more than I could earn working flat out for three days. I bent down to give him a kiss.

But as I did so, he turned his face around so that I kissed him smack on the lips.

I jumped back, surprised, but in that moment the whole table erupted into laughter and wolf whistles. Embarrassed, I grinned awkwardly and the man grinned back. I felt a light fluttering in my heart.

'I know you, don't I?' he said, narrowing his eyes. 'Don't you go to the same school as my son, Fergus?'

'Yes.' I had seen him a few times at our school, dropping Fergus off in a beautiful green Bentley. 'Your son is in the same class as me.'

'Well, why haven't you been round to one of his parties?'

'Erm, I'm not really part of that group,' I replied awkwardly.

Fergus was practically the leader of the cool kids. He came into school wearing the latest DM boots, his tie slung cockily over his shoulder and his pockets bulging with cash. I knew that Fergus invited other kids over to his place for parties and, judging by the rumours, he lived in a beautiful, big house on the other side of town. But I wasn't allowed to go to parties and, besides, I wasn't cool enough for him to invite me anyway. In his eyes, I was a geek: I studied hard, played sports and basically did what my parents told me.

Fergus rubbished all of that. He had no respect for the teachers and it was clear he planned to drop out after his O levels, whereas I had big ideas of going to art school. One time he had asked me bluntly why I was such a square and I'd informed him, quite primly, that I needed to study hard if I wanted to get a good job.

'That's rubbish!' he'd scoffed. 'My dad's got loads of money,

Bentleys and Jaguars and he didn't even go to school. He can barely read or write! You're wasting your time.'

Now his dad was right in front of me and he seemed very different from his brash, spoilt and immature son. He was quiet and spoke to me in a way that made me feel like I was the only person in the room.

'Well, I don't know why Fergus hasn't brought you back to our house. I really don't. I mean, out of all the girls I've met from his school, you're the best-looking one by far. Why don't you come over to our place sometime?'

I hesitated for a second then, looking down at my feet, and replied: 'No, I don't think that's a good idea, Mr Kelly. Like I said, I'm not in your son's group.'

'Please don't call me Mr Kelly. It's Stuart to you.'

I looked up then and in that second I felt that same fluttering in my heart.

'Sorry, Stuart.'

'And you're Dawn, aren't you?'

'Yes.'

'Well, it's a real pleasure to meet you, Dawn.'

Stuart. Stuart. I smiled to myself as I cleared away the rest of the plates, his name like a mantra running rhythmically through my head. For the remainder of the evening, I kept catching him looking at me as I served all the tables in the dining room, bringing out desserts and drinks and refilling glasses. Every time he smiled at me, my stomach did a little flip. Here was a confident, sophisticated businessman paying me a lot of attention. It was thrilling and a world away from the young boys like Dominic with their needy, grabby hands and their boring small talk.

After that day, I bumped into Stuart more and more often. He was at the hotel most days and frequently gave me lifts when he passed me at the bus stop. He happened to be passing me a lot from then on – usually when I was on my way home from tennis in my white skirt and shirt. Every time he saw me, he told me what a beautiful girl I was and that if only he were twenty years younger, he'd take me out.

'I never knew anyone as beautiful as you when I was a young man,' he'd say as he drove slowly towards the hotel. 'My wife and I, well, it was all a bit of an accident. She fell pregnant when we were teenagers and in those days, you didn't have any choice. You had to get married. It's been a struggle since then. I've got to be honest, I never really loved her.'

As for me, I had developed a massive crush on Stuart. He asked if it was okay if we were friends and I said yes. I wanted him to be my friend.

'That's so sweet,' he sighed. 'You've got a lovely nature, Dawn. Really, because some people would be suspicious of a man of thirty-seven being friends with a fourteen-year-old. They wouldn't understand. They would think it was all a bit sordid, and they might not approve, so best not to tell anyone . . . okay?'

I had a secret admirer! It was so exciting! Weeks passed and now suddenly my life had an exciting new element. Some days I'd open my curtains in the morning to find Stuart's Jaguar parked right in front of my house. When I asked him why he had been there, he just looked at me with sadness: 'I don't know, Dawn, I guess I just want to make sure you're okay. You're such a special person, I want to watch over you, to look after you. Is that okay? If I could, I'd marry you and I'd spoil you so much, you would never have to work. You're so precious, I wouldn't let any other man even look at you. We'd travel the world, I'd buy you nice clothes, shoes and take you to all the best restaurants and bars. I would be the envy of every man in Glasgow!'

It was too much! I blushed with delight. Everything he said was amazing and I couldn't believe that this important and rich man was paying me so much attention. Was this love? Was this how it made you feel? Mum had told me you'd know when it was right; you would feel as if you could walk on air. Well, this must be it, I thought. I'd never had this feeling before, so what else could it be?

'You can wave to me if you like,' he added. 'When you see me outside your bedroom window. But be careful not to let anyone catch you. Some people might think it a bit odd and get the wrong idea.'

School started up again at the end of August, and during that first week Stuart picked me up from tennis on my way home and asked whether I was going to the school disco on Friday night. He'd heard all about it from his son.

'Maybe.' I shrugged. 'I haven't really got much to wear for a disco. There's a nice pair of shoes I've seen in Dolcis, but they're quite dear.'

'How much?' Stuart said without missing a beat.

'Oh no, I don't mean that!' I said hurriedly.

'Don't worry about it,' Stuart insisted. 'How much do you need?'

'They're £19.99.'

Stuart unfurled a clutch of twenty-pound notes from his large cash wad.

'Here, take sixty quid,' he said. 'Get yourself a nice outfit.'

I just stared at the money, gobsmacked: 'But . . .'

'No arguments,' said Stuart. 'Just take it. You deserve to treat yourself.'

I was flattered, overwhelmed, in awe of this man. No one had ever told me that I deserved to treat myself; no one had ever said nice things to me. It seemed like he truly wanted to look after me.

By this time, I had almost completely buried the memories of what my brother had done to me as a young girl. Then John came back home for a few days, after Mum persuaded Dad that he was truly sorry for flunking his exams and wanted to make it up to them.

John hadn't changed one bit, though; he was still a complete pothead and party animal. He hadn't been home more than one night before he sneaked out to a club and came back in through my bedroom window in the wee small hours. I didn't have any trouble now telling him to get lost. This time I was angry, and no longer scared of him. I knew what he had been doing all these years was so wrong. I didn't want to be reminded about having sex with my brother; it made me feel sick to the stomach thinking about it. This time he didn't fall into my bed, but shook my shoulder and asked me to move up. It was like he was testing the ground. He knew I had rejected him the last time and wanted to know if I would change my mind – or had his little sis truly grown up?

The next day, Stuart gave me a lift to hockey practice.

'What happened last night?' he asked me, in a demanding tone, as soon as I got in his car.

His question took me by surprise as I clicked my seatbelt into place and settled back against the luxurious leather seats; I far preferred travelling in Stuart's elegant Bentley to my dad's clapped-out old Saab. 'What do you mean?' I asked, confused.

'I saw a boy crawl into your window at about three in the morning. Who was it?'

My heart began to beat faster. *What can I say? How can I explain this?*

'Oh, that's my older brother John,' I said, in what I hoped was a light tone. 'He went clubbing and it was his only way of getting back in the house. We don't see him much, he lives in London.'

Despite myself, I felt colour rising to my cheeks as I talked of John and lied about why he was in my room. I looked out of the window to hide my discomfort.

'Is that all there is to it?' Stuart probed.

Silence filled the car as I counted the trees that whizzed past the window.

'What do you mean?' I asked, casually, certain he could hear my guilty, pounding heart.

'I mean, is there anything else you want to tell me about John? It just seems strange to me, that he should go through your bedroom.'

He seemed so caring, so gentle, that I felt I could trust Stuart; that of all the people in my life, he would understand. We'd been friends for months by then, and I trusted him completely.

Little did I realize that this was the very moment everything changed for me. Years later, I would be told that my 'revelation' to Stuart had been crucial, that it told him so much about me and my world; not least that I was capable of keeping a secret.

'Grooming' – that's what they called it. But at the time,

aged just fifteen, I had no idea. I simply thought he was my friend and he cared deeply about me.

I stared across at Stuart in the Bentley. He gave me a re-assuring, oh-so-kind smile that brought an involuntary smile to my own lips, like we were mirror images: two sides of the same coin. *You can do this, Dawn*, I told myself. It felt right.

And so, for the first time ever, I opened up. I told him that John had abused me in the past, when I was a little girl. I told him everything. I told him how I hated John, even though the abuse had stopped some years before. I told him how much it had hurt.

I was shaking with emotion by the time I'd finished talking and Stuart took me in his arms in a huge embrace.

'That's terrible,' he whispered. Now he took me by the shoulder: 'That's really awful what he did to you, Dawn. I want to beat the shit out of him for what he did . . .'

'No! Don't!' I looked at him in alarm.

'I won't, Dawn, not if you don't want me to. Don't worry – your secret is safe with me. I won't tell a soul.'

There was a pause then, as though he was thinking hard. He gave me another easy smile as he rubbed my arms gently with his big, grown-up hands. 'You know that I care *very* deeply about you, don't you, Dawn?' he said, smoothly.

I nodded.

'I can't help it. I know I'm a married man and you're still only fifteen and at school, but . . . I love you.'

He loves me!

'If I were single,' Stuart continued, 'I would marry you tomorrow. I've never had feelings like this for anybody before. All I want to do is run away with you and look after you for the rest of our lives.' He looked me deep in the eyes. 'Tell me, do you feel the same?'

I nodded shyly. I was blown away by Stuart's kindness, and this declaration of his love was overwhelming. I felt myself swept up in a tornado of emotion. *He loves me!*

Well, I loved him too. We would be together forever, I knew that now. Stuart would love and protect me and keep me safe. *I have nothing to worry about*, I thought happily. *Nothing at all.*

And then, for the first time, Stuart leaned in close towards me. It felt incredibly intimate. His face loomed closer to mine and I knew before he did it what was about to happen. I closed my eyes, anticipating – sweetly anticipating. Locking his lips on mine, Stuart kissed me passionately, then whispered into my ear as his hands started to explore my body with an excited, urgent pace.

'I know this is going to be hard, Dawn, but I'm prepared to be there for you and to protect you, always,' he murmured as his palms roved my body. 'We mustn't let anybody find out about us, though, because you are underage.

'This is going to be our little secret. Okay?'

Chapter 6

Stuart

Stuart wanted sex straight away – of course he did. I assumed that this was normal because it was all that I had ever known. Never mind what I wanted, when men wanted sex they got it: that was just a fact. And Stuart had been at pains to re-assure me that sex wasn't a bad thing, even though my brother had abused me. It was a natural and beautiful thing between two people who loved each other. Sex was nothing to be ashamed of and if it was with the right person, it was the best thing in the world.

That was what he told me, at least, but my first time with Stuart wasn't what I expected from his passionate declarations.

Not at all.

I had agreed to meet him after school at one of the buildings he had just bought in the centre of town. Stuart was a real wheeler-dealer businessman, with interests in cars, jewellery, antiques and property. From the way he had described this new venture, I had imagined a glamorous high-rise building with luxury flats; a real 'party place' he'd called it. But when I arrived at the address, I was surprised to find a grim sixties office block with an entrance through an underground car park.

As I picked my way through the subterranean parking lot, my satchel banging against my knees, I felt a prickle of fear on my skin. There were no lights and I couldn't see if anyone might be hiding in the shadows, ready to jump out at me.

Should I go back? I wondered. *No, I can't. I promised I would come. But what's that smell? Eurgh – urine!*

The stairs were filthy and littered with cigarette ends and cans of Special Brew. *Do people really have parties here?* I thought in disgust.

As I came up into the main stairwell of the building, I spotted a door to the left which opened onto a large room with graffiti on the walls. *This can't be it, surely?* It was less like a party place and more like the beer cellar in our hotel: dirty and grim, with a pervasive musty smell.

A neon strip light illuminated a pool table in the centre of the room and I could see an old television on a wall bracket. The minimal furnishings consisted of a couple of battered lamps on upturned beer crates and three mismatched sofas. I was just about to turn around and leave when I heard Stuart's voice cutting through the gloom.

'So you made it then? Fancy a drink, Dawn?'

'Erm, okay. Coke or Fanta if you've got it.'

'Don't be silly. I mean a proper drink.'

'Oh no, I don't like alcohol,' I replied.

'That's because you're drinking the wrong drink,' he said, grinning, as he handed me a brimming glass.

'What's this?'

'Cointreau. Try it.'

The sickly sweet liqueur tasted like oranges. I was so nervous I knocked the whole lot back in one go and he quickly refilled my glass from a dusty bottle. I started to giggle apprehensively as he pulled me close to him.

'Don't worry, Dawn. I'll drive you home if you're a little tipsy. I can't drink myself or I'll get done for drink-driving. Now, come here, gorgeous!'

Suddenly my stomach lurched. A wave of nausea slid up my throat. If this is what being drunk is, forget it! It's terrible. Why would anyone want to make themselves feel sick?

'Can you take me home now, please?' I asked in a small voice, but Stuart didn't hear me because he was kissing my neck and exploring my body with his hands – or maybe he chose not to hear me.

'I feel a bit sick. And dizzy,' I went on. I felt so ill my head was spinning, and the last thing I was thinking about was being amorous. I was trying to compose myself and not vomit all over Stuart, to save myself from further embarrassment.

'Shhh!' he said as he eased off my Clarks shoes and pulled down my thick black tights, leaving me standing there in just my pants and my school uniform.

'You're very hairy down there,' he remarked as he put his hands inside my underwear and groped me. 'You should get waxed. My wife always gets waxed.'

What does he mean? What is that? What is waxing? Strange, disjointed thoughts chased themselves round my head as Stuart unzipped his trousers and took his penis out. My stomach heaved again. His penis was really big and hard. *He has more hair than me. Maybe he should get waxed,* I thought dreamily. Now my head felt thick and fuzzy.

'Go on. Touch it, Dawn,' he urged in a low voice. I took the penis in my hand. It was very fat, as if it was swollen, and in my hand it seemed to throb. Then he forced my head down and made me suck it, thrusting his pelvis with rhythmical movements, his pace quickening, his grip hardening around my head. I did my best not to gag as he stroked my long blonde hair.

'Yeah, that's it. Suck harder,' he murmured. 'Good girl! Doesn't that feel good? This is really good. My friends want to do this to you but I won't let them, I'm keeping you all to myself. Good girl, good girl. Oh my God! And that school uniform . . .'

'I'm going to be sick.'

I gasped as I stood up. Somehow, I managed not to retch but it took every effort to stop myself from throwing up.

'Don't worry,' he soothed as his hands roamed over my breasts and down into my pants again. 'Don't worry. I'm not going to hurt you. Only people that love each other do this. It's a special bond between us. Now, turn around.'

Stuart spun me round then hitched my skirt up over my hips. I felt so ill I couldn't do anything to resist. His breath quickened as he yanked down my pants, exposing me. I felt like a rag doll as he bent me forwards. Taking a deep breath, I braced myself, knowing from what John had done to me that what was coming would be painful.

But Stuart had something different in mind. To my shock, he stuck his penis in my bottom.

'Ow!' I cried out with the sudden and unexpected pain. *This can't be right!* I thought, as tears stung my eyes. *This can't be right! This is horrible!*

'I have to do it this way so you don't get pregnant,' he whispered from behind as he thrust himself inside me. My body was now jammed up against the brick wall and the smell of urine was worse than ever. Stuart grunted as he slammed me against the wall over and over again: 'This is our secret. I love you, Dawn. I love you.'

I was sick into a plastic bag all the way home. As we pulled up in front of my house, I was overcome with fear. *Will Mum notice something is wrong? How on earth am I going to hide this from her?*

I stumbled in the front door that evening, hoping she wouldn't smell the alcohol on my breath or notice that I could barely walk. But Mum was too busy cooking to notice anything. I went straight to my room and curled up in bed.

Is this what it's going to be like with Stuart? I wondered. Though he had hurt me, I still trusted him; he loved me, after all. *God, I hope it gets better*, ran the scattered thoughts in my head, *because this will kill me.*

I guess you could say it got better. From that point on Stuart wanted sex with me all the time but, to my relief, he used condoms – which meant that he didn't try to have sex with me in the bottom again. We did it in his car, in his empty properties and in various car parks around town. He couldn't get enough of my body – and I thought that meant he really loved me. I was giving him what he wanted and so we had a good relationship. I hung on his every word, besotted with this older man who had promised to spoil me for the rest of my life. But, as he warned me time and again, we had to be careful.

'Your mother is an old woman. She's losing her looks and she's probably very jealous of you, jealous of your beauty and your youth,' he'd tell me. 'You can't let her find out about us or she'd probably put an end to it.'

I was his special girl, he said, and one day we would be

together forever. My head was filled with dreams of the won-derful life I'd have when we finally ran away together.

If it wasn't for his stupid wife, I could have it all right now, I reasoned. But there she was – Maria Kelly – standing in the way of what I believed was true love. *They aren't in love, so why does she insist on staying together? If only she'd just let Stuart leave to get on with his life . . .*

But no: according to him, she had threatened to ruin him financially if they ever split up and he needed time to 'secure the businesses' before we went public. Besides, there *was* that small matter of my age. At fifteen years old, I was still a minor, not that it was a big deal to me at the time. In 1984 no one had heard of 'grooming'. There were dirty old men, sure, but then there were sexy older men like Rolling Stone Bill Wyman, who was dating teenager Mandy Smith. She was fourteen, and he was thirty-four years older than her but nobody batted an eyelid. Those were 'wild girls', young teens who went out and took what they wanted from life. I imagined myself as another Mandy Smith. I felt that Stuart was giving me my freedom. It was the freedom to do what I wanted without my having to ask permission for every little goddammed thing, or so it seemed.

He would let me drink – encourage it, even. My friends were saving up to buy a bottle of Diamond White to share before the school disco whereas I had an endless supply of anything I wanted. I was soon taking their orders for Sweet Martini, Peach Schnapps and the newest liquor on the shelves, Midori.

It was great. I was no longer one of the geeky girls but the one everyone wanted to hang with. The cool boys and the grade-A girls soon welcomed me into their group. I was invited to every party. A space was reserved for me at the top table in the dining hall. I started to realize that money talked, and was all people were really interested in. Money had the power to make you popular, to buy you friends, to buy you freedom, to buy you anything, and Stuart was now moulding me into someone who would not want to lose the power that came from money.

As the weeks passed, Stuart and I had to think of new places to meet, away from prying eyes. As such, he arranged a few get-togethers for us in The Schoolhouse, which suited me because I'd been so desperately curious about what went on there for months.

It was easy enough to sneak out of my bedroom window and creep into the basement through the fire exit. And there my eyes were opened to a truly depraved way of life. The girls who rented rooms were all addicts and prostitutes, 'lost girls' with vacant expressions who would do anything for their next hit. Jim's friends and business associates all flocked there for the wheeling and dealing, the drugs, but most of all for the sex on tap.

At first, I felt very different from these girls; superior, even. I wasn't an addict or a prostitute, I had a good home and I was still at school. Besides, Stuart said he'd never let any of the other men do anything to me, but the way they talked about these girls! And the things they did to them . . . it was like they were less than human.

'What can I do with this one, Jim?'

It was a Thursday afternoon and four middle-aged men were sitting round the reception, drinking whisky and coke, while Jim held forth in a half-open bathrobe. I'd refused his offer of a 'hit' of cocaine, but the others had snorted it up their noses in powdery white lines. Drugs didn't interest me at all.

The man who'd asked the question was known to everyone as Wolfie because he had wiry black hair all over his body, even on the backs of his hands. Now, he was drooling over a girl standing at reception.

'Well, Wolfie, this one likes it up the arse, don't you, darling?' said Jim, gesturing towards the girl who wore a tiny red miniskirt, cream vest top and no underwear. She looked about seventeen and was clearly high on drugs. She barely noticed when Jim slapped her hard on the behind.

'She likes to be tied down, don't you, honey?'

She didn't say anything, just smiled absently.

'It's only fifty quid and you can do what you want. Tie her up, put her against that door and all three of you can fuck her up the arse and she won't mind. Might be an extra tenner each. Is that not right, honey?'

'Yeah, that's right.'

I recoiled inside.

These girls were so desperate for money they would do anything for cash. It scared me.

One time I met Stuart at The Schoolhouse, I passed a girl being fucked in a corridor. The girl's empty hollow eyes fixed on mine as she bobbed up against the wall, her legs lifted around the bloke's waist whilst two other men stood waiting for their turn. Drugged up to the eyeballs, she looked about the same age as me, with straggly bleached blonde hair hanging limply over her shoulders.

Could that be me one day? I felt a shiver run down my spine. I had to get out of there.

'I don't want to meet you at The Schoolhouse again,' I told Stuart later that day. Something about Jim's world felt very wrong and I was frightened that if I spent any more time

80

there I would become corrupted by it. I was convinced my love for Stuart was different from the ugliness I'd witnessed at The Schoolhouse. That was real and pure.

With the change of venue, my meetings with Stuart were now mostly in the mornings and afternoons, before and after class. The rest of the time, I filled my hours daydreaming about him. I confided in my friend Simone about our 'affair' because I was desperate to share my excitement at the new life that we had planned together. It was always on my mind, day and night. Nothing else mattered; not even my education anymore.

'You don't have to do that stupid homework,' Stuart had insisted one night when I told him I was too busy working on an essay to meet him for sex. 'A girl like you can get anything you want. You're bright, you're beautiful and you can use your looks and charm in life. You'll never go without.'

'But what about art school?' It had been drummed into me that I had no option but to study hard if I wanted to get on in life.

'Look at your mother!' Stuart had reasoned. 'Your mother had a good education and where is she now? Slaving behind a stove in a hotel kitchen fourteen hours a day. What kind of life is that? She's miserable and, frankly, I don't blame her. You're not going to end up like that because you're going to have it all. Don't be a mug, Dawn. Trust me, you don't need school to get on in life.'

Stuart frequently made disparaging remarks about my family. He said that my sister was jealous of me, my mum was bitter about losing her looks and my brother would disapprove because he had lost me. He even managed to slip in some insults about my father. He said my dad would feel inferior that a man more successful than him could show his daughter a real life, one he should have given his own wife but could never afford. Little by little, I began to feel isolated from my family, and Stuart encouraged this. I didn't need them, he insisted. I didn't need to work hard at school. I didn't need anything or anybody apart from him.

It worked. I became completely convinced that Stuart was my destiny, my true love and my salvation from a predictable and boring life of misery. Before long my grades began to slip and I started to flunk all my tests. So, when I was called in to see the head of the girls' department at my school in early October 1984, I thought I knew what it was about.

Oh flip, I thought, as I knocked on Mrs Crowthorne's door. I'd managed to conceal my falling grades from my parents but there was no disguising it from the school and now I was in for a real ear-bashing.

Mrs Crowthorne was sat behind her large mahogany desk when I came in, a look of intense concern on her pinched features. She pushed up her reading glasses and leaned back in her creaky wooden chair as I shuffled into her office, pressing her hands together and resting her chin on her fingertips.

She studied me for a moment, then she drew in a deep breath and began. 'Dawn, I want to talk to you about a very delicate matter. The fact is, you have been seen having dinner in a restaurant with an older gentleman, Stuart Kelly, and another man. It was brought to our attention by another guest in the restaurant because there were just the three of you there.'

I was taken aback. Stuart had indeed taken me for a Chinese meal the week before; it was a special occasion because I was meeting his cousin Adam Kelly. The two men were best friends and business partners and, to me, this was the first step on the road to becoming the next Mrs Kelly.

'Oh aye, she's stunning alright!' Adam had nodded admiringly when we were introduced. 'You've landed yourself a right catch there. Good on you, Stuart. I'm really happy for you both.'

At that moment, I had felt honoured to be accepted into Stuart's inner circle and simply sat quietly for the rest of the meal, eating my chicken in black bean sauce as the pair discussed business. Why did the school care if I went out for dinner with them?

'I was only out with Fergus's dad and his cousin,' I said innocently.

'Yes, we know who he is, Dawn, but why were you with these men?'

'It was only a meal!' I shot back defensively. 'Where's the harm in that?'

'Well, Dawn, we don't understand why a girl of fifteen is going out for dinner with two older married men *on her own*. It's not like you were with your parents or Fergus. It was just you. From the school's point of view, this looks like an unhealthy relationship. Is there anything you want to tell me about this, Dawn?'

I shook my head vehemently.

'Right, well, if you're seen with him again, we'll have to call your mother.'

I was outraged by this intrusion by the school into my private life and I ranted at Stuart when I saw him later that day.

'I mean, what right have they got to go poking their noses in?' I seethed.

'It's because of your age,' Stuart muttered, looking far more worried than I felt. 'We've just got to get you to sixteen, then everything's going to be okay. I'm going to divorce Maria and we're going to get married but none of this can happen, *none of it*, if we get caught and I go to prison. So look, if anything happens, you have to remember this: you are entitled to one phone call. Got it?'

I nodded.

'You're a bright girl, Dawn, you know what I'm saying, don't you? If you get nicked, you call me. Don't say anything to the police. Nothing! Because if they find out we're having sex before you're sixteen they'll put you in care and I'll be locked up. And it won't be me responsible for getting us into trouble because I know how to keep my mouth shut. It's your own mouth that will get you in trouble so you have to deny it. If you don't admit anything, they can't prove anything.'

So we carried on as before, only this time we tried to be more discreet. I slowly dropped out of all of my after-school sports clubs and spent more and more time at one of the flats Stuart owned opposite my school. I thought we were being really clever, outwitting my parents, the school and the authorities.

Only I hadn't banked on Mrs Maria Kelly. I was so wrapped up in my own little world that I completely failed to take account of the fact that Stuart was now spending all his time with me, and not at home. As any wife would, she started to wonder about his long absences.

It was just before 9 a.m. one morning in March 1985 when a pupil from another class came to the door of my classroom and spoke to the teacher.

'It's Dawn McConnell,' she announced. 'She needs to come to Mrs Crowthorne's office straight away.'

My form teacher nodded at me so I got up and followed the girl back along the corridor, fully expecting to be disciplined about my mock-exam results. I'd failed all of them, except Art, and I hadn't had the guts yet to tell my parents. So I was surprised to see two tall, young policemen standing in the room when I arrived.

'Dawn,' said Mrs Crowthorne grimly. 'We've had another report about you, this time from Mrs Maria Kelly, that you're seeing her husband. She's had a private eye following the two of you for the past three weeks and she has shared this information with us.

'Dawn, I warned you previously. You're not sixteen. Legally, you're underage and that's why you're going to be taken to the police station for questioning. You have to go with these gentlemen here.'

It was a shock, but in that moment I didn't feel frightened, I felt angry.

'I need to make a phone call,' I said defiantly. I was ready for this – Stuart had prepared me for this moment.

'Why do you need to make a phone call?' asked Mrs Crowthorne suspiciously.

'I need to phone my mother.'

'No, I'll phone your mother.'

'No, I want to. I can make a call, can't I?'

'You can call from here.' The head gestured to the large black telephone sitting on her desk.

'No, I want to make a private call,' I insisted. 'I'm entitled to a private call.'

One of the policemen now spoke up: 'Who told you this? Who's put this into your head?'

'It's my rights. I know it's my rights,' I practically shouted, and with that I stomped out of the office and towards the payphone in the corridor. The two policemen bolted after me: 'You're going to run, aren't you?'

'Don't be ridiculous!' I snapped back. 'Where do you think I'm going to go? I'm going to the payphone!'

They followed me all the way to the payphone where I managed to make a call, leaving a message on Stuart's pager: *Just been arrested from the high school.*

And when I'd finished, that's when they put the handcuffs on me. Right there, in the corridor of my school! The bell had only just gone so everyone was still milling about and they all got a good eyeful of me being marched down the corridor between two hulking policemen in my school uniform. I was embarrassed and ashamed, but mostly angry.

How dare they treat me like a criminal! What do these imbeciles know about love? I thought, as they ushered me into the police van, parked in the courtyard of the school. I kept my eyes locked in front of me, but I couldn't help noticing the crowds of students and teachers who had gathered to watch the spectacle unfold.

My mum was at the police station when we arrived. She was sitting in a plastic chair, dressed in a smart navy Betty Barclay suit and holding a hanky to her face, as if she was at a funeral.

'What's *she* doing here?' I snapped at the young policeman at my side.

'She's your mother,' he said, though this was self-evident.

'I don't care. Get her out of here. I don't want to see her.'

By now I had nothing but resentment for my mum and everything she stood for. She could cry if she liked, but it was her who had welcomed Stuart and his friends into the hotel.

It was her who had stopped me seeing Dominic and insisted I spend the whole summer in the hotel. What did she expect? That I wouldn't find my own amusement somehow? She was a blazing hypocrite as far as I was concerned and probably jealous, just like Stuart said. It was all sun and roses when they were offering to run away with *her*, so why not the same for me?

In the interview room, the policemen finally took the cuffs off and let me sit down. Now two plain-clothed policewomen came in, carrying a wad of papers and a cup of tea each. They sat at the desk opposite me.

Nobody had offered me a drink, I noticed. I know such situations would be dealt with differently now, but back in those days there was no sympathy or even a perception of me as the innocent victim: I was assumed to be guilty and made to feel like a criminal. It had only one effect: it steeled my nerves to protect Stuart, who – in stark contrast to these people – had always treated me so kindly and so well.

The older policewoman, who looked about forty, examined the papers on the desk in front of her and then, still looking at them, she spoke: 'We've had a report from Maria Kelly. You know who she is?'

'Yes.'

'We've had a report that you're having sexual relations with her husband and you're under sixteen, you're a minor.' Finally she looked at me. 'Do you know the consequences of this?'

I just stared silently at my feet. Stuart had drilled it into me to say nothing and I wasn't going to let him down. I wasn't going to be responsible for sending him to prison. If anybody could stay quiet, it was me: I'd had a lot of practice at it, ever since I was five.

I remembered what Stuart had told me, too: as long as I kept quiet, they had nothing that could split us up.

Now the two policewomen took turns to fire questions at me.

'How long have you been seeing Stuart Kelly?'

'Are you having sex with Mr Kelly?'

'Where do you meet him?'

'How often do you meet him?'

'What do you do with him?'

'Where do you go?'

'Are you having sex?'

'Are you using a condom?'

I didn't say a word. I just stared at them both, my arms folded, with one eyebrow raised and a cocky smirk on my face. Fuelled by self-righteous rage, all I could think was: *I hate these bitches.*

What right do they have to treat me like this? I thought indignantly. I couldn't see that they were trying to protect me, that they were trying to gather evidence for what was, at the end of the day, a crime that Stuart had committed. On and on it went, the questions and the interrogation. They wanted to do a test to check if I was still a virgin. Would I submit to this test? No: I shook my head. Finally, exasperated, the older policewoman sat back and sighed.

'You know you're going into care, don't you?'

Silence.

'Your mother has told us that she can't ensure your safety from this man and wants you to go into care.'

I didn't speak but inside I was raging. *Was this true? Mum wanted to put me into care? What a bitch!* Every inch of my fifteen-year-old body seethed with anger.

'We've arrested him too, you know. He'll go to prison and you'll go into care so you might as well talk to us, Dawn.'

But the only time I spoke was to ask to go to the toilet. When I got back, I was surprised to see a smart man in a beige suit and tortoiseshell glasses sitting on my side of the table.

'You've got a solicitor here now,' said the older police-woman testily. 'A criminal lawyer. Who called him?'

I just grinned knowingly at her.

'Well, anyway, you can speak to your lawyer now.'

The policewomen both got up and left the room. Once the door was firmly shut, the lawyer turned to me.

'My name is Michael Turner – call me Mike. I'm Stuart's lawyer and now I'm going to represent you. It sounds like you've done well, Dawn, by not telling them anything.

'Now, once we finish up here, I'll speak to the police and they'll release you back into the care of your parents. You've got a few months till your sixteenth birthday so you have to be very careful. If you and Stuart are seen together, you'll get arrested on the spot. Maria's got a private investigator follow-ing Stuart. She's given times and dates of where you've been seen. So just be really smart about this, okay?'

Mum was still in the station reception when I came back out; still sobbing into her hanky. She walked me to the car outside where Dad was waiting for us.

'Look what you've made your mother do,' he said, as I slid into the backseat. He started the engine and, as he drove us all home, Dad told me there would now be a new regime. He was going to drop me off and pick me up from school each day and I'd have to sign in to each class. If he got a report that I'd missed any classes, I'd be in serious trouble. And, naturally, I was grounded.

'Go to your room,' Dad muttered when we got home. 'Nobody wants to speak to you.'

That was ironic: I hadn't spoken a word the whole time. My only thought now was: *how on earth am I going to last six weeks without seeing Stuart?*

For in my mind, nothing had changed. The dream lived on: once I turned sixteen, we would run away together and I was going to be treated like a queen. Just two months, that was all, and then everything would be different. I'd leave this miserable hellhole and move into Stuart's house. We'd get married, have children and I'd spend the rest of my days as a lady of leisure. Just two months, and it would all be mine: a happy, loving future with the man that I adored.

Or so I thought . . .

PART II
LOST

Chapter 7

Trouble in Paradise

'Dawn, what are you calling for? We're going to have to cool it,' said Stuart in an urgent whisper. 'I could get arrested, I could lose my whole business! My children aren't speaking to me. I'm sleeping in the spare bedroom, for God's sake!'

I didn't understand. I had expected Stuart to compliment me on how well I had managed to keep my cool under pressure in the police station. I had been holding out for his warm words, for since that day I'd been a virtual prisoner in my own home, under constant observation. After school each day the police were round at the house, making sure I didn't go out. Meanwhile a journalist from the local paper hung around the school gates all day, hoping to get a juicy titbit about the 'private schoolgirl who'd copped off with the married businessman'. Nobody talked. After all, what could they say? Without my confession there was no story and I wasn't about to start blabbing. I had thought that Stuart would be proud of me – and impressed that I had managed to escape the surveillance to snatch this phone call with the man I loved.

My opportunity had been my chores. A week after my arrest, I'd managed to get to the payphone three streets away from my house under the guise of taking the dog for a walk. Excitedly, I had dropped in the coins and paged Stuart the number of the phone box.

Straight away the phone rang – I had been delighted, thinking it a sign of how much he had missed me – but instead of showering me with praise for my silence in the face of hostile questioning, Stuart seemed irritable and uneasy.

'What do you mean, "cool it"?' I said now. 'I don't understand.'

'Look, the shit's hit the fan big time here and I can't see you.'

'What do you mean?'

'I can't see you until you're sixteen!'

'Stuart, I have to see you,' I insisted.

'Oh, don't you get it, you silly girl?' he snapped. It was the first time he'd been so angry with me and I was taken aback. 'I'm getting followed!' he went on. 'The police are looking for me, Maria's going to divorce me, she wants all the money, all the business and she's planning to bankrupt me. You need to go back to school and get your O levels.'

What?! This was the complete opposite of everything that Stuart had been saying to me. Do my O levels? How could I, now? I'd stopped working months ago, which meant I was bound to flunk them completely.

'But I don't want to do my O levels,' I said pathetically. Suddenly, I felt lost and very alone.

'Just do them,' he grunted. 'Do your exams, don't contact me and I'll see you when you're sixteen.' With that, he hung up. I was shocked and very angry.

I lay in bed that night, staring at the ceiling and wondering what to do. Suddenly, I was gripped with cold, white fear.

Had I ruined my whole future for a stupid schoolgirl crush? Oh God, I had been silly and foolish. But it wasn't too late! Nothing terrible had happened. I could still turn this situation around.

I was filled with determination but gradually, day after day, it got harder to believe I could get my life back on track. Home was unbearable with neither of my parents speaking to me. At school, I heard the students whispering behind my back, though no one seemed to want to talk to my face anymore; no doubt they had been warned to keep away by their appalled mothers. Meanwhile my exams were looming and I had done no work at all. *Did Stuart really love me?* I wondered, hurt and confused. He'd shown no affection in that last call; he'd treated me less like a queen and more like an inconvenience. A 'silly girl'.

Is that what he thinks of me? Is that all I am to him?

As the weeks passed, I knew I needed help. Eventually, one day after school, I screwed up my courage and went through to the kitchen where Mum was ironing. I slid myself up onto one of the Formica kitchen counters and watched her silently for a minute, swinging my legs.

'Mum, I've got something to tell you,' I said eventually, my voice quivering with emotion. She didn't look up, just kept ironing. 'Mum, I *have* been seeing Stuart Kelly, but I don't like him anymore and I need you to help me.'

With that, she put the iron down and looked at me with cold, unsympathetic eyes. 'Well, Dawn, you made your bed, you can lie in it.'

'Mum, I need help here. I'm really sorry. I know I've made a big mistake, but I've got my O levels coming up and I need you to help me. I don't think I'm going to pass them and I don't know what to do.'

I heard my own voice then, pleading with my mother, begging for her help. I knew I'd taken things too far but I wanted to get back on track and I couldn't do it on my own. I was still only fifteen; the problems before me seemed so huge I had no idea how to handle them.

'After what you put me through, I don't want anything to do with you,' Mum said, shaking her head in disgust. 'Haven't you brought enough shame on this family? I think it's time you left, don't you?'

How can she be so cold, so heartless? Now the tears welled up and I couldn't stop them landing in big splashy drops on my thighs. I just needed a hug; I wanted her to take me in her arms and tell me it would all be okay.

'It was a mistake,' I sniffed, wiping at the tears. 'I know it was a silly thing now. It was a crush and it went too far but I want to stay at school. I want to go to college.'

Mum had returned to her ironing and now she smoothed out the sheet in front of her on the board. 'Dawn, all married men are the same, you should know that. They tell you what you want to hear. It's disgusting what you did. You put a lot of pressure on us, on the family, and it has caused a lot of arguments between me and your father.'

'Oh, you're always arguing anyway!' I spoke angrily through my hot tears. Didn't she care? I was reaching out for her help and her love but, like she always did, she was pushing me away, making me pay for her public humiliation in the police station.

'Fine,' I said. 'Fine! If you don't want me here, I'll just leave then.'

'Good.' She smiled acidly. 'Why don't you leave home? I think that would be best for all of us, don't you?'

Stunned, I stomped off to my bedroom, where I slammed the door and crawled under my bedcovers, pulling the duvet tight over my head so she couldn't hear my sobs.

I thought over my situation. There seemed no way out, and I realized that I had no choice now. Mum had said I had made my bed and that I had to lie in it; there was no help coming from that quarter. I felt trapped, scared and alone. Most of all I was confused. I didn't know who I could trust anymore and, in desperation, I turned to the one person I believed could help me now.

I called Stuart again.

This time, I told him Mum knew everything and that she wanted me to leave home.

'But I've got nowhere to go,' I sobbed. 'I thought you loved me! I thought we were going to be together.'

'I *do* love you, Dawn.' Stuart's voice now softened. 'And we *are* going to be together. We just have to be smart until the heat is off.

'Look, I've got an idea. I'm going to go away for a few weeks, just to let everything calm down. I think it would be a good idea if you went away too. How do you fancy a trip to London?'

This was just what I needed to hear! All was not lost – Stuart *did* love me and now he was proving it. Like that – just like that – I was back in his thrall.

A couple of weeks later, Stuart met me and Simone at the station cafe with train tickets and £500 in cash. I'd managed to persuade my friend to come along for the adventure. Her family wasn't as strict as mine; in fact, her mum didn't seem bothered that she was going away for a fortnight, just weeks before her exams.

I didn't even tell my parents I was leaving. Instead, I penned an angry note for my mum: 'I've left and I'm never coming back so don't tell the authorities and don't try looking for me. I hate you and I never want to see you again!' After the way she had abandoned me – the memory of that acidic smile as she told me to leave was burned into my brain – every word I wrote was true.

We were sent off with strict instructions that we could do what we liked with the money as long as we managed to stay in London and out of trouble until my sixteenth birthday in two weeks' time. It was a marvellous holiday and Simone and I had the time of our lives!

At first we stayed with my sister Susy, who was studying design, in her shared flat in Baker Street but, after a couple of days, Susy said we had to go because her flatmates weren't too impressed at suddenly having two young houseguests. We weren't close any longer and she was so much involved in her own life and her own boyfriend issues that she really didn't have time to try and bang some sense into me. Her advice was basically to sort out all the commotion I had caused and try to salvage anything left of my education. Of course I thought I knew better so laughed it off, and Simone and I left and went to stay in a variety of different B&Bs and hotels. We spent our days strolling round Carnaby Street, Oxford Street, Sloane Street and Camden Town. At night we drank in pubs, danced at clubs like the Hippodrome in Leicester Square and caught a couple of West End shows. Simone teased me because I insisted on buying a black trilby, just like the one worn by Sally Bowles in *Cabaret*.

We kept moving from place to place, just in case the police were looking for us, and I stayed in touch with Stuart by leaving messages on his pager. Eventually, after two weeks skiing in Switzerland, he came to London. By now, Simone was due back home so on the day I turned sixteen, I waved her goodbye at London's King's Cross Station.

'When are you coming back to Glasgow?' she asked.

'Never, I hope!' I grinned as I gave her a big hug and then saw her off.

If I sounded confident, it was more than I felt. Inside, I was a mess, not knowing where my future lay or what I was going to do. Stuart had promised me everything would be different once I turned sixteen and I clung blindly to this belief, but in my heart I didn't feel at all certain about it. He had been cold and distant since everything blew up, despite this trip to London. My confidence in him was shaken and I didn't know if I could trust him anymore. Bit by bit, the perfect future I had dreamed of for us seemed to be drifting away. And the more I reached out to it, the further it seemed to get.

'We're going to Guernsey,' he announced that night when he met me at the Sloane Square Hotel. I had been anticipating a happy reunion, but Stuart was moody and distracted. We'd had sex very quickly after he arrived, but it felt almost perfunctory and didn't cheer him up like it used to. I expected so much more from him now that I was sixteen. I expected him to be so happy that we could now be seen in public without people staring at us, wondering if I was of age. But now he was distant; he didn't even appear to fancy me. People had warned me that as soon as I was sixteen the attraction would wear off, but I never believed them.

Afterwards, we went out for dinner in Chinatown.

'It's Maria,' he said sullenly. 'She's chucked me out and now divorce is on the cards. I've got to secure the assets or she's going to take everything and leave me with nothing. So I have to go to Guernsey and now that you're sixteen, you can come too.'

'Why? What's in Guernsey?' I asked innocently.

'Well, for one thing, my mother's there. And for another, Adam and I have got business interests in Guernsey. If we can get those sorted out quickly, I just might be able to walk away from this marriage without losing my shirt.' He spoke through mouthfuls of sweet and sour pork balls.

I just sat there, trying to work out where I fitted into all of this. *Where is my life heading now?* I asked myself. I wondered, too, why Stuart's attitude towards me seemed to have changed so much. *Wasn't this what we always wanted? Him getting divorced so we could be together?*

'Are you going to eat that?' he asked gruffly, as he grabbed a pork ball from my plate.

We got the train up to Edinburgh the next day and, from there, we met Adam at the airport, where we all took a plane over to Guernsey together. The two men discussed business all the way while I kept quiet and looked out of the window. I got the impression that Adam did most of the talking while Stuart mainly listened and agreed with him. He was a genius, that's what Stuart had told me about Adam, a master in business, and he had learned a lot from his older cousin. 'You could learn a thing or two from him,' he said. 'Trust me, Adam knows what he's doing!'

Once we got to Guernsey, Stuart hired a car and drove us to a small estate just outside of the main town. I was surprised because it looked like quite a poor area. After all, Stuart was such a successful businessman. He owned tons of properties in Glasgow – so what were we doing in this run-down, council semi? It made no sense.

I was even more surprised when I finally came face to face with his mum, Gladys.

'Hello, dear!' said a gnarly old voice as she opened the front door. I had been expecting a well-dressed, elegant woman but Gladys wore a stained, shabby housecoat; she was short, and skinny as a bird. Her leathery hands clutched the handles of her Zimmer frame and she seemed to wobble precariously as she looked up at us.

'Mum.' Stuart bent down and pecked her on the cheek before going through to the lounge, followed by Adam.

'So this is her!' Gladys exclaimed as she saw me hovering behind the men. 'Come in, dear, don't just stand there! Well now, you're a lovely-looking thing, aren't you? Close the door. That's right.'

She hobbled to the lounge, every step a massive effort, and there she eased herself into a dilapidated floral armchair. The whole place looked like it had been decorated forty years ago and there was a damp, musty smell, as if the windows were rarely opened.

'Ohhh!' she sighed gratefully as she sat down. 'Don't mind me, dear, I've got terrible arthritis so I'm not very good on me pins. Now, let's look at you. Yes, she'll do! Much better than that silly old bitch Maria.'

The swearing shocked me, but I pretended not to notice.

She sighed and rubbed at her legs. 'Oh, my legs are killing me. I don't suppose you know how to make a pot of tea, do you, dear?'

I felt sorry for her. The poor woman seemed in terrible pain so I jumped into action and made tea while the cousins got on with their business. They pulled out several documents and rested them on the little laptray in front of Gladys.

'Here, sign this, Mum,' Stuart ordered, producing a fountain pen from his suit pocket. 'And this, and this . . .'

She seemed to have trouble holding a pen but with a great deal of grunting and groaning, she managed to sign her name on several blank cheques, a dozen sheets of headed notepaper and a few official-looking documents.

'Here,' Stuart said, pointing to each place in turn. 'Here . . . Here . . . Here . . .'

'Is this part of your business?' I asked Adam as he sank into the sofa next to me and drank his tea, while we both kept our eyes on Gladys as she slowly and carefully etched her name on the documents. Canned laughter from an afternoon quiz show blared out of the TV next to us.

'It's like this, Dawn. Guernsey is a tax haven,' explained Adam patiently. 'Here, you're not subject to the same taxes as you are on the mainland – but there's a catch. You have to be resident here to open a bank account, so that's where Gladys comes in.' He took a big slurp of his tea as he nodded at the feeble old lady in front of us.

'Gladys is a resident and she's got a bank account so, basically, we put all our business through her. And that way we don't have to pay tax on the profits we make. It's a loophole. Everyone would do it if they could.'

102

'I don't understand,' I said. 'What happens to all of the money in Gladys's bank account?'

'Oh, it doesn't stay there!' laughed Adam indulgently. 'Once it's gone through her account, the money gets transferred into a couple of companies based in Panama, another tax haven. These companies invest in properties, cars and other items like antiques, first-edition books, fine wine . . . that sort of thing. They're our companies, of course – we own the shares – but on paper it doesn't look that way. On paper, we have no assets. So nothing's in my name, nothing's in Stuart's name. Again, a little loophole which is designed to protect us both from losing it all to the taxman, or thieving fucking wives like Maria.'

We didn't stay long – just a couple of hours – enough time for the cousins to get all the signatures they needed. Then, as we were leaving, Stuart handed Gladys an envelope stuffed with cash.

'Here you are, Mum,' he said. 'A little something to keep you going. Don't spend it all at once!'

The old lady's eyes lit up – it was clear from the economy packets in her fridge and the old furnishings in her home that she was only just getting by. I was glad Stuart had given her some money because she obviously needed it. But as the door closed behind us, Adam muttered, 'She's only going to waste it on booze, the degenerate old cow!'

It was a shock to hear him talk that way about her. After all, she was doing them both a huge favour, letting them use her bank account.

'She seemed really nice to me,' I offered limply.

'Ha!' barked Adam.

'Well, Dawn, you don't know her very well,' said Stuart

bitterly. 'What that nasty old witch got up to in her day would make your hair stand on end. Put it this way – she couldn't stay in Glasgow any longer; she'd exhausted every avenue she had. Sucked all the good will dry from every single person she knew. Honestly, that silly bitch could cause trouble in an empty house. We did her a favour, getting her out and into this place.'

'So you moved her over here?'

'Yeah; not that she's grateful. Complains all the bloody time, doesn't she, about how she doesn't see anyone and how lonely she is. Well, she's got no one to blame but herself for that!'

'She's pleased you're on the scene,' Adam said, smiling at me.

'Yeah, fresh blood for her to sink her fangs into!' laughed Stuart. I was taken aback but I tried not to show it.

For the rest of the day, we holed up at one of the hotels in town and Stuart and Adam drank the bar dry. It seemed so strange to me, the way they talked about Gladys, as if she was some kind of mother from hell. I'd been brought up to respect my elders and it never occurred to me that someone who was a grandmother could be a sinister character.

Well, I didn't care what they thought. Right now, she was my future. I wanted her to love me, to be my new family. I decided to do everything I could to make sure she accepted me.

For the next two months, Stuart and I lived in a small, unfurnished flat in Edinburgh; one of Stuart's empty properties. Stuart told me that I had to keep away from Glasgow while he got everything sorted out with Maria and that I had to stay put. But the same curfew didn't apply to him; I felt increasingly uneasy about the many nights he failed to come back to the flat.

'Where are you staying when you're not here?' I demanded, paranoid that he'd gone back to his wife.

'It's none of your fucking business,' Stuart shot back. 'A man is where he wants to be, got it? So if I'm here it's because I want to be here and when I'm not here, I'm also where I want to be.'

'Are you seeing your wife again?'

'Don't talk stupid! Why the fuck would you even ask me that? After all this shit I'm dealing with, I could do without the third degree from YOU!'

I hated him shouting at me. This wasn't how it was supposed to be. But he was my only future now. I didn't have any choice in the matter – I had to trust him. Stuart was all I had left in the world. My family was gone, my education was over and everything rested with him.

Now that we were back together as a proper couple, I thought my life with Stuart – the one he had promised me at the start – would begin. And when he announced that he was taking me away for a holiday to Rhodes in September 1985 I was so excited. This was a 'boys' trip', he warned, so I wasn't to embarrass him. Of course I agreed. Now that my family had well and truly turned their backs on me I knew I had nobody but Stuart, so I would do everything in my power to please him. It was to be our first holiday abroad as a real couple, and I thought I knew what to expect: fast cars, night-clubbing and expensive jewellery. I thought it was the start of my glamorous new life. I thought wrong.

When we arrived at the hotel, Stuart asked me to show him what I planned to wear for our first night out. I pulled out a pair of turquoise culottes and a stylish white blouse.

'For fuck's sake!' he exclaimed, shaking his head. 'We're going out to a club afterwards, not a fucking school disco. Come on, let's go get you something to wear.'

Upset at Stuart's rejection, I let him drag me downtown where he bought as many clothes that made me look like a hooker as he could find. There were short PVC miniskirts in black and red, sheer blouses in an assortment of colours to wear with my two skirts and a white PVC minidress with zips up either side. Two pairs of high heels, one white and one red.

Yuck.

'You don't need to put on underwear,' he grinned, as I squeezed myself into my new, uncomfortable plastic clothes. 'Not tonight.'

I felt a jumble of mixed feelings as Stuart led me down the stairs and out to the poolside bar to meet his friends: excited about making my appearance, but also nervous about my new attire which made me feel so awkward.

My boobs bobbed about for the whole world to see under the sheer blouse, my miniskirts rode far too far up my legs and I could barely walk in the towering stilettos. I clutched onto Stuart's arm like a baby giraffe as we entered the bar, but then he suddenly pushed me aside and headed off in the direction of raised pint glasses and the sound of his name being chanted.

Approaching the bar I noticed the four men were accompanied by five women. Five, I wondered. Why five? Stuart barely glanced in my direction as he handed me a Malibu and pineapple and he failed to make any introductions either, so I was left in the dark as to who everyone was. These women seemed sophisticated and elegant. One now had her arms draped around Stuart and was nibbling his ear as he flung his head back in laughter at what she had just whispered to him.

I tried to look away, pretending I hadn't noticed, but I felt the sting of tears behind my eyes as I realized with shame that they were lovers. *Why had he brought me here?* I wondered, as I watched them flirt in front of me. I felt humiliated but trapped by the situation.

Finally, after the fourth Malibu and pineapple I wobbled over to a seat recently vacated by a young couple and kicked off my horrendous shoes with relief. Nobody had batted an eyelid when I left. It was as if I had become invisible. As 'Reet Petite' started to blare above my head from the large black speakers, Stuart and this woman took to the dance floor.

'Hello, darling.' One of the women from our group had come over and was smiling at me sympathetically. 'My name is Pippa. I can see you're new to all of this. Why don't you let me fill you in a little?'

Nice as she was, Pippa clearly enjoyed furnishing me with all the sordid details of the last six years of the boys' trips to the Greek island. Every man was married and every woman here was his 'holiday friend'. Stuart had been seeing Susan for all this time, and she really loved him but knew he was married.

'We'd heard about you, doll,' drawled Pippa, trailing her finger in her cocktail then sucking it. 'But you're not quite what we had expected. Nice girl from the suburbs, expensive private school, all jolly hockey sticks . . .' Her voice trailed off as she looked me up and down. No, I didn't look very impressive, did I? I was a teenager in cheap PVC who resembled a hooker.

I sat alone and watched them all until it hit midnight, then I went back to the hotel room alone. Stuart stayed out and when he arrived the next day his first words to me were, 'Don't even fucking start!'

So I didn't. In fact, all I wanted to do now was go down to the beach and start soaking up the sun, but when Stuart looked through my daytime clothes, he just shook his head. Finally, he grabbed my peach one-piece and a short beach dress and flung them at me.

'Right, put these on,' he commanded. 'So we are going down to this beach where we always go. There is this bar where we will eat lunch. But not you, well, not yet. When the boys are seated and the girls have joined us you will walk towards the beach shower and start showering. What you are going to do is start peeling down your costume to your waist and start washing your tits, rubbing them for about two minutes. You're then going to take your costume off totally, ring it out and walk up to the bar, lean on the bannister where I'll be sitting and ask if there is any moussaka going. This is going to make the boys so fucking hard through their speedos it will be so fucking funny!'

I nodded. I wanted to please Stuart, I really did, and I thought this would make him happy. So when I got down to the beach and saw Stuart sitting having lunch with his pals, I started the show. I pushed the costume down to my waist and that is where it ended. I saw them all watching me, jaws dropping. I just couldn't take it off, I just couldn't, so I pulled up my costume and ran over to where Stuart was sitting and asked him what we had rehearsed.

He looked at me with cold eyes, then he took off his shirt and turned his back on me to show me the aftermath of his night with Susan. Bite marks and scratches covered his back, then Susan bent over to him and kissed his shoulder, promising that tonight she'd go easier. I was mortified and, without a word, retreated to my sunlounger with no moussaka. Ignored again, I spent the whole afternoon on my own, and eventually walked back to the hotel alone and cried myself to sleep. I didn't see Stuart again for the rest of the week. I only ate crisps, as that was all there was. There was no money. Staring at the sign above the bathroom sink, which informed me not to drink the water, I realized that I could not disobey Stuart again. I would have to do exactly what he asked of me, otherwise I wouldn't even have food, never mind the riches he had promised me. He would just starve me. I wouldn't even survive.

Meanwhile, during our trips to Guernsey, Gladys became more and more demanding. I wanted to do everything to help her so that she loved me and thought of me like a daughter, but quickly I realized that she was taking advantage.

At first she asked me to do simple things like put the Hoover round or wash the dishes and I was happy to oblige because I could see how much she struggled on her own. But, gradually, her gentle requests morphed into commands: 'Put the TV on!'

'Clean the car!'

'Weed the garden, Dawn!'

There were no 'pleases' or 'thank yous' with Gladys. She treated me like her personal slave and I soon got fed up with being ordered about.

In fact, I was getting fed up with the whole situation. I knew from telephone calls with my friend Simone that everyone was asking about me in school and they all had their plans to go to college. I was jealous. Their lives were moving on and I was getting left behind.

On one particularly awful business trip to London, Stuart

had done something so horrendous I can't even think about it now without feeling sick. We had been on our way to see an antiques dealer in north London, someone who apparently dealt in stolen goods, and I was sat in the back of Stuart's Bentley with him on my left side. In the front was Wolfie and another of Stuart's associates. They were talking about girls in that way they had – like they weren't even human beings – and I tried not to listen, instead looking out the window at the new and unfamiliar scenery.

Suddenly I heard Wolfie say, 'Go on, Stuart, take her clothes off. Let's see what this girl has that is so special. Let's see why you are prepared to lose half your wealth and give up your family for this girl. What's she got that is so great?'

Stuart turned to me idly and said, 'Take off your top and show them your tits.'

I was mortified. I didn't want these men ogling me. I shook my head, begging Stuart silently not to make me do this. But then he exploded. 'Fucking take it off and show them!'

As I looked out into the bleak day I lay my head on the coldness of the window, the sleet making it even colder. I gulped. The rush-hour traffic was at a standstill. I lifted off my top and undid my bra and closed my eyes.

'Great tits. Great tits!' said Wolfie appreciatively. Then he spoke to the driver. 'Open the window, Pete, so she's cold and her nipples go hard.'

Then, totally out of the blue, Wolfie leaned towards me and twisted my nipples until they were sore. I flinched but I didn't make a sound. I was freezing cold now as the icy air chilled my bare skin and, at the same time, I felt myself freeze inside. I knew I was powerless in this situation and there was nothing I could do, so I had to just endure it.

'Okay, Stuart, take off her jeans!' Pete called from the front seat. 'Come on, mate! Give us a proper show!'

I looked at Stuart in fear. My eyes filled with tears. *Please don't make me . . .* He just nodded and I knew I had no choice. I had to obey him or there would be hell to pay. I knew from my experience in Rhodes that I couldn't afford to piss him off. Cold wasn't as bad as hunger.

So I slipped off my jeans. The cold wrapped itself around me completely now, since all the car windows were open. The only protection against my modesty was the cigar smoke that swirled around me as both men sitting in the front kept turning around, jeering. A young man in a Vauxhaull van in the next lane thrust his hips in approval and shouted, 'Go on! Don't stop now!'

Wolfie was so excited now, he got his dick out. 'Move in the middle, darling, so we can see. Fuck! Stuart, she's so hairy!' Then he thrust his hand between my legs and I nearly screamed in shock. His rough, aggressive hand felt so alien.

'Dry as fuck!' Then he spat on his hand and rubbed me. 'Right, my old son, you gonna just look at her or fuck her?'

Stuart laughed, then he pulled his hard cock out and lifted me on to it. Straddled on him, facing the two men and with an outside audience, Stuart fucked me, quick and hard. I bounced up and down, and closed my eyes so I wouldn't have to see them watching me, watching me and wanking. Wolfie squeezed my nipples and shouted, 'I'm next!' At that Stuart came.

'No you're fucking not, Wolfie,' he growled as he zipped himself up. 'You can watch but you don't get to fuck her.'

I wriggled off Stuart and hurriedly put my clothes back on. As I did so, I looked over to see the van driver wiping himself with a Kleenex. For the rest of the journey I curled into the corner, trying desperately to forget what had just happened. Later, at the hotel, Stuart warned me not to give him any shit for 'that little performance of yours'.

'I could have let them fuck you, you got that?' he snarled. 'I could have let them all have a go, but I didn't. I protected you. So I don't want any fucking moping around from you. You're mine and you'll do as I say.'

Could I possibly go back home? I wondered now. *Have I burnt my bridges with my family?* Stuart had lured me with promises of riches and a life of idleness. He had been so kind and warm at the start, and had made me feel like the most important person in the world. Then, as my teenage crush faded, and as my friends and family all fell away, he had changed. I was his now. I had to obey him and do everything he said. And that was true because he was all I had. I chewed my fingernails, turning my situation over and over in my mind. *What if I wanted to start again? Was it possible?* I knew that it would take a lot for Mum to forgive me but I hoped that Dad, with whom I'd always had a good relationship in the past, might be able to see things my way. At the very least they might let me back in the house so that I could sit my O levels. After all, I'd left school with no qualifications whatsoever.

But just as I was beginning to think of how I could try to recover some of my old life, I got a shock. And now I knew there was no going back.

'I think I'm pregnant,' I told Stuart one day in October.

'How do you know?'

'I did a test. It was positive.' I was strangely numb about having a baby. I should have expected it; after all, Stuart had stopped using condoms months ago.

'If you and I are going to make a go of this, you have to get pregnant straight away,' he'd told me. 'So you can forget using contraception from now on.'

It hadn't been my choice but I was getting used to the fact that I didn't have choices anymore. Stuart had said that's what we needed to do in order to make the relationship work so I just went along with it at the time, never really considering what it meant. At that time, too, I would have done anything he said.

'Well, that's good,' Stuart now remarked in a businesslike tone. 'That's what we wanted, wasn't it?'

'Hmm . . .' I responded noncommittally. *Was that what* I *wanted?* I wasn't sure anymore. Stuart smiled at me then and gave me a hug. I grabbed him back, tightly: it was rare now that he gave me much affection, though we still had sex as regularly as ever, so when he threw me a bone, I lapped up his hugs and kisses like a dog.

'I hope it's a boy,' he said into my ear. He pulled back, kissed me once on the cheek, briefly, and squeezed my shoulders just a touch too hard. 'It had better be a boy.'

Chapter 8

Showdown

I lay on my bed and stroked the small bump between my hips. It was hard to believe I was now five months pregnant, but that's what the doctor had said when Stuart had finally allowed me to see a GP. At first he had kept me away from the medical professionals.

'Look, the truth is we don't know when you got pregnant,' he'd reasoned. 'If you got pregnant when you were fifteen then that's me in prison for sure. Is that what you want for me? No? Right, well, let's not go to the doctors just yet, shall we?'

I didn't mind at first, but after a while I began to worry. I needed to know that the baby was okay, that everything was normal and so, finally, I'd managed to persuade him to let me see a doctor. Since I was living in Edinburgh now there was no reason a doctor would connect me to Stuart and I wasn't about to tell them who the father was.

So I went along on my own for my first GP appointment. He measured my tummy and said I was five months gone which meant that I was due in April. Relief flooded my body – so I had definitely fallen pregnant after I turned sixteen in

May. I was pleased that I had some good news for Stuart. He'd been so grumpy recently, so hard to please.

'You'd never guess,' the doctor had remarked. 'I mean you're barely showing at all.'

It was true; I was as skinny as before. If anything, I'd lost weight in the past few months. And that's the way I wanted it. Stuart had warned me early on that if I got fat he would leave me. Besides, he planned for me to give birth in Guernsey so that our child would have Guernsey citizenship and that meant I couldn't look obviously pregnant.

He had explained it all to me one morning: 'Adam and I have talked it over and the way we see it, if you give birth in Guernsey, we can open a bank account for the child and we can keep doing business there once dear old mum pops her clogs. But they won't let in female tourists who are obviously pregnant, otherwise everyone would be at it, wouldn't they? So you've got to stay slim, got it?'

I'd felt honoured that Stuart and Adam already had plans for my baby; it made me feel important and seemed to cement my place in Stuart's world. But now, as I lay in bed in the grotty flat in Edinburgh, I felt lonely and desperately sad. Stuart hadn't been to see me in weeks. I kept hoping he would turn up but these days he didn't even get in touch himself when I needed more money; he usually sent one of his cronies to drop off some cash. They'd hand me an envelope with £30 or £50 in notes and that would have to last me for as long as possible. Once it ran out, I had to call Stuart again and then he was moody and cross for making him spend all of his money.

Apparently, things weren't going well with the business and this was why cash was tight. So I tried to make it last as long as possible. No wonder I was so thin. I barely ate! I didn't even go out much – what was there to do? I knew no one in Edinburgh and I got tired of wandering round town. Without money, it was no fun going into shops. So I spent most of my time just lying on my bed, watching TV.

Where's the fairytale I was promised? I wondered, as the now-familiar tears welled up behind my eyes. This flat was a hellhole, with broken, boarded-up windows, stained carpets, peeling wallpaper and no furniture except the TV and bed. I'd trusted Stuart to whisk me away to a life of luxury and love, that was all he had talked of as his hands had eagerly roamed my body, but there was none of that here.

More to the point, I thought, *and more importantly to me, where is Stuart?* I wanted him to stay with me – I was lonely and I missed the happy times we'd used to share – but these days I barely saw him. He kept telling me he was out there, fighting fires, trying to shore up his business so that Maria didn't fleece him in the divorce, but I didn't understand why he had to stay out every night. He said he was sleeping in the office, just to make sure she didn't try to break in and steal the files, but I was beginning to have my doubts.

Money was so tight he'd even asked me to sign on, something I would have considered unthinkable and degrading a year before. But now that Stuart was struggling to hang on to his assets, he said I had no choice: I had to try to support myself. I gave in and went to the benefits office to beg for a state hand-out. After getting a ticket and waiting on a blue plastic chair with half a dozen other miserable-looking people for ages, I was finally called to speak to a woman through a plexiglass window. Even though it was barely 10 a.m., the woman looked exhausted and harassed as she tapped on her computer.

Finally, she stopped typing and peered at me over the half-moon glasses perched on the end of her nose.

'Dawn McConnell, is it?'

I nodded.

'Your parents own a hotel, Dawn,' she said to me with a frown.

'So?'

'So you could go home, darling,' she sighed, rubbing her forehead.

'I can't go home,' I muttered.

'Right, well, can you tell me who the father is?'

I just shook my head and walked out. This was too humiliating.

'You what?' Stuart had growled after I related this encounter on the phone. 'Why the fuck did you walk out?'

'They weren't going to give me any money!' I insisted.

'For Christ's sake! I don't need this. I've got a family to take care of. I don't know why I need to give you cash as well! You better not give me a hard time because I'm getting sick of all your demands. I could leave, you know, and then you'd be totally alone. Is that what you want? You want me to leave?'

'No,' I'd said. 'No.' And 'I'm sorry'. 'I'm sorry.'

I said that more and more these days.

And I *was* sorry. Sorry for myself; sorry for this whole depressing situation. Now I stared bitterly at the Artex swirls on the ceiling, wondering: *how on earth have I got myself into this mess?* I couldn't believe how much I'd screwed up. Here I was, five months pregnant, and the man I'd thought was going to love and support me for the rest of my life barely wanted to know me. I couldn't go home now even if I'd had the courage to call Mum and Dad. I was too ashamed and embarrassed about my situation – and Stuart knew it.

All I could do was wait: wait until the baby arrived and hope that everything would get better after that.

I'd never expected to hear from my mum ever again so when Simone mentioned that my mother wanted to visit me, I was unsure. It was a bitterly cold winter day when they had bumped into each other in Glasgow town centre. Mum had heard the rumours and asked Simone to confirm if I was pregnant with Stuart's baby. Simone saw no reason to lie and that's when Mum had asked to see me.

'Oh, I don't know,' I said to Simone. 'I can't say I relish the idea of seeing my mother right now.'

'Look, she's your mum. She seemed genuinely worried about you,' said Simone. 'I think she just wants to make sure you're okay. Where's the harm in that? Just meet her once, okay?'

So I reluctantly agreed to lunch at a little Italian restaurant near Queen Street. I didn't want to take her back to the flat; I was too embarrassed at the state of the place. I wanted her to think that everything was okay, that I was fine.

When she walked in that day, nine months after I'd last seen her, she looked exactly as she always did when she was going out: smart suit, leather gloves, elegant heels and all wrapped up in a fur-trimmed coat. Her golden hair had been recently styled and set at the hairdressers and she wore a slick of red lipstick across her lips. Bundled up in my thick woollen jumper and parka, I couldn't help feeling like a child again in her presence.

'You look well,' she remarked as she sat down opposite me. 'You're pregnant?'

I nodded.

'Well, you wouldn't know it,' she said coolly. Over lunch we spoke generally about the hotel, about Dad, his drinking and how well Susy was doing in London, studying design.

'So, you're with Stuart now?' she said primly, dabbing at the corners of her mouth with her napkin.

'That's right,' I said, with a confidence I definitely did not feel. Simone had reported that he'd been seen out and about recently with Maria and it made me worry that they had got back together.

As if she could read my mind, Mum followed up with: 'Are you sure he's left his wife?'

'Of course!' I retorted.

'Are you sure he's going to support you and the baby?'

'Yes, Mum.' I sighed. 'You don't have to worry. I'm not going to come and bother you and Dad for money.'

She looked up at me sharply, one eyebrow raised, then she put down her cutlery and fixed me with one of her most scrutinizing looks.

'Dawn, are you happy?' she said carefully.

'Yes, of course I'm happy, Mum,' I insisted and then, with tremendous effort, I grinned for her. I really hoped it looked genuine. I had too much pride to admit when I was wrong.

'Well, that's all good then.' She smiled too, and picked up her cutlery again. Here we were, both of us pretending, for appearances' sake, that everything was fine. It seemed so false, so unreal.

Isn't a mother supposed to know when her sixteen-year-old daughter is struggling? I thought. *What's that thing they call it – 'a mother's instinct'? Ha! So much for that!* But there was too much water under the bridge for us to be honest with each other. Looking back now, even if she had fought to help me (which would have been very out of character) I probably would have turned her down flat, my foolish teenage pride stopping me from accepting what I so desperately needed.

I know the real reason you're here, I thought next, angrily, with my defences rising like hackles. *You just want to make sure I won't embarrass you any further. Well, don't worry, Mother dear, I won't be darkening your door again.*

My face betrayed nothing of these thoughts. I nibbled sedately at a side salad as she rambled on about her financial problems at The Drayton Arms. She said it helped that they didn't have any more school fees – naturally, with that comment she gave me a pert and meaningful look. I wanted to leave then and there, but I was too polite for that. She kissed the air either side of my cheeks when we finally got up to leave, brushed my collar and told me to look after myself.

She didn't invite me back home to visit or mention bringing Dad to see me. No, to her mind I was definitely better off out of the picture, away from the neighbours and all the gossips in Glasgow. I could see how it would have embarrassed her: the sixteen-year-old private-school dropout, now a single mum. The shame of it all! It was very convenient for her that I was out of the way in Edinburgh. I wasn't her responsibility any-more and that suited her just fine. I watched her walk away, the click-clack of her heels fading as she went out of sight.

That night, I felt more lonely and isolated than ever before. Nobody wanted to know me, not even my own family. And Simone had more bad news for me – she'd heard through Fergus that Stuart and Maria were back on and now running a pub together in Glasgow. Fergus was telling everyone at school how embarrassing it was that his parents were like a pair of love-struck teenagers again, smooching and holding hands in public.

Of course, Stuart denied it all when I confronted him. He said it was lies, utter nonsense and I should know better than to listen to idle gossip. But the rumours simply wouldn't go away and my confusion and misery grew by the day. So, finally, I decided to find out the truth for myself.

It was raining heavily on Valentine's Day 1986 as I stood in Princes Street to hail down a taxi – the kind of horizontal rain that hits you from every angle. Within minutes I was soaked, but I held tight to the wad of notes in my pocket. I had been saving my money for weeks now, only spending £20 a week on food, and now I handed over the lot to a taxi driver so that he could drop me at the pub in Glasgow that Stuart denied even hearing about, let alone owning.

For two hours, we drove through the beating rain and hazardous fog and I fixed my mind on Stuart, on the father of my child, on the man I had given up everything for. Christmas had come and gone while I stayed home alone. Now it was Valentine's Day: *he should be with me*, I thought. He hadn't called or contacted me recently at all – so where was he? One way or another, I knew I needed to know the truth, as painful as it might be.

The taxi pulled up at last and I lumbered out into the rain. For a moment, I stood outside the pub, listening to the noise from the boisterous crowds inside. *Am I really going to do this?*

I had worn my tight jeans, the ones that showed off my baby bump, and a polo-neck sweater. My hands were shaking but there was no going back now. I pushed open the large wooden doors.

Inside, a party was in full swing, red heart-shaped balloons decorating the bar, couples were dancing while 'That's Amore' blasted through the stereo speakers. Less romantically, drunken women puffed on their fags and shrieked over the music while old blokes leered at them. I stood there for a moment, just looking around. It seemed no one had noticed me come in.

I walked towards the bar – and that's when I spotted the two of them, Stuart and Maria, serving customers from behind the bar while their son collected glasses. She was laughing and he was smiling at her warmly. Then he bent down and kissed the top of her head.

It looked so natural, so affectionate. There was no mistaking the affection in that tiny, tender moment. Nobody else clocked it, nobody else even saw it, but in that moment of intimacy I felt all my hopes and dreams evaporate. With one last exhausted sigh, I knew it was over.

Maria's eyes scanned the room and that's when they met mine. Instantly, her smile disappeared and the colour fled from her face. Stuart had been talking to one of the customers, but when he saw Maria freeze, his eyes followed hers and he too stopped dead.

From then on, everything seemed to happen in slow motion. I didn't feel anger or pain. I didn't feel anything at all. It was just as I had suspected for some time and now the truth was out, I felt calm. I hardly even noticed as Stuart lifted up the hatch of the bar, grabbed my arm and marched me back outside. His wife was right behind him, and their son behind her.

'You told me it was over!' Maria yelled at him once we were outside. 'You said she was out of the picture completely!

What the fuck is she doing here?' She turned to me: 'What are you doing here?'

In answer, I opened my coat.

There was silence. For a moment Maria just stood there, open-mouthed, not quite able to process what she was seeing. It was obvious to me that Stuart had been lying to us both.

'You're pregnant?' she finally stammered. 'She's pregnant, Stuart? IS SHE FUCKING PREGNANT, STUART, WITH YOUR FUCKING BABY?'

'What are you doing here?' Stuart demanded, shaking me by the arm.

I didn't speak, just stood there as the rain beat against my face and the wind wrapped itself around me like a blanket. I felt frozen inside. There was nothing left for me to say. He had betrayed me; he was a coward. He had deliberately got me pregnant and then gone back to his wife. He didn't even have the guts to tell me it was over. He had just treated me like crap, assuming I would get fed up of him. But I had caught him out in this monstrous charade and now I knew I could never trust him again.

'Yes, I'm pregnant.' I spoke to Maria in a calm voice, shrugging off Stuart's hand. 'I'm due in about two months but now that I know how Stuart feels about the whole situation, I think I'll be better off on my own.'

Maria seemed too perplexed to speak so I went on, now addressing Stuart: 'If you'll kindly give me £115 for the taxi fare back to Edinburgh I'll be on my way.'

I looked him up and down. His mouth was opening and shutting like a fish, but no words came out. He was pathetic. He'd lied to me over and over again and she could have him!

'I don't want him now,' I said tonelessly. 'I don't even like him anymore.'

My words seemed to break her. Maria burst into tears and flung herself at Stuart's chest, beating on him and screaming out: 'You bastard! You fucking bastard!'

'Wait, Maria. Please . . . Please, Maria!'

'No, Stuart! NO! You can get stuffed. I've had it.' And with that she straightened up and looked at me, her face a picture of misery. 'I don't want him either. You're welcome to him.' Then she turned and stomped back into the pub, Fergus following her.

Nearly seven months pregnant, I had no education and no place to live. I was the very person my mum had warned me I would become. I was too exhausted mentally to worry about Maria, who at least had a roof over her head and food on the table. She could also drive, while I didn't even have the bus fare to get back to Edinburgh.

For a moment, neither Stuart nor I moved. What would he do now? Would he run after her or stay with me? Who did he really want?

I didn't much care either way now. I just needed to get back because I was so cold and wet. The way it was all unfolding, it didn't feel like my life at all, more like a movie I was watching from the outside. I was detached, watching it all take place around me, almost like I'd had to do when I was twelve, when John had snuck into my room and forced himself on me.

'Oh fuck!' Stuart said now, bitterly. I watched his mouth form the words, feeling nothing. Then he looked at me. 'Well, come on then. I'm not forking out a hundred fucking quid on a taxi. I'll drop you back.'

Neither of us spoke on the return journey to Edinburgh. I just stared out of the window, watching the orange street-lights flash past. There was nothing between us now: no feelings, no love. Nothing. It had been a fling to him, that was all. I got it now. He had used me for sex and now it was over, he just wanted me to disappear.

How stupid I'd been! And how much I hated this man sitting next to me. I had seen him now for the weak, pathetic individual that he was. Well, there was nothing else for it now: I had to have this baby and then try to figure out what to do next.

Stuart drove us both back to the flat and he stayed over that night because it was too late for him to leave. The next day, he took me to a Chinese restaurant for lunch.

'You've probably just cost me millions with your little stunt back there,' he said as he guzzled down mouthfuls of special fried rice and noodles. Of course, it was all my fault!

There was no apology, no admission of guilt. I could barely eat. All night long, I had lain awake planning what I would do. I felt nothing for this baby growing inside me and I didn't want to be a teenage single mum – so there was only one way forward. I had decided I would put the child up for adoption once it was born. There was no other way.

In the meantime, without any other means of support, I had no choice but to stick with Stuart, but it was purely out of financial necessity. I had nowhere else to go.

After lunch, Stuart opened his wallet and took out two fifty-pound notes: 'Here, this is all I've got. It will have to last you because I won't be coming back this way for a while. The business is probably fucked and I've probably lost everything. You don't know how these things work – I was trying to play happy fucking families so she wouldn't try and fuck me over. But I guess that's all blown out of the water now. So just . . . just lay low. Okay? I don't need any more fucking dramas for now.'

The next time I saw Stuart was the beginning of March when he picked me up from the flat and drove me to the airport. He handed me a flight ticket to Guernsey and a little blue jewellery box with a pretty pearl ring inside that brought tears to my eyes when I saw it.

'Good luck,' he said, as he waved me off at the departure gate. 'Just do what Mum says and you should be fine. I'll see you on the other side.'

Chapter 9

My Black Eyed Boy

'Please let me call the ambulance, Gladys! I really think I'm in labour.'

It was 8 a.m. on 12 April 1986 and I was lying in bed after a night of being sick in the toilet and now the tops of my thighs were killing me.

'My legs are hurting,' I called out.

'What are you talking about?' Gladys grumbled from her bed on the other side of the room. We'd been sharing her bedroom for the past four weeks and I was sick of running around after her. She seemed not to notice that I was nine months pregnant!

'You don't get sore legs when you're in labour,' she went on. 'Why would you have sore legs?'

'I don't know!' I replied. 'I haven't given birth before, have I?'

I'd never been to any antenatal classes. I didn't even have a book on pregnancy or giving birth. The only time I had seen a doctor was when I was four months pregnant so I was completely in the dark about how this was meant to go. The plan was just to turn up at the hospital when I was due to give birth.

'Look, have your waters broken?' Gladys asked.

'What does that mean?'

'Is your bed wet?'

'No. But my legs are so sore.'

'Listen, dearie, my legs have been sore for twenty fucking years. I've got chronic arthritis and I'm on a Zimmer so don't tell me about sore legs! Now stop whining and make me a cup of tea!'

Somehow, I managed to heave myself off the bed. I was very big now so I waddled to the kitchen, made Gladys a tea, took it through to her and then got dressed and went downstairs. It was the middle of April and I was due to give birth this week, according to the doctor I'd seen. It couldn't come soon enough! I was fed up being so big, fed up living with Gladys and her endless demands and fed up waiting for this baby to come out.

Stuart hadn't been to see me the whole time I'd been here, though we'd talked on the phone and he'd said he'd be by my side the moment the baby came out. Despite everything, I hoped so. I was scared and although I still had my dreams of putting the baby up for adoption and starting over, I had no idea if I could do it alone. With my hormones flying all over the place and my fear of the future sky-high, despite myself and my big ideas, as the birth grew closer, my naive sixteen-year-old self held onto the faint hope that everything would be fine once the baby arrived.

The night before, I'd complained to Gladys that I was bored to death of being pregnant and I wished the baby would just hurry up and come.

'I know how to get this baby out,' Gladys had told me. 'You need a bottle of castor oil, fresh orange juice, a curry and some wine. Then you'll definitely give birth!'

So we went out for a curry and Gladys ordered me a chicken vindaloo which burned like fire all the way down my throat. Then she made me drink the cheap red wine we'd bought from the off-licence. By the time we were on our way home, I was already feeling queasy but Gladys wasn't finished with me yet. Next she'd ordered me to mix half a glass of castor oil with half a glass of orange juice.

'Drink that!' she'd ordered.

'I can't drink it!' I'd giggled drunkenly as I watched the two liquids separate in the glass. It looked and smelled disgusting. So Gladys got a spoon and mixed the drink up, swirling it round and round until the two liquids had formed a sort of brown gloop.

'Now drink it!' she shouted. 'Quickly!'

I knocked it all back and half an hour later I was violently sick in the toilet. In fact, I'd spent most of the night with my head down the loo, Gladys cackling away like an old witch.

Now, at 11 a.m. the following morning, I still felt as rough as anything. Gladys eventually got up and dressed and came hobbling into the living room. I begged her once more to call the ambulance and, finally, she agreed. We arrived at the hospital at 11.20 a.m. and the midwife checked me over.

'I'm afraid you're only three centimetres dilated,' she said.

'What does that mean?'

'It means you could be here for hours.'

'But I'm in labour?'

'Yes, but the very early stages. Why don't you go through to the waiting room and get yourself a coffee?'

I shuffled back into the waiting room where Gladys was sitting, peeling hard-boiled sweets from their wrappers. She gave me a questioning look.

'They say it could be hours. I'm getting a hot chocolate.'

'Tea for me,' she said as she popped a bright yellow sweet in her mouth. I waddled over to the machine and took out some change. Just as I was putting the money into the machine, I felt a warm, flowing sensation down my legs. I looked down, horrified to see I was leaking water everywhere.

'Oh dear,' I breathed. 'Gladys! Something's happened! I think it's the waters breaking. Oh God, Gladys! Do you think I should clean it up?'

I felt so embarrassed at the mess I was making but the nurses and midwives swung into action. They put me in a wheelchair and whisked me straight through to the delivery ward. There, they measured me again. Now, I was eight centimetres dilated, which surprised everyone because apparently it was very unusual to go from three to eight in under ten minutes. I didn't care about their stupid numbers, all I knew was that I was now in agony.

'Can I get something for the pain?' I begged the nurse as they laid me down on the bed. There were people everywhere now. They had put some pads on my stomach to measure the pain.

'No, your pain levels are very low, just a two on the scale,' she said. 'You only get pain relief if it's over seven. Relax, you'll be okay.'

'But it's very painful . . .' I couldn't go on. There was a heaving sensation in my stomach and bile filled my mouth. I turned my head to the side and threw up all over the floor.

'Did you have a curry last night?' someone asked. *Christ!* I could have died from shame. Even I could smell the curry and the castor oil. The pain came again and, once again, I was sick over the side of the bed.

'You've given birth . . . to a little boy!' someone announced.

'What?' I said groggily, wiping the spit from the corner of my mouth. 'Already? While I was throwing up?'

A minute later, Gladys came in.

'You look alright for being in labour,' she remarked with a grin.

'Gladys, I've had it. I've had the baby.'

'I hope it's a bloody boy or they can put it back.'

'Yeah, it is a boy.'

'Oh thank goodness! We'll call him Stuart Michael.'

'No, we're not calling him Stuart Michael.'

'Well, whatever. So where is he then?'

Strangely enough, I hadn't even thought about where the baby was.

'Just coming . . .' called out a midwife. 'We're just cleaning him up. You won't believe this but she gave birth while she was being sick! She didn't even feel him coming out!'

'Aye, that's because she drank a bottle of castor oil last night. He slipped out!'

'Really? Oh dear, that's really not advisable . . .'

Someone had pushed up the bed so now I was sitting up and, finally, the midwife placed a little bundle into my arms. My son. I looked at him – he had a strange, squashy face and a mass of dark, curly hair.

For a moment, I was confused. Was this my baby? Really? I felt like giving him back. Stuart hadn't even made an appearance, and there was no family showing any interest in my predicament. What was I really doing? I was so consumed with how, at sixteen, I would survive and look after myself that I couldn't imagine how to do it for two people. I didn't have a plan for me, let alone another person who really couldn't look after themselves. His eyelids flickered open and now all I could see were big black eyes. *Oh my God, he looks like Damien from* The Omen*! I thought. Where did those black eyes come from? I've got grey eyes and Stuart's are blue.*

'Why are his eyes black?' Gladys asked sharply. I just shrugged. I couldn't speak. I couldn't quite believe any of this was real. After all, at sixteen, I was just a baby myself.

'Come on,' the midwife said. 'Let's get you onto the ward, shall we?'

She took the baby away and helped me off the bed. Just as I was edging my way towards the wheelchair, I felt something fall out of me.

'Ahhh!' I screamed. 'What's that? Is it another one?'

'No, that's the afterbirth.' The midwife smiled reassuringly. 'Don't worry, it's perfectly normal.'

They put us on a nice ward with several other new mums and over the next few days, I watched from my bed as throngs of visitors came and went from the ward: husbands, parents, older children, brothers, sisters, nieces, nephews and friends. The noise levels rose and sank with every new batch of arrivals and there was a great deal of cooing and clucking among the women.

But it was strangely quiet on my side of the ward; my only visitor was Gladys. It gave me time to get to know my son a little better. The adoption option was very much at the forefront of my mind. But with all the nurses and midwifes constantly reminding me how wonderful motherhood was and how privileged I was, I hardly had the opportunity to discuss adoption with anyone. Luckily, my little boy latched on quite easily so I figured I would breastfeed him. It seemed like a lot less hassle than faffing about with bottles. That first day, I managed to hobble over to the payphone.

'I've had the baby,' I told my mum on the phone. 'A little boy. He was born at midday.'

'Congratulations, Dawn,' she said. 'How was the birth?'

'Everything was fine. It only took half an hour. He weighs eight pounds exactly. The nurses say we're both doing well.'

'That's good. I'm glad you're both healthy.'

And that was that. She didn't ask when I was coming back or when she could see him. I could sense her disappointment in me from hundreds of miles away. I knew I was a failure in her eyes, a miserable failure. I slowly replaced the handset and hobbled back to bed.

Over the next few days, the nurses were great, showing me how to hold, feed and bathe my son. I wanted to call him Callum – it was a name I'd always loved – so I just started calling him that and everyone else did too. He was a sweet little baby and I liked him well enough, but I could see I didn't have the same bond that the other mums on the ward had with their newborns. *Is there something wrong with me?* I wondered. These women seemed smitten but to me, Callum was just like a cute puppy. Nice enough – but not terribly interesting. I couldn't see how our futures might fit together.

Three days after the birth, Stuart arrived. I sensed immediately that things weren't much better between us; in fact they seemed worse than ever.

'Where is he then?' Stuart demanded and I pointed to the

Perspex cot next to my bed, where our son was sleeping soundly. He looked at him and nodded a couple of times.

'I've named him Callum,' I said.

'Right, well, when you get out of here we'll get his birth certificate sorted out,' he said as he pulled up a chair to sit by my bed. For a while he just sat next to me, elbows on his knees, hands clasped together in front of him, rocking. It was obvious he didn't want to be here. Once, I had felt I could tell him anything, but now we had nothing to say.

I noted he was wearing a new black-and-white leather jacket.

New clothes? I thought. *That's odd. Why is he buying himself new clothes? I thought he was broke.*

'So, Mum tells me everything went fine,' he said eventually. 'And you're breastfeeding? That's good. It'll help your stomach to go down.'

I felt awkward and uncertain as he stared at the other mums on the ward. He didn't seem interested in me at all and I didn't know what to say to engage him.

'Look, erm, not many people know about the baby right now,' he started.

'Why not?'

'Well, it just wouldn't help with the divorce, would it? But I've bought a flat in Glasgow for us to stay in when you come back and I'm trying to stay on good terms with Maria to make everything go smoothly. We had a meeting the other day.'

'Why did you need to have a meeting with her?' I asked quickly. I'd thought things were finished between them.

'Oh, you're not going to start giving me a hard time, are you?' he snapped at me. His anger sprang up so quickly I was cowed into silence.

As we sat together, saying nothing, I thought over what he'd said – about the flat in Glasgow he'd bought for us. Sadly, it reminded me a little of our old plans. I'd been so determined after catching him out in his lies to try to make my life my own after the baby was born – but, as I looked at Callum in his crib, I realized that I now had no control over my life anymore. What could I do? I was only sixteen, I had nobody I could turn to and no one I could rely on. Though it was Stuart who had put me in this position, he was also the only one offering help: a place to stay, a future of sorts. It felt like I had no choice but to do as I was told.

Twenty minutes later, he was gone. He hadn't even picked up his son.

A few days afterwards, Stuart came to take me back to his mother's house; I needed another week to recover before I could fly back to Scotland. We registered the birth and then he insisted all three of us go to the pub, to wet the baby's head.

It was all smoky in there. I was sure it wasn't good for the baby, but Stuart insisted we stay so that he could have a pint. Finally, we got back to Gladys's – she was out shopping. Clocking the empty house, no sooner had Stuart put down the cot in the living room than he turned to me and said: 'Right, come on, let's get your clothes off.'

Really? He wanted *sex*?

'What? Now?' I asked quietly, taken aback. Before the birth, as my body had grown fatter, he'd left me on my own, not even visiting the flat in Edinburgh for weeks at a time. He had made it very clear that his attraction to me visually was very important. Now, it seemed he wanted to get back to 'normal'.

135

'Did you know that sex is the first thing women refuse when they have children, did you know that?' said Stuart evenly. 'You're not refusing me, are you?'

I felt so weak, but at the same time I didn't want to upset him. His anger frightened me and it seemed his fuse was shorter than ever.

'I'm really sore,' I began, trying to plead my case. 'It hurts when I go to the toilet to pee. I don't think I want this right now. Not yet.'

'I'm not asking you to *think*,' said Stuart crossly, yanking me into the bedroom and closing the door. 'You haven't had stitches, so you have nothing to worry about.'

It was the same situation it had always been. Why did I think I should have any say over what happened to my body? I should have known better than to speak out against his demands. After all, I had learned from a young age: when men wanted to have sex with me, it happened, no matter what I wanted or what I said.

Stuart undressed me and then pushed me down onto the bed, where he had rough, painful sex with me. It was so sore, I could barely move. I just lay there, obediently, cowed into place. How had the last two months of my life spiralled out of control? The one thing that I thought I had control over Stuart with was sex – now he didn't care about my feelings. There was no life in his eyes, no passion, no excitement. He was hurting me and he had never done that before. It was almost as if he was punishing me for giving birth and putting him in the situation he was now in. That was it – he was punishing me for his situation, and he was certainly letting me know.

I woke up in the dark four hours later in terrible pain,

alone, with a crying baby. The sheets were covered in blood. There was a note on the sideboard: 'Gone to the pub with Mum. Make sure you clean these sheets. If there ever is a "next time", make an effort!'

Chapter 10

Neither Here Nor There

A week later, I arrived back in Edinburgh. Stuart was waiting for me in the airport arrivals hall, leaning casually against a pillar, spinning his car keys around on his finger. As I struggled through with my two-week-old son, the carrycot and all the other baby stuff, he didn't make a move to come and help. On the contrary, as I got nearer, he turned and moved away so that I had to follow him. There was no kiss on the cheek to welcome me home; no sign of excitement at seeing his son.

This does not bode well, I thought.

In the car, he barely spoke. It was more than I could bear so after fifteen minutes I blurted out: 'Why are you so quiet?'

There was a slight, uncomfortable pause. Then Stuart turned to me and said: 'I'm back with Maria.'

It was a shock and I burst out crying.

'Look,' he said. 'Maria and I have talked this over. We've agreed to let you stay in the flat until you get on your feet and we'll give you fifty quid a week for expenses. That should see you through until you sign on for housing benefit.'

He was so cold, so calculating – he had it all worked out.

'I'm not staying in your flat,' I sniffed angrily.

'Yeah, you are!'

'No, I'm not.'

'Look, you've just had a baby, all your hormones are hay-wire. Give it a thought, but I'm back with my wife.'

I couldn't speak; I was crying too hard. That was it. I was officially a loser, a dreg of society who would soon be leaching off everyone else, claiming benefits. Everyone who had said 'I told you so' was right. I could see my mum and dad's faces now, the regulars of the hotel shaking their heads as they stared into their pints, commiserating with Dad's story. What a let-down I'd been, how much promise I had shown, how I had thrown it all away. And, to top it all, Stuart had lied to me and I had fallen for it! He clearly didn't care about his son or what became of him, and just wanted rid of us as quickly as possible.

'Ah, for fuck's sake, Dawn!' He lost his temper. 'You *knew* I was married and you tried to trap me by having my baby but it's not going to work!'

Through my heaving sobs, his words sank in and left me stunned. *I* tried to trap *him*? He was the one who had insisted on not wearing condoms and trying for a child!

'I'm back with my wife,' he went on, talking down to me patronizingly as if I was a child. 'It was always going to happen. You're young and we have nothing in common. I already have a family and you knew this. So we had our little fling and now it's over. I want you to stay at the flat, stay away from us and everything will be fine. I let you put my name on the birth certificate – but don't think it means anything. GOD, STOP CRYING!'

He hit the steering wheel in frustration and I was shocked into silence.

Without another word, he drove me to his new flat – this was where we were meant to be starting our new life together. Instead, I was now a single parent with no money, no prospects and no qualifications. It couldn't get any worse.

'Right, I'm off,' he said after taking the cot upstairs.

'Where?'

'Dawn, you don't need to know where I go anymore because we're not together. But, actually, if you must know, I'm off to Amsterdam with Maria; we need a holiday and now that you're back in town, we need to get away from all the eyes.'

It was like my insides had been cut up. I just didn't know what to do anymore. I wanted to run away from everything – but I couldn't because now I had a two-week-old baby to look after. At every point in our relationship together, Stuart had convinced me to do things that just made my life worse and worse. To sleep with him; to stop studying; to have a baby when I wasn't much more than a child myself. He'd broken every promise he'd ever made and his latest attempt to rewrite history, accusing me of tricking him into having the baby, made me realize once and for all that I'd run out of options with him.

But without Stuart, where could I go?

There was only one thing for it.

'Dawn?' Dad answered the phone at the hotel.

'Dad,' I said in a very small voice. 'Dad, I'm in Glasgow. I'm not with Stuart though – that's over. Will you come and get me because I've got to get out of here?'

'Course I will.'

Dad didn't say anything when he came to collect me that

afternoon. It was the middle of the week, mid-afternoon, so there was nothing much on at the hotel. Mum was shopping in town so she didn't know anything yet.

'So, where's ma grandson, then?'

I showed Dad up the stairs, to where Callum was sleeping soundly.

'He's got a really big nose, hasn't he?'

Dad didn't say anything else, just carried all my things into his battered old Saab. It was bad enough getting taken home by Dad, having to admit I needed help, but when I walked back into the family home, I was enveloped by a crushing sense of failure. Here I was, back in my old room with my old single bed, surrounded by all my old things. It felt like walking back in time – but everything had changed.

'So, has the penny dropped, love?' asked Dad with a twinkle in his eye. I just nodded sadly, feeling a sob welling up inside.

'Here, come here,' he said and wrapped me in a big bear hug. 'Don't worry, Dawn. It'll be alright. It'll all come right in the end.'

Later, when I heard Mum's key in the door, I felt myself tense up. At first, though, she seemed genuinely happy to see me and to meet her grandson.

'Oh he's lovely,' she cooed at him. 'What are you doing here, Dawn?'

Dad answered for me: 'She's moved back. I picked her up this afternoon. She's not with him anymore. She's with us now.'

I could see that this did not sit well with Mum. She pursed her lips, blinked a couple of times and said slowly: 'I see . . .'

Then she straightened up and put a hand on her hip: 'Well,

I'm not looking after him if that's what you were thinking. Don't think you're coming home for an easy ride. You'll have to work; you'll have to earn your keep.'

Here we go . . . I knew my mother and I knew she was only just getting started.

'Don't think I'm going to babysit him,' she went on shrilly. 'And you, young lady. You'll have to figure out what you're going to do with your life.'

'We don't need this conversation now,' I said hesitantly, trying to keep the peace. 'You just walked through the door.'

'We *do* need this conversation – otherwise when are we going to have it?'

'Urgh, forget it. I'm going to my room!'

As I stormed off, I felt every one of my sixteen years, but I was no longer a typical teenager.

It was strange living with my parents again. So many things were just as I had left them, when I'd gone off to London with my head full of dreams that Stuart had planted there. But so many things were different, too. Now there were four of us, with Callum.

Luckily, he was a very good baby. He slept soundly in my bed from the very start, didn't cry much and never seemed to get ill or nappy rash. He couldn't have been easier but, even so, I struggled to show him the love I knew he deserved. After everything I had been through, I didn't know if having Callum had been the worst mistake of my life; when I looked at him, I saw only a lifetime of drudgery ahead.

I told myself firmly not to get too attached – after all, if I was going to try and pick up the pieces of my ruined life, I would have to have him adopted. With Stuart out of the picture, my head cleared and I returned to what I thought was a sensible, straightforward plan. I knew I couldn't go back to school as a single mum, it just wouldn't work. My parents were pretty resolute about not helping me, refusing to take him for a couple of hours here and there, so adoption seemed the only answer. Mum had made it very clear that he was my responsibility alone, and as for Dad, well, he'd hardly been a model parent the first time round!

My parents stuck rigidly to their working routine at the hotel, which meant I was stuck at home pretty much all day and night. The highlight of my day was usually when Simone dropped in after school.

Simone adored Callum. Her eyes lit up whenever she saw him and she loved to pick him up and plant soft little kisses all over his head. Frequently she turned up with little Baby-gros for him because she loved to dress him up. I often thought she was more motherly than me.

Together, we'd stroll through the park with Callum in his buggy and stop at the gates for ice cream. One day, on the way back from getting ourselves a 99 each, I confided in her about my plans to have him adopted.

'Oh, but you can't!' she said, wide-eyed. 'He's adorable. How could you abandon him like that?'

'I'm not abandoning him,' I said defensively. 'I can't look after him on my own. What am I supposed to do? Stuart doesn't want him. My parents don't want him. How am I meant to provide for him if I've got no qualifications? I mean, what choice do I have?'

As far as Callum was concerned, Stuart had more than once reminded me on that journey home in the car from the airport that he didn't really want to get involved with a child that age. 'When he's about two, he'll be more interesting and have his character,' he'd said. He thought his input for a child so young would be a waste of his time. 'When the boy is old enough to know who I am I'll catch up with him,' he told me.

One morning I came downstairs late, just as Mum was putting down the phone.

'That was him,' she said, gesturing at the telephone.

'Who?' I asked, groggy after a sleepless night with Callum.

'Stuart! I told him not to call again!'

The calls continued though. Stuart would always call in the mornings because he knew that my mum would be at the hotel doing the breakfasts. She had made her feelings about Stuart pretty clear from the start.

'I don't want you speaking to him. Don't take anything from him. Cut your ties with him completely.' Of course, she had seen all this coming. But although she thought I'd been foolish, she still despised Stuart for stringing me along and leaving me alone with his baby.

And then, one afternoon, *I* answered the phone in the hallway.

'Please don't hang up!' said Stuart at once.

'What do you want?'

'I'm so sorry, Dawn.' His next words made my mouth drop open in surprise. 'Look, I've made the biggest mistake of my life. I still love you. I want to be with you. I only went back to Maria to save the business but she's tricked me and I can't believe I fell for her plan. It was all a big mistake. I'm so sorry, Dawn. I've left her for good now.' And then he wheeled out an old trick: 'I promise.'

'I don't believe you,' I replied dully. I'd heard his lines too many times before.

'It's true. I *promise*.'

'Yeah, well, even if it is, I don't want to see you again. I hate you. You've been horrible to me and you lied to me. It's over, Stuart. I'm going to put Callum up for adoption, then I'm going back to school.'

There was a strange noise on the line then. Was he *crying*? I couldn't believe it. He'd only seen Callum for a few hours his whole life. He had no bond with him at all.

Even so, he said: 'You can't put Callum up for adoption.'

'I can. I'm only sixteen and I'm not going to be a single parent.'

'I love you, Dawn. And I want to get back with you and I want us all to be a family together.'

'How can I trust you?'

'I give you my word,' he said solemnly. '*Please*, Dawn. *Please* give me one last chance. I won't let you down again, I *promise*. *Please*.'

Is this the truth? After so many lies and let-downs I wondered if I could truly trust him. But he was begging me – I could hear his desperation and his passion even on the phone. I felt the armour I had built up around me start to crack.

And it wasn't just Stuart's words that were chiselling at me, wearing my defiance and my determination down. In the past few weeks, Callum and I had become much closer: I was starting to fall for his cheeky little smiles and the way he held his pudgy hands out for cuddles. I was starting to miss him when he was asleep, and had to fight the urge to wake him up. The past few weeks, I had finally admitted to myself that I didn't really want to put Callum up for adoption. I just hadn't thought that there was any way of keeping him on my own.

Could we really make this work? I wondered. Despite all the lies from Stuart, deep down I wanted this more than ever. I wanted to keep my little boy, I really did, and part of me still longed for that happy-ever-after that Stuart had once promised me. Hearing him beg for my forgiveness, his voice soft and kind, like it used to be, brought it all back to me. I played with the telephone cord, thinking it over.

'Okay,' I said reluctantly, in the end. 'One last chance.'

My bags were packed when Mum and Dad returned from the hotel that night. I'm not sure how I thought my parents would react. Dad laughed when I told him and shook his head, amused by the absurdity of it all. But Mum glowered at me, hardly able to believe my stupidity.

'Don't call us again,' she warned. Then she kissed the top of Callum's sleeping head and walked away.

When Stuart picked me up that night he explained that he had taken steps to ensure Maria couldn't get her hands on his money. It was all now safely locked away in Adam's name in a company in Panama. He laughed as he bragged that she wouldn't get a penny and I laughed along with him. We moved into the flat in Glasgow that he'd planned for us to live in after Callum was born.

From the word go, Stuart made it clear he wasn't going to be a hands-on dad.

'Don't even ask me to change a nappy!' he announced as he threw the baby bags down on the floor that evening. 'It's absolutely disgusting! That's a mother's thing.' But I'd been coping on my own ever since Callum had been born; I was used to changing nappies and doing everything else by myself. I took it all in my stride as I took in my surroundings: our new home.

Our flat was actually very nice. Stuart had bought some lovely furniture from Heal's, too. He impressed on me that we had to keep the place tidy because he was going to be bringing his business pals back from time to time. As I settled in, though, it became clear that he spent most of his days at his new pub.

In May I turned seventeen but, still, I couldn't go into the pub because I was underage. So I stayed at home most days with the baby while Stuart went out into the world.

'Once you're eighteen, Dawn, we'll get you into work,' Stuart had assured me. 'You won't be bored at home all day, I promise.'

One morning, about two months after we moved back in together, he left for the day while Callum and I lingered in bed, listening to Madonna sing 'Papa Don't Preach'. For the first time in ages, I felt content with my life. So I lay back on the bed and lifted Callum above my head. Then I brought him down and blew a raspberry on his tummy to make him laugh.

'Shall we go out for a walk?' I asked him and he giggled some more. 'Shall we . . . go for an ice cream!'

I placed him in his cot, took a quick shower and then we left the house. For a few pleasant hours, I pushed him round town. Now that Stuart and I were back together and he seemed to have sorted out his business problems, I was given money to spend on Callum, so that day I bought him a couple of new tops.

As I wheeled the buggy into our road, I was surprised to see Stuart's car in the car park, but genuinely happy. *Perhaps we could go out shopping together*, I thought, *or go out for dinner this evening?*

I bumped Callum up the three flights of stairs, opened our front door, and then reversed into our flat, excited at seeing Stuart in the middle of the day. Then . . .

Bang!

The punch to the side of my head sent me reeling sideways. Luckily, Callum was still in the pram so he didn't even see what had happened. I staggered for a moment, then righted myself and looked around. But I couldn't see him anywhere. My head ached with pain from slamming off the door frame and, since the pain was so sharp, I checked my head for blood. Nothing. The swelling came up immediately; a massive egg on the side of my head, hidden under my hair, was throbbing. I was okay. I was stunned and shocked but I had more important concerns. Callum – was he safe? My instinct as a mother took over and all my pain was shoved to one side for that moment.

Where is he? Where is Stuart? Shit! What do I do now?

Carefully, and very quietly, I lifted Callum out of his buggy and put him down in the cot in the bedroom, wanting him to be safe. But the room offered no comfort: the wardrobe-door mirror was smashed to pieces.

My heart was beating like crazy now. The living room door was ajar so I knew Stuart must be through there; he must have punched me and then, while I was still reeling, gone through to wait for me. I stood outside the door for a moment, wondering how to behave. *How is one meant to act after getting punched?* I thought frantically. *Do I storm in and shout: 'What is your problem?'*

No, no: I don't have the guts to do that. Walk in normally and greet him with a kiss and a hug, ignoring the punch?

Or sneak in unnoticed? But that would be hard to do.

The TV wasn't on, which wasn't normal for Stuart. *Shit. Shit. Shit. What's he planning?* I felt myself start to shake, so I made myself take a deep breath and then I counted to ten in my head: *One . . . Two . . . Three . . . Four . . . Five . . . Six . . . Seven . . . Eight . . . Nine . . . Ten. Enter!*

The bottle of red wine whizzed past my head and smashed onto the wall. I ducked just in time and looked around to see Stuart sitting in the centre of the blood-red chesterfield, his face like thunder. He glared at me, his chin resting on his hands, which were holding something, and his foot tapping away uncontrollably.

What's that he's clutching in his hands? I wondered. I looked closer. *My knickers? Why is he clutching my knickers?* I was lost now. *What's happened?*

He got up and went to the bathroom. Then, without warning, he stormed back in the room and quickly punched me in the stomach. I doubled up in pain. He grabbed me by the hair and dragged me back down towards the ground, so that I was on all fours. And he led me like that towards the bathroom. The pants he'd been holding were now on the floor and he pushed my face towards them.

'I brought a business partner back here today,' he growled, his voice full of menace. 'And he needed the bathroom, and guess what he found when he got there? Your filthy, dirty pants on the floor!' And with that he smashed my head into the bath panel, then pulled my head up so fast I fell over backwards.

149

'And what's this?' he bellowed. 'WHAT THE FUCK IS THIS?'

There was a dirty nappy that had been folded up and left in the corner of the bathroom.

'ARE YOU TRYING TO EMBARRASS ME?'

Releasing me from his grip, with his head angled away from the smell he bent down and opened the nappy.

'You want to act like a dog? Well, you know what happens to dogs when they mess, they get their nose shoved in it.'

Now he wrapped my hair around his hand so I couldn't pull away and shoved my head into the dirty nappy on the floor, over and over again. I tried to resist, but he was far too strong for me. Callum was now crying and the contents of his used nappy were up my nose and in my mouth. Clumps of baby poo stuck to my hair and face. Over and over again, Stuart pushed my face into the nappy until eventually he shoved so hard that the nappy ripped and my nose scraped on the floor.

Finally, he let go, pushing my head away.

Ow! I felt a sharp kick in the ribs as he booted me while I lay on the floor.

'You disgust me!' he spat.

He knelt down and looked at me with utter contempt.

'Look at you,' he breathed, his face inches from mine. 'Look at you, covered in shit! I don't even want to hit you. You make me sick. You think you can embarrass me in front of my business partners? This is the *last time* I tell you. Understand? When you leave this flat it will be in showroom condition!'

Then he left, slamming the door behind him. I was so shocked and traumatized, I had forgotten how to cry. I hardly felt the pain from the blows he'd landed; it was the stink of the poo in my nostrils that I couldn't stand. That wheaty, sweet smell which didn't seem too bad from a distance was revolting in my nose and mouth.

I pulled myself unsteadily to my feet and washed the shit from my face; gargled some mouthwash. But no matter how hard I scrubbed nor how much mouthwash I used, I would smell nothing but poo for days.

That evening, I made sure the flat was spotless. I kept hearing Stuart's angry words over and over in my head as I cleaned. They made me feel worse and worse. I'd embarrassed him in front of his business partners . . . I wondered if they were all talking about it now, in his pub. *Dirty nappies, dirty knickers. On the floor? Shameful!* I cringed just thinking about it.

I had shown him up, humiliated him. I felt so bad; so dirty; so in the wrong. It was the first time Stuart had been physically violent – but I didn't think any less of him for it.

After all, I had deserved it, hadn't I?

I was too young to see then how wrong I was. It took many years before I understood that Stuart's behaviour that day had crossed a line; a line no man should ever cross. But I was barely seventeen and I had lost my sense of where that line should be many years before, when my brother had taken me for my bath aged five and taught me that women are merely playthings for whatever a man may want.

As I vigorously cleaned the flat until it sparkled, I felt, alongside my shame at letting him down, a sincere determination that I would try harder, do better in the future. For, as I had always dreamed, for better or for worse, I was now firmly part of Stuart's world.

151

As such, I was about to be taught a new way of thinking. I was about to learn Stuart's rules for life.

I was truly out of my depth – but I didn't know it. I knew nothing of the world, nothing about people and nothing about myself.

But worst of all, I thought I knew it all.

Chapter 11

A Cash Business

The girl who came to the door was in her early twenties. She had long, straight brown hair, and a soft, gentle smile that radiated genuine warmth. Even so, she was a perfect stranger and I wasn't happy that she was going to be looking after my son all day long, taking my place in his world. Stuart had insisted that hiring a nanny to take care of Callum was the only way forward and, besides, he said it wouldn't be all day, just 9 a.m. till 4 p.m.

'Look, if you want to learn a trade and get on in life, you need to start work,' he reasoned. 'I'm giving you a once-in-a-lifetime opportunity so come on, buck up! Life isn't a free ride.'

It did seem an exciting prospect, running my own bar at the age of eighteen, and I was definitely ready to get back into the world. The problem was that I'd really grown to love spending time with Callum in the past thirteen months and I knew it would be a horrible wrench to be apart from him. I would miss everything about him from the way he smiled to the way he smelled. I had breastfed him for the whole of that first year so the bond that had been missing between us in the first few weeks of his life was now firmly established.

Our new nanny, Hannah, was the daughter of a friend of Stuart and had worked as an au pair abroad for the past few years.

'Don't worry, Dawn.' She smiled at me as I left for my first day at work. 'Callum will be fine with me. I promise.'

I had no choice but to put my baby from my mind as I got to grips with my new job. It was a steep learning curve. Stuart had bought the lease of The Queen's Head pub from the brewers and told me I was a joint partner (though he never asked me to sign anything so there was nothing official). I was too young to be the licensee, so Stuart asked his old pal Dave to show me the ropes and put his name above the door.

I'd had a small amount of experience serving the guests in my parents' hotel bar, but this was different. Now I learned how to change the kegs, change the gas bottles, pour pints, pour the Guinness, arrange stocktakes, hire and fire staff, serve people and ban people. It was a busy pub – Dave said they were taking around £14k a week before Stuart took it over – so I had to pick it up as we went along.

Some aspects were fairly mechanical, like ordering and restocking the fridges. Other parts were administrative, such as learning about the licensing laws, banking, dealing with environmental health and the licensing police. Luckily, I was a quick learner and enjoyed the challenge of getting stuck into staff rotas, accounting and ordering. Though it felt like a long time since I'd used it, I'd always had a good brain on me: I may have left school with no qualifications thanks to Stuart's inter-vention, but had I stayed and studied, I knew I would have done well. It felt empowering, now, to realize I could do this.

But there were some lessons that came directly from Stuart as the official owner of the bar.

'This is my till,' Stuart explained, pointing to a small green till at the back of the bar. 'You put most of the takings through this till. And this . . .' He pointed to the large till out front, which was hooked up to our ordering system. 'This is the till for paying staff wages, stock and the brewers' bills. Got it?'

In the first week, I saw how it all worked. We took in money and then, once a day, Stuart would come and empty his till, taking between £100 or £200 at a time. By the end of that week, he'd probably had over £1,000 in cash. I knew that this was 'skimming', not strictly legal because it was un-declared earnings, but Stuart argued that this was his rightful wage from his investment and, besides, it was a cash business. Everyone expected this kind of leakage in a cash business, he said, it was the way the pub trade worked.

But the problem with this system became apparent straight away.

'I don't have enough to pay the brewers' bill,' I complained to Stuart in week three, just as he was fishing handfuls of notes out of his till. 'Can't you leave some in there today?'

'No!' he said. 'And don't fucking challenge me about how I run my bar ever again. If you're short, find the money! Why don't you try working harder?'

It was a quiet afternoon in the pub but there were still enough punters for Stuart's words to draw an audience. I felt the colour bloom in my cheeks as he raised his voice, louder and louder: 'This is my fucking pub and if you don't like it you can fucking get out! I didn't put you here to complain or to give me fucking problems. Don't ever, EVER defy me again in my own pub. If you can't make it work, you can fucking LEAVE!'

155

Too embarrassed and humiliated to argue, I quietly backed down. It was the one and only time I tried to stop him taking money from the till.

So I had no choice but to cut staff hours, picking up the extra shifts myself, to free up enough cash to pay our bills. Very quickly, we lost staff and my hours increased further, so I was now at The Queen's Head twelve hours a day. We invited Hannah to move into our spare room so she could look after Callum full time. After all, she was very loving and gentle with him and now we depended on her constantly. I didn't call my parents and they didn't call me either. Mum had warned me not to get in touch and I knew they weren't interested in helping out with childcare. Still, it saddened me that Callum didn't get to see his granny and grandpa.

So I struggled on alone but no matter how many hours I worked, we were always short and my life became a juggling act, putting off one bill after another to try and scrabble together the money to stay afloat. Nevertheless, I ploughed on, convinced that I could do a good job of running this pub. In fact, I was pretty good with the books, the ordering and the administrative tasks but I didn't yet have the people skills to know how to deal with customers. Every time someone was rude or challenged me, I banned them.

'You don't like the food I serve? Well, you're banned!'

'You don't like the way I run things? Banned!'

'Did that woman just look at Stuart? She's banned!'

I went power-crazy and within a few weeks, I'd scared off half of our clientele. The other half left of their own accord, muttering about how the place had gone downhill since 'the stroppy teenager' had taken over. Dave wasn't much help – after midday, he liked to stand on the other side of the bar, drinking with Stuart, leaving me to do most of the work. Tired, irritable and fed up, my attitude with the customers only worsened.

One morning, I went in to open up and Dave failed to show up for work. *Typical!* I thought angrily as I restocked the fridges and changed the kegs. Dave had become completely unreliable over the past month. And on top of everything, money was going missing all over the place. The brewers' bill was due today and the £3,000 I'd put inside the safe was now gone. Things were so tight we were barely making £5,000 a week. In the space of two and a half months, the business had practically collapsed. After another slow day, I got a call on the bar phone.

'Hi Dawn, is everything okay?' Stuart slurred drunkenly.

'Fine. Where are you?'

'We're in Portugal.'

'What? What do you mean you're in Portugal?'

'Me and Dave – we've gone to Albufeira for a wee break.'

'What are you talking about? And where's the money for the brewers?'

'We took it and we're in Albufeira. We'll be here for a week. Look, what's your problem?'

What was MY problem?! Fucking bastard! I was too enraged to speak so I hung up. That was the first time I'd hung up on him but I was so mad I could have punched him. I mean, what was the point of putting me in charge of a pub if he was going to tie both my hands behind my back? I couldn't run this place without cash.

When I finally got home that night, long after my son had been put to bed, Hannah asked if I was okay. I was upset; she noticed and offered to make me a cup of tea. Gratefully, I accepted her offer and as we sat together at the kitchen table that night, I told her what Stuart had done.

'What a bastard!' she cried out, outraged on my behalf. 'Well, let's teach them both a lesson. Let's go away to Albufeira ourselves. Why not? If he can do it, so can we!'

I was so angry at shouldering the burden for our failing pub, I readily agreed. I had missed my son desperately over the past few weeks and resented all the hundreds of hours I'd clocked up in The Queen's Head while Stuart just seemed to sit around, enjoying himself. His little trip to the Algarve had been the last straw.

The next day, I took £200 out of the till and bought flights for the three of us, due to leave on the day Stuart and Dave returned. *Two can play at that game*, I thought as I pocketed the tickets. *Why should I be bothered with this crappy old pub if the owner is determined to skim it to death?*

Of course, he was livid when he found out. He was back a day earlier than I expected so I informed him that Hannah, Callum and I were off the next day for our own 'wee break'. It was our first proper big fight and he threatened to do terrible things to me if I got on the plane the next day.

'I'll kill you if you leave!' he shouted. 'I'll take Callum away. I'll cut off your hair. I'll throw acid in your face so no man will ever want you. Mark my words, I will destroy you, Dawn! If you go on this holiday you'll never get back in this house. You will never see your baby again. Never!'

It was utterly terrifying and yet, weirdly, Hannah, who had heard all this from her room upstairs, didn't seem bothered by Stuart's vile threats.

'Oh, let him shout,' she said blithely, as she packed all our things in two small cases. 'He's only got himself to blame.'

Hannah's father was one of Stuart's oldest friends so she'd known him all her life and this familiarity meant she wasn't frightened of him the way I was. I took comfort from her strength and resolved that I wouldn't let Stuart scare me into staying. Even so, I shook uncontrollably all the way to the airport, sick with fear and worry.

Once there, however, Hannah turned to me. 'I can't wait any longer,' she said. 'It wouldn't be fair.' And she handed me a card. There were penguins on the front and, inside, in Stuart's handwriting, it read: 'Sorry you're leaving! I'll see you when you get home. Enjoy your time in the sun!' He'd also stuck in £100 cash.

Oh, thank God! I kissed Hannah with relief! Now I could relax, knowing that my life wasn't over. But as the hours passed, the card left a sour taste in my mouth. This wasn't his gold seal of approval but the start of what were to be his mind games. There was no way in a million years he was happy with me being away. This card was for Hannah's benefit and that was all.

In fact, the three of us had a wonderful time in Albufeira. Hannah and I were so close in age, we were practically like sisters. It felt great to be away together. Between us we looked after Callum, went to water parks and sunbathed on the beach. It was bliss, my first adult holiday abroad, and a much-needed break from all the stress of the past three months.

Only one cloud hovered on the horizon. *Why had Stuart used Hannah to make his feelings known?* I wondered. *Why couldn't he just tell me himself?*

'Oh, you know men!' Hannah tutted when I asked her. 'So full of pride. They can never admit when they're wrong.'

I lay on my sunlounger, thinking things over. I knew

Hannah was my friend but an ugly thought suddenly went through my head that maybe Stuart was also using her as a spy, making sure I didn't get up to any mischief while I was away. *Oh no.* I shook my head. *That is surely too cynical.* I breathed in the warm Portuguese air and let all my worries go.

'So, what's going to happen to The Queen's Head?' asked Hannah.

'No idea,' I said as I stretched out my long legs. I genuinely didn't care anymore. 'S'not my problem.'

But it soon was. By the time we got back, the liquidators were in and Stuart's special till had disappeared. He warned me not to talk to them and I knew what he meant by that: no word about his 'skimming'. They kept me on for a few weeks to run the pub on their behalf and then I was let go. There were huge debts, apparently. Thirty thousand pounds were missing from the takings and Stuart was in big trouble with the brewers as he had failed to pay them any rent in the whole time we had been there. What a disaster! Between my inexperience and his stealing, we had run the business into the ground.

It wouldn't have been too bad, only Stuart and I had over-stretched ourselves financially. It had all been Stuart's idea, of course. Some months ago, he'd said the flat was too small for all of us and so he had found a nice four-bedroom house in need of renovation. He sold his flat and put the house into my name, explaining that all his assets were going to be seized by the Inland Revenue for unpaid taxes, which meant that he would be declared bankrupt. (Of course, most of his assets were already in Adam's name anyway, but if the house was in my name, the Inland Revenue couldn't touch that either.) He had bought the place with £40k cash, then he marched me to the bank to take out a £40k mortgage, in my name – which all went into Stuart's pocket. So now he had his cash, and I had a huge mortgage.

At the time, I'd been ecstatic at the move – my own home! What other eighteen-year-old could boast of owning a four-bedroom house? But once The Queen's Head went bust I became terrified. How could I keep up the mortgage repayments now without an income? I didn't know where my next pay cheque was coming from. And it wasn't just the mortgage that concerned me. How could we pay the food bills, for the Sky TV, the electricity?

And that's when Stuart and Adam came up with a new plan. Between them, they bought a pub called The Old Bell – outright. This time, there were no brewers and no rent bills to pay. It was going cheap because it was in need of a complete refit and, worse, it was in a bad area. They laid out their idea: I was to borrow £100k from the bank to pay for refurbishments and then I'd lease the pub from the cousins, paying them a monthly rent, just as I might do if they were the brewers. But the advantage from my point of view was that I didn't have to buy beer from a brewer at inflated prices, I could run the pub exactly as I wanted and, if I managed to make it a success, then everyone would win.

'So I get all the debt, all the risk and all the work?' If I sounded sceptical, it was because it seemed like a better deal for the cousins than it was for me. I had just taken on £40k of debt. Did I really want another £100k round my neck? I was still only eighteen and it seemed like a massive responsibility.

'Yeah. That's right!' Stuart said firmly, with a nasty undertone in his voice. 'You can have all of that. Or you can have nothing, Dawn. What do you think: something or nothing? Because if you're going to take nothing, then I'll need to know how you intend to pay your way. Tell me – how are you planning to keep up with the mortgage? How do you propose we keep the cash coming? Because I'm not doing it.

'Let's get one thing straight, Dawn, I make my own money and I expect you to make yours. What else have you got going on at the moment? Anyone else offering you the lease of a pub? A business on a plate? No? Thought not.' He sneered at me. 'Now I'm offering you a chance to be part of something or nothing.' He leaned over into my face, challenging me with his eyes. 'What's it going to be?'

I ducked my head, cowed, as I always was, into submission. He knew what it was going to be, and so did I.

Just as it had been since I'd very first been seduced by him, it seemed I didn't have a choice.

PART III
GROWING UP

Chapter 12

My Bar

What a miserable place, I thought, as I surveyed the practically empty bar. The only customers in The Old Bell this afternoon were a couple of dirty drunks but later on, I knew, the prostitutes would be in for a quick nip of whisky to warm themselves up. Stuart had told me the pub was in an area that was up-and-coming. New office blocks were opening round the corner and soon, he assured me, it would be teeming with young, trendy office workers. It was hard to believe – right now, it felt like the back of beyond, a run-down and lonely part of town where nobody wanted to hang out, least of all me!

But, I told myself, *this is only day three so there's no need to panic*. After all, I had to get a feel for the place before I made any drastic changes. Right now, I had my elbows on the bar as I scrutinized our food menu. Scampi and chips, pie and chips, gammon and chips. *Urgh! Who eats all this deep-fried rubbish?*

Just then, the large double doors swung open and a pair of tall men in blazers and jeans sauntered in, both of them scanning the room as they approached the bar.

'Two pints of lager, please,' said the tallest one. They looked to be in their mid-forties, well turned out and with slicked-back blond hair.

'Two pounds forty, please,' I said as I placed the pints down on the counter.

The first one looked at me, dead-eyed, and in a low monotone said: 'We're not paying for that.'

'And why is that then?'

'Because we don't pay for drinks around here.'

'Why?'

I was confused and not in the least bit intimidated, even though I was on my own today. I had the courage of a lion when it came to anyone but Stuart. He had taught me well. If you stand up to someone, they most likely back down. My association with him would scare most people off, and if they dared touch me they knew that any assault on his girl or property would not be taken lightly. I was protected and I knew it, but most importantly they knew it.

'Surely you know who we are?' said the second one, his eyebrows raised.

'No, I don't know who you are,' I replied smartly. I wasn't really in the mood for this game.

'Who's here then? Who else is working with you tonight, or are you on your own?' said the first one again, taking a new tack.

'No one.'

'Okay, so this is what's going to happen,' he said. 'I'm Jason Mead and this here is Len Hamilton and we ran this bar for years. We're going to come round once a week and we're going to collect everything you've got in the till.'

He spoke calmly but the menace in his voice was clear. However, I wasn't about to let myself get pushed around by this guy; I had enough of that at home. Who the hell did he think he was?

'No, you're not,' I said, equally calmly. 'Why would I let you do that?'

'Well, look . . .' He grinned, talking slowly, as if to an idiot. 'You see these nice windows here? We're going to smash them. We're going to smash them every week and you're going to give us money not to smash them.'

At eighteen years old and with so little experience, I'd never even heard the word 'extortion'. I didn't know what a protection racket was. I had no idea that these were two of the biggest criminals on this side of Glasgow and that they were famous for shaking down all the local businesses. I didn't know *any* of that. All I knew was that they were being rather unpleasant, and – unlike with Stuart, who had such power and sway over me – I wasn't going to stand for it.

'I don't understand,' I said. 'Why don't you just *not* smash them?'

By now, the one called Len was fed up and asked impatiently: 'Look, how much have you got in the till?'

'Five pounds. You want that? Five pounds?'

'I know you,' said Jason suddenly. 'You're Stuart Kelly's bird, aren't you? Why don't you get him on the phone, tell him Jason Mead's here and we'll see where we go from there, shall we?'

I shrugged and went through to the kitchen, where I called Stuart and told him what was happening.

'You're not going to give them any money, are you?' he said.

'No, there's no money to give them. Are you coming to help me here?'

'Erm, no. I'm watching *Family Fortunes*. Anyway, I've had

a bottle of wine so I can't drive. You'll just have to deal with it on your own.'

'Okay, I'll deal with it,' I said. I hadn't really expected him to help me; Stuart never did.

So I walked back into the bar, my brain whirring, and said to the men: 'Right, I've told Stuart and he told me to get the money from the safe, in the back office.'

'Good girl! Well, off you go then . . .'

And I did – I went to the back office and, from there, I called the police. Then I returned to the bar and shrugged. 'Sorry, lads, there's no money in the safe. We've only been open a week.'

At that moment, Jason lunged over the bar and grabbed me by the scruff of the neck, pulling me back over to his side of the bar with extreme violence, and snarled: 'Get the fucking money!'

Just then, two policemen walked in. *Thank God! Not a moment too soon*, I thought, as Jason quickly let go of me. I'd never been a huge fan of the boys in blue after my treatment at their hands when they'd tried to lock up Stuart (even then, I still didn't think he'd done anything wrong in sleeping with me underage), but right at that moment, I couldn't have been more pleased to see them.

'Jason!' the policeman shouted. 'Jason, what the hell are you doing? You've not been out more than a month. I can't believe you're back here at your old haunt trying the same thing!'

'You called the fucking police?' Jason's eyes bulged.

'Yes,' I said calmly. 'And I'll testify too.'

That was the end of that.

When I got home later that day, Stuart was lying on the

sofa, pissed. He saluted me with a mock toast of his wine glass when I told him what had happened.

'Great! I knew you'd handle it,' he grinned, bleary-eyed. *Hmm . . . no thanks to you*, I thought crossly. Those guys could have seriously harmed me – yet he seemed completely unconcerned. I was beginning to learn that Stuart's idea of protection was very different from mine. Well, that meant I had to toughen up and learn how to look after myself outside of this house.

It was clear to me that The Old Bell didn't just need a refit – it needed a whole new identity. So I started researching bars and pubs in the area. I realized that the ones I liked best were the real-ale pubs, the unusual, quirky pubs with character. We needed to look different, to stand out from the crowd and I'd had an idea of turning the pub into something that was desperately needed in Glasgow. A sports bar. So I started scouring the web for all sorts of memorabilia. I loved American sports and so the walls were adorned with baseball caps and bats, a Montreal Canadian ice hockey stick, a New York Ranger goalie helmet, basketball strips, you name it we had it. A Babe Ruth signed ball took centre stage behind the bar and we covered one wall in old cigarette sports cards.

The lounge area was home to good old English sports memorabilia. I tried to stay away from showing support for Rangers or Celtic as that would be asking for trouble but instead I collected a Jimmy Connors tennis top, a signed Wimbledon McEnroe tennis ball and a Lendl tracksuit top. I even managed to acquire a Björn Borg tennis racket. Cricket stumps from when we lost the Ashes and Scottish rugby tops from when we beat the All Blacks sat above the old casks of real ale that we used as tables. An old replica

Formula One car hung from the ceiling and a book case was filled with sports autobiographies and trophies.

Before long, the place was transformed. People were amazed when they walked in for the first time and I could see that, visually, I had achieved the right look. I felt so proud of myself. Art had always been my passion and with The Old Bell I'd turned a blank canvas into my own personal work of art. But, still, the product itself wasn't right.

We had been open two months and there were no customers, thanks to our old-fashioned menu and standard beer. I was doing the same as every other pub in town. Why would anyone come to my pub to be served the same pre-packed crap that was bought in from suppliers, pretending it was home-made?

When I examined the contents of our fridges, I was shocked. The eggs had a shelf life of three years! Sauces were bought from the cash-and-carry in gigantic tubs, all the fish was pre-battered and frozen, as were our pastry pie tops. The cheesecake lasted six months when defrosted and tasted of plastic. It was cheap, nasty rubbish and a huge con for the punters. I knew I had to shake things up, do things my way.

So, I designed my own food menu. Firstly I kept on the basics, as there were still a few who loved their scampi and their steak pie, but then I created a special burger menu. With the American sports theme, what could be better than a mouthwatering burger menu. Nobody else was doing fresh home-made burgers at that time and so my only competition was McDonald's.

Oh, it was great fun – I worked together with the local butcher and Hannah and Callum helped me to taste-test all the different burgers. Before long, we'd thrown out all the frozen rubbish and had an attractive and appetizing menu full of fresh ingredients.

My other big change was to move away for the mainstream brewers and use a real-ale brewery instead. This was a pretty radical move in our area – the men here only seemed to like Tennent's and McEwan's and I was warned by Stuart that if I didn't serve these I was doomed. But I didn't want those old customers anyway – I wanted young people, families, workers and trendy students: people with money. And I needed to entice them in.

Fortunately, the brewers I chose were a young, ambitious company who wanted to be involved in new businesses like mine and they invested their own money in ripping out our old fonts and supplying a bank of eight new real-ale pumps. They sent me on training courses, so I learnt how to tap real ales and after six months of sweat and tears, throwing out lots of real ale that had gone off because no one was drinking it, my idea began to catch on.

First, the students came, attracted by the drinks and our 'giant nachos' sharing plate. I'd also started live music afternoons with jazz musicians that attracted a fun, bright and young crowd. Then the families came in at the weekends for burgers, knowing their children would be happily distracted by all the curious wonders on our walls and ceiling. Finally, the businessmen came for the real ale. By the time the new offices in the area finally did open up, we were the hottest pub in town.

Within a year, The Old Bell was transformed from a failing pub into a bustling, successful enterprise. We were now taking nearly £15k a week. I'd made all my mistakes with The Queen's Head and this time I managed to get things right. I took on young, enthusiastic staff and paid them well, on time. Instead of cutting staff hours, I increased them so that we could cope with the rise in trade and I learned how to manage tricky customers instead of throwing them out. Now it was hard to get a table for Friday or Saturday lunch or dinner as they were all booked out.

My confidence grew as the money started rolling in – I was thrilled my vision had taken off and motivated to keep working hard. So I spent almost every waking hour at the pub, working to make it a success. It was my name above the door now, and I wanted to build a strong reputation.

Of course, my absence was hard on Callum and I always felt horribly guilty about having to leave him every day, but Stuart insisted that I was a natural at business and I had the knack, so I should run with it. He was still taking money from my till, once a week, but thankfully I was making enough money to keep him happy and still pay our bills.

It confused me that Stuart didn't pay anything towards our household expenses from his own business ventures; after all, he made his own money through buying and selling antiques, jewellery, art, property and cars. But it seemed all his money went to Guernsey. This, his business empire, paid him a monthly 'dividend'. But he said it was only enough to cover his own expenses. It wasn't enough to pay our household bills: that was up to me. And, I suppose, this didn't bother me at first because I was so driven to succeed.

Certainly, it felt important to prove to everyone that I wasn't the miserable failure that I had appeared to be three years before when I had returned to my parents' house, a broke, single, teenage mum without one O level to my name. More importantly, I felt I had to prove to my mother that I had turned my life around, that I had made the 'right' choices after all. So, once the pub was up and running, I took driving lessons and, after passing my test, I bought my first-ever car. It was a very battered, 1960s Ferrari. It was so old and knack-ered it was the price of a clapped-out Ford, but to me it said something to the world, something important about where I was going in life.

With the car keys in my hand, I was ready to stage my comeback. And so, when Callum was three years old, I drove him round to The Drayton Arms in my new car. This time I would make the effort and sit in their company and introduce them to Callum. The last three years with them had been tense, and I could count on one hand the times we had seen each other.

'Oh hell, what do you want?' Mum exclaimed when she saw me. 'Do you want me to look after Callum? Is that why you're here?'

I had to smile. She never changed.

'No, Mum,' I replied. 'I've just come to see you. I'm doing fine, everything's fine. I just thought it would be nice for Callum to get to know his grandparents a bit.'

'Yes, well, we're pretty busy right now so maybe you can go through to the kitchen to help out there and I'll catch up with you when I get a minute.'

I wandered through to the kitchen where I found Dad perched on a stool, peeling potatoes. He was fatter than ever but it was still lovely to see him after all this time. He seemed much happier to see us than Mum and we spent a long time catching up on what I'd been up to. He'd heard that I was now running The Old Bell and he said, with no small amount of pride in his voice: 'Aye, it's getting a good reputation, that place. I'll have to swing by some time, see what all the fuss is about.'

'Yeah, that would be really nice, Dad,' I said with a shy smile.

'Ah, I always knew you'd be alright,' he said. 'You're a chip off the old block. There's warrior blood in yous, Dawn. Aye . . . I never really worried about you, ken?'

'Thanks, Dad.' I grinned at him. Then he heaved himself off his stool and lumbered over to the cupboard, where he got out a chocolate bar for Callum.

'Well, now,' he said with a smile for my little boy. 'Does ma grandson want a special treat from his grandpa then?'

From then on, I was back in touch with my parents and I was grateful to find that, although Dad was now suffering quite badly with his health due to years of over-indulgence, he was more than happy to take Callum on days out to the park or the zoo. It meant a lot to me that my son had a good relationship with his grandpa. Dad walked slowly but that suited Callum's little legs and Dad loved to spoil him, buying him treats like ice cream and fish and chips. Dad even started to come to The Old Bell regularly for his lunch, which was really nice. Although I was often very busy myself, I liked to have him there and it made me feel like he was proud of me and what I had achieved.

In fact, I was growing up every day and learning how to deal with customers and difficult situations better. Now twenty years old, I had experience under my belt and my confidence was growing by the day.

I often needed it. One quiet Monday night in January, I was behind the bar polishing the glasses when a man wearing a raincoat came in and ordered a pint. He took it and sat down in the corner booth opposite me. Now, the raincoat wasn't unusual, and neither were the wellies, but, if I wasn't mistaken, didn't he have bare legs? *Strange attire for January*, I thought.

Then he stood up, opened his coat and, to my horror, I saw he was completely naked underneath and sporting a rather large erection. Then he started masturbating in front of me. *Oh hell*, I thought. *What do I do now? What is he going to do with that?* I didn't want to be raped. *Fuck! Okay, deep breath . . . Deal with it, Dawn! This is your bar and you are in charge here.*

So, summoning up all my courage, I walked over to the gentleman, took his pint, walked to the sink and poured it away. Then I turned back to him.

'I suggest you leave now,' I said coldly. 'The police are on their way.'

To my utter astonishment, it worked. Hurriedly, he tied his mac up at the front and left. He didn't even challenge me. At The Old Bell, I was certainly the woman in charge and everyone knew it.

At home, though, it was a different story. There, Stuart was the boss and I had to do what he said. This was the choice I made every day because I thought it was easier on me and my son. I didn't love him, I knew that. Stuart controlled every aspect of my life. I had no bank account, and if I did I would have to explain why I needed one. I was never allowed to open my own mail, he opened everything. Every daily event was timed and every minute away from him had to be properly accounted for or he would punish me. Car keys would be taken first, followed by the house keys and my purse, so I couldn't make a quick exit. He would be very careful not to show any signs of violence that would be noticeable to anyone but liked simple tortures like coming up behind me when I was making a cup of tea and twisting my arm around my back for minutes on end until I begged for him to stop. He also liked to pour boiling water on my hand just as a reminder that he was in charge or to yank my hair in a tight knot and hold my head in place whilst he kept pulling until my scalp bled at the roots. This would happen if I was late home or refused to answer his calls, but most of the time it was for no reason at all, just to keep me in check.

There was no time to visit friends, no time for anything apart from work and home. Every waking minute was controlled by Stuart. So when he told me to stop wearing skirts and dresses because I was fat and had tree-trunk legs, I stopped wearing skirts and dresses. He said make-up made me look like a drag queen so that was out too. When he told me to take him and his friends out for the night, driving them round from pub to pub, that's what I did; and when he called the pub five times a day to check up on me, I was expected to answer or I knew there would be trouble. I was completely under his control. Stuart liked to know where I was at all times so it suited him well that I worked at The Old Bell from first thing in the morning till last thing at night.

And God forbid I should be somewhere else! Then his temper would flare up and he'd scream down the phone at me or leave threatening messages on the answerphone: 'If you don't pick up the fucking phone in the next thirty seconds I'll come over there and fucking kill you, you silly bitch!'

I was a twenty-year-old woman and he was afraid I would go off with someone else. He had often commented that I needn't think about leaving him for someone younger, since men were all the same in bed. The truth was I didn't know any different, so I assumed that this was normal. Looking back, I can see that my life with Stuart was very far from normal, that a partner isn't meant to control every aspect of your life – choose your clothes, keep money from you, stop you going out – but I was so young and naive, I accepted it. And this kind of behaviour is insidious, destroying your self-esteem, making you feel powerless, and brainwashing you until you simply cannot see any other way to be.

Today the bullying, threats and intimidation would be interpreted by the law as coercive control, which carries a prison sentence. Because we understand so much more about domestic abuse now, we know it's not just about one or two incidents, but about a pattern of abusive behaviour that can trap someone in a prison created for them by their own partner.

And his threats were so scary, I always did as I was told. He owned everything in my life and he could take it away in a second. The fact was, we had a child together and I thought I had to make it work for the sake of our little boy. Yes, there were many times I thought of leaving Stuart but then, to my mind, what sort of a mother would I be if I took Callum away from his father? Though Stuart hurt me, he never hit Callum. Also, there was the unavoidable fact that Stuart and his cousin owned my pub. And, oh yes, he liked to rub that in my face.

Frequently, he would stand at the bar, getting steadily drunker throughout the afternoon, reminding me that I was just a worker, that he was the real brains behind our success and so I had better show him the respect he deserved.

'I could take all this away tomorrow if I wanted to,' he'd slur. 'I'm the fucking owner. You're only the licensee. Remember that. I could easily replace you, close the doors, change the locks and that would be you – out!'

'Shhh . . .' I'd try to placate him, afraid of what others thought. 'Please don't shout.'

'Well, don't make me angry then!' he'd shoot back. The fact was, Stuart loved to make a scene and embarrass me in front of people, whether it was, on the street or in a posh restaurant. He knew I was too afraid of what people thought to challenge him in public – just another way he liked to control and dominate me.

'I own this fucking pub and I own you, Dawn McConnell. Don't fucking forget it!'

Almost without me noticing, years passed. The work at the pub got harder as we got busier and the council regulations for bars and restaurants were changing all the time, which I had to keep on top of. Though I hated to, I seemed to spend more and more time there and less and less time at home. Though at first I had enjoyed making my mark on the pub and using my brain and my creativity to build a successful business, I realized with horror that, instead of the life of leisure I'd always imagined for myself, I'd only managed to replicate my mother's life, the life of a workaholic. I grew to hate the daily drive to the pub and the long, long shifts I was forced to put in.

The constant work was even taking a toll on my body – I'd been diagnosed with kidney stones and some days I was in almost constant agony. But the physical pain was as nothing to the emotional distress I suffered. For, as the years passed, I noted with sadness that my baby was growing into a little boy and I was missing all this wonderful time together. It wasn't even as if Stuart spent much time with him either – he was Hannah's little boy now. When he was sick, it was Hannah he asked for; when he wanted something to eat, he asked Hannah to feed him; and when he cried, it was Hannah's arms he wanted to comfort him. I felt that he was slipping away from me and there was nothing I could do about it.

One evening in 1991 our solicitor dropped in an official-looking letter for me at the pub. I was too busy serving during our weekly quiz to look at it, so I slipped it between the orange and lime cordials while I dealt with the customers. Later, as I cleared up at just gone 12.30 a.m., I noticed it sitting there, so I wiped down my hands and opened it.

For a moment, I couldn't quite believe what I was reading. Then I pumped the air with my fist and screamed: 'YES!'

Stuart, sipping from a bottle of Miller at a bar stool, looked up.

'Whassup?' he slurred.

'We have an offer in from Scottish and Newcastle Brewers to buy the freehold of the pub,' I told him excitedly. 'I'm outta here. Thank God for that!'

'You aren't seriously considering taking it, are you?'

Normally, I would never answer Stuart back. I would never question his judgement or challenge his decisions. But on this one occasion, I just couldn't hold back. This was my call to make, not his.

'Are you kidding?' I said. 'I don't see my son. I work sixteen hours a day and on my one day off a week, I clean the house and do the laundry. I have no life. I don't go anywhere because you are so jealous and think I'm going to run off with the first person I meet. I'm stuck here all the time and I hate it. I hate this damned pub.'

179

Stuart just sat there, staring at me, as I carried on, ranting, years of frustration finally bubbling to the surface.

'On top of the regulations becoming impossible, I have a son who is now five years old. Someone else has the privilege of looking after him at my cost. Don't you think I would rather be looking after him while the nanny works in the pub? I'm twenty-two and I want to see my son grow up before it's too late. So yes, I'm the licensee and I'm selling.'

The thought of having free time to see Callum gave me the strength to stand up to Stuart. I couldn't stop the words coming out, and it was only later I realized what I had done. I had stood up to him for the first time.

He just looked at me, took a sip of his beer and then hurled it against the wall. Then he got up and left.

I sold the pub that year for a little over £700,000. Stuart and Adam took the agreed £200,000 cut from the proceeds for their share, I paid off the remaining £50,000 loan from the bank and with the leftover £450,000 I purchased flats to let. These flats were mine – I owned them and they were in my name. I knew this was important; I knew I had to build up an independent source of income for myself. After all, Stuart had told me so many times that I couldn't rely on him for money, so I needed my own safety net. Just in case.

I began spending more and more time visiting my parents, helping out at their hotel. Mum talked a lot about Susy and John when I was there, who were both living in London. I noticed she had pictures of them up on the mantelpiece but there were none of me. It irked me, and if I was honest with myself it hurt me, too, but there was nothing much I could do about it.

Given where they lived, I rarely, if ever, saw my siblings. And that suited me just fine, especially when it came to John. The fact was, I didn't think about my brother and what he had done to me anymore. Out of sight, out of mind, that was my attitude: an attitude I had to stick to in order to stay safe; to stay sane. It was all in the past as far as I was concerned and that was where I wanted it to stay. *Forever.*

Only things didn't quite work out that way.

Chapter 13

Revelations

I stood at the kitchen window and poked my tongue out at Callum, who was on the front lawn of the hotel grounds, kicking his football. It was a sweltering day in July 1991 and I'd brought my son over to The Drayton Arms to play while I helped Mum out with the catering for a funeral.

A smartly dressed little boy from the funeral party stood watching my son from the gravel pathway. I signalled to Callum to invite him to play and, happily, Callum lobbed the ball over to the boy in the waistcoat and tie, who kicked it straight back. Then they were off, the pair of them zigzagging round the lawn.

He didn't need much encouragement, I realized with wonder. My son was a very sociable little boy and always looking for new playmates. There was so much I was learning about him, now that we had some time together at last.

I turned back to the kitchen counter where I was buttering bread for the sandwiches, hopping up onto a bar stool to continue my work. Mum was stood next to me, filling the sandwiches and cutting them into neat triangles before arranging them carefully on large silver platters. Once they were ready, her ancient waitress Phyllis shuttled the trays to and from the dining room.

The local news on the radio was the only sound in the kitchen as we all worked busily to finish the order, mindlessly listening to the news reporter's words.

'. . . He was sentenced to fifteen years in jail for the abuse. Summing up, the judge said the defendant had shown no remorse for his abominable actions which had damaged his own daughter for life. The family thanked the police for their cooperation and said that the interest of justice had finally been served.'

'Och, that's terrible what happened to that lassie,' Phyllis commented sadly as she waited for Mum to finish off the smoked-salmon platter. 'Being abused like that all that time. And no one did anything about it.'

'I know, it's absolutely shocking,' Mum agreed, lining up the triangles on the platter. Then she straightened up and put a hand to the small of her back. 'I mean, how can something like that go on in your own home and you don't know it?' she went on. 'In your own home. Right under your nose!'

'Aye, but they say it's more common than you think,' remarked Phyllis, picking up the tray. 'They say the victims always know their abusers. It's never a stranger.'

I sat there on my stool, hot blood pounding in my ears, still buttering bread mechanically. Mum's words were circling in my head like piranhas, eating me up. 'How can something like that go on in your own home and you don't know it.' *How can she say that?* I thought numbly. *How can Mum say that after what happened to me?*

But then, I thought to myself, had *Mum known about it?* Maybe that was the whole point, the point she was unwittingly making – for I had been abused for years 'under her nose', and she had never made it stop. Was it because she had not known? But no – I had told her that day, I had said 'John's hurting me'. Surely she had known what I'd meant?

I watched as Mum added a sprig of parsley garnish to the smoked-salmon sandwich platter: it was the finishing touch. Phyllis scooped up the tray and tottered out of the kitchen with it in her patent black court shoes. Mum and I were left alone.

I sat quietly for a moment, slowly spreading the butter up and down a slice of white bread. As though from a great distance, I watched my own hand as it moved backwards and forwards, feeling slightly detached from it, as if it was someone else's hand. Then I stopped. I took a deep breath. As an adult I'd never broached the subject of my abuse with my mother, but now it had come up, I couldn't ignore what she'd just said.

'Mum, I get what you're saying to Phyllis,' I said evenly. 'But you remember: this happened with John and me?'

I felt my cheeks burn hot with shame as I said the words. I hadn't spoken about the abuse for years, not since I was a teenager, when I'd told Stuart what John had done to me. And even though I was now a fully grown woman and it was all in the past, it still felt wrong to bring it up; it still made me feel so dirty and ashamed. 'I mean, how could you say that to Phyllis about it going on in your own home and not knowing?' I continued.

Mum had been clearing away the sandwich things, putting cheese slices back into plastic tubs, wiping down surfaces and returning tubs of butter and egg mayonnaise to the fridge when I spoke. But as my words sank in, gradually her movements slowed and then, very carefully, very precisely, she screwed the lid onto the top of the mayonnaise. Finally, after a long and heavy pause, she stopped and looked at me.

In a querulous voice she asked: 'What? What did you say, Dawn?'

'Well, you know it happened to me, Mum. You know that John abused me for all those years.'

Mum's face seemed to collapse. As if to steady herself, she put a hand out to a bar stool before gently lowering herself onto it. Her hand went to her mouth and her eyes brimmed with tears. 'Oh Dawn, I'm sorry. I'm so sorry.'

For a moment I was dumbstruck, horrified at what I'd done. I had somehow expected Mum to come back with a smart reply, like she always did in any conversation, not to fall apart in front of me.

There was a sharp tapping of black court shoes. Phyllis was now back in the kitchen, and a couple of the other serving staff members also came in, looking to fill the giant urn for the teas and coffees. Mum was perched on the stool, looking small and fragile and crying properly now, her shoulders shaking with emotion.

Phyllis looked at me questioningly and I suddenly felt horribly guilty. I hadn't meant to upset Mum like this and now look, she was crying in front of her own staff.

Ashamed and embarrassed, I walked quickly to her side and whispered: 'It's okay, Mum. Really. It's fine. Please, please don't cry.'

Mum took out a hanky from her pocket and squeezed her nose with it. She sniffed a couple of times and then looked at me through red-rimmed eyes.

'We'll talk about this later,' she said. Then she adjusted her apron, dabbed at her eyes and carried on working to finish up the funeral lunch.

For the next forty minutes, I helped to refill sandwich platters, arrange biscuits on plates and load the dishwasher with the crockery. I tried not to let myself think about John and the mindless tasks helped a lot. Keeping busy had always helped me to block out my most unpleasant thoughts; I found work focused my mind and let me forget about the things that bothered me. Perhaps that was partly why I had worked myself to the bone in the pub, missing out on time with Callum in the process, just to make sure that every hour of my day was filled.

Because it was during the quiet moments, in the silences, that my head was filled with the dreadful memories of my past.

As I worked in the hotel kitchen, I occasionally looked out the window to check on Callum – he had found two more friends to play with and now the four of them were having a full-on football match, with my dad refereeing. The kids ran about, knees pumping up and down, all with ruddy cheeks, so full of energy, so innocent.

They were the same age I had been when my brother first gave me that 'special' bath.

The news story on the radio had been familiar to me: it was about a case involving a young girl who had been abused by her father. It was a big local story and the community was shocked that someone who was such an upstanding pillar of society had turned out to be a vile paedophile – but it was happening more and more these days. Or, at least, we were *hearing* about more and more cases as historic accounts of abuse now came before the courts, with survivors speaking out about the traumas they had suffered long ago.

As they did for my neighbours, each one filled me with fresh horror at the thought of what these girls went through. But for me there was a double whammy, as the women's words resonated with my own experiences, reminding me of my own secret childhood shame.

Nevertheless, I had never considered going to the police about John myself; never considered telling my own story. It all seemed too public and I had no desire whatsoever to rake it all up again – for my own sanity as much as anything else. No, I had decided that it was in the past and that's where I wanted it to stay.

In fact, I would never have said anything to Mum at all if it hadn't been for her comments to Phyllis. It was the way she had spoken, her voice laden with judgement, dripping with condescension, as if she couldn't possibly imagine such a thing in her own home. If she *had* known, it was hypocrisy, plain and true, and I couldn't stay silent anymore.

Finally, service was finished and Mum instructed the staff to take a break. Then she made us each a cup of tea and we sat silently on the stools in the kitchen for a while, lost in our own thoughts.

Eventually, Mum spoke: 'Dawn, I'm so sorry about what happened with John. But I thought I stopped it.'

My pulse began to quicken. So she *had* known. She had known exactly what he was doing . . . I swallowed hard.

'Yeah, well . . . it didn't stop,' I mumbled. I felt so embarrassed talking about this with her. It was excruciating.

'I can't believe you're bringing this up again, after all this time.' Mum held her tea with both hands and blew over the top of it to cool it. 'Do you think about it a lot?'

'Yes, I do,' I said. No matter how much I tried to block it out, those kinds of memories can never be bricked up. 'Especially now I've got a child of my own. I wanted you to stop it, Mum, but after I told you, it just kept going.'

The tears sprang from her eyes again.

'I thought I did stop it,' she said in a voice thick with emotion. I sat in front of her, unmoved. I wasn't upset myself, just curious for answers. *Who is she crying for?* I wondered, in a detached way. *Is she crying for me, or for her?*

'So you do remember then?' I went on. Now that it was finally out in the open, I couldn't let this point go. 'You remember when I tried to tell you what he was doing? And you *knew* what he was doing?'

'I remember very clearly,' said Mum. 'And yes, I *did* know what you meant. You told me he hurt you – and I just knew. *I knew* – but I thought I stopped it. I told him to stop hurting you.'

'Well, it didn't stop,' I said bitterly. I was staring out of the window now, unable to meet my mother's eyes. On the lawn, Callum was trying to do keepy-uppys on his knee. The ball bounced once, twice, three times, and then slipped sideways and rolled away. I watched him run after it.

'Well, why didn't you come back and tell me?' Mum asked suddenly, almost accusingly. 'Why didn't you tell me it hadn't stopped?'

I shrugged, still looking out over the lawn. I didn't know the answer. I had only been five. I'd asked for her help and, when it didn't come, what more could I have done?

But my mother's tone set my mind ticking, peeling back

the years to the same old guilt I'd always felt. *Is it my fault it went on so long?* I wondered now. *Is that what she's saying? Am I to blame?*

Mum had her hanky out again and she was now talking into the space in front of her, gesturing with it.

'I just thought that it maybe happened once or twice and then I put a stop to it. You never said anything else! So then, I thought you'd got over it. You were into your sports and you did tennis. I mean, look at you, Dawn, you're such a strong person. Look how well you're doing now! I didn't think . . . I really didn't think you had suffered.'

There was a challenge in her eyes, one I had to counter.

'Well, I did, Mum. I did suffer.'

Other than that, I hardly knew what to say. A tornado of emotions and thoughts ran through me so fast I couldn't catch a hold of any of them long enough to put them into words. After trying to bury these memories for so long, I didn't know how to even begin to talk about them. But I knew I had to say something, to let her know the truth.

Mum sat in front of me, quietly sniffing back tears as I battled with my shame and embarrassment. Finally, I let the words slip out quietly, like a sigh: 'It went on for years, Mum. It only stopped when he went away. Except then he did it one more time when he came back. I was twelve. And he raped me.'

There was a sharp intake of breath and Mum looked away. For a moment I felt like a little girl again, and inside I could feel my heart hammering so hard it felt like it would explode out of my chest. *Look at me, Mum!* I cried inside. *Look at me!*

Just like the child who had tugged on her apron so many years before, I was reaching out to her. I wanted her to see me, to acknowledge my pain.

189

But no. There was nothing. For a long while, I just listened to the whirring of the draft extractor above our heads. Finally Mum said: 'Well, I'm going to speak to Jenny about this. I'll talk to your aunt.' Then she got up off her stool, squeezed my shoulder once and left.

I couldn't get away from the hotel quick enough that day. I gathered Callum up, threw a breezy 'goodbye' in my dad's direction then marched my son off down the road so fast his little legs had to run to keep up.

I was very confused by how that conversation had gone. Though I'd imagined talking to my mum about the abuse one day, this had been a very different conversation to the one I'd expected. So Mum *had* known what was happening, even though I'd never expressed in words exactly what my brother was doing.

So why hadn't she stopped it? I thought angrily. *Why did she think it was over?*

I thought of my mother: her elegant outfits, her sense of superiority to our neighbours, her obsession with us kids doing well. Was it just too unpleasant for her to bring up again? Could she just not face the truth?

Questions flew through my mind. After all this time, I felt more confused and ashamed than ever about what had happened. And Mum's reaction and her questions made me feel so guilty, too. *Was* it my fault it had gone on so long?

I was so upset, I just wanted to get home and try and get things straight in my mind. But that same evening, Mum called.

'Your aunt flew up to Scotland tonight,' she said at once, with no preamble.

'Why?' I asked dumbly. I still couldn't make sense of anything that was happening.

'Because we need to talk about things. I think you better come over, Dawn. We have to talk to you.'

It felt rather like I was being summoned to my own execution. *What is this about?* When I walked into my parents' house at 8 p.m. that night, I had no idea what to expect.

The kitchen was dark except for the low central light which hung over the kitchen table. There, Mum sat nursing a Scotch while Jenny paced the kitchen. Dad was nowhere to be seen; he was probably still working at the hotel.

'Dawn!' Jenny ran towards me and threw her arms around my neck. She held me tight, as if I'd just escaped some terrible accident. 'Are you okay, Dawn? Sit down, Dawn. Sit down. Your mum told me everything. Oh, it's awful. Awful! We haven't stopped talking about it for the past few hours, have we?'

Mum shook her head.

Jenny was in full 'crisis management' mode: 'Dawn, sit down! Now look, do you want to tell me what happened?'

'Erm, er . . . well . . . not really,' I mumbled. Actually, I felt like running away. Jenny was so over the top and melodramatic it was difficult to know how to act. After all, this hadn't *just* happened. I'd lived with this for seventeen years now and all her hysterics were a bit baffling and unsettling.

Jenny stopped pacing for a minute and came to sit opposite me. She took both my hands in hers and, with an earnest look, she said: 'Dawn, we need to know – do you want to take this any further?'

'What do you mean?' I asked.

'I mean, do you want to report John to the authorities?'

191

I pulled my hands away now and sat back on my wooden chair.

'Well, yeah, I've thought about it . . .' I started. Though I was scared of the publicity and scared of speaking out, ever since Callum had been born five years previously my memories had been a little like a pickaxe, chipping away at my resolve to lock it all away, reminding me over and over that there were innocent children in the world and that it might be my responsibility to keep them safe. When Callum was born, these fears had begun to haunt me: I'd suddenly realized that John was still out there, still the same person he'd been years before. On late, dark nights when I couldn't sleep, I worried that he might find other vulnerable children to abuse.

I opened my mouth to tell my mum and Jenny all this – but I didn't get the chance.

'Yes, well, we know it's an awful thing that's happened to you,' Jenny butted in. 'I can't imagine the pain you went through as a child. I really can't. It must have been *horrendous* for you. But, I wonder, how that would make *you* feel?'

'What?' My head was buzzing now. How would *what* make me feel? I couldn't follow her.

Perplexed, I looked over to Mum for guidance, but she wouldn't look at me. She just sat there, head bowed, a Kleenex to her nose, occasionally shaking her head as if too distressed to talk.

'Look, if you go to the authorities we'll back you,' Jenny went on. 'A hundred per cent, we'll back you. But I'm wondering: how do you think that's going to help the situation?'

'What do you mean?'

'Help you mentally, I mean?'

'I don't know.'

'Well, we don't think it will. Think about it. If you bring a case like this against your brother you're going to have to go over what he did to you in great detail not just to the police, but in court, in front of dozens of people. And that's going to be reported in the papers. That in itself will be very, very difficult for you.

'But then imagine he pleads "not guilty"; then the jurors will have to decide – who is to be believed? You or John? And you know what? That's going to be very tough for you.'

Jenny barely paused for breath before continuing: 'Even if, in the *best* possible outcome, you manage to convince the jury that he's guilty and he gets sent to prison, his defence barrister is going to tear into you. He's going to bring up your whole past and everything to do with Stuart and the school and everything else. Your personal history, with Stuart and Maria and their marriage, will be used against you, to discredit you, to make you look like a liar. Whatever happens, whatever the outcome, your name will be dragged through the mud, in the interests of justice. In the interests of giving John a fair trial.

'Think about it, Dawn! You've got Callum to look after now. He starts school in August – if this comes out it's going to be humiliating for him. You might have to take him out of that school and put him in boarding school so that his education isn't affected.'

She paused for a beat now, letting that sink in. 'Even so,' she went on, with a troubled sigh at all this distress I would be caused, 'it's going to be very traumatic for you, and very traumatic for him too, no matter what. And that's imagining the *best* possible outcome.

'Now imagine for a minute you bring this case against John and you lose. We're not just talking about humiliation now, we're talking complete bloody annihilation. Your character, your good name, your reputation, your mum's reputation, your dad's, Stuart's reputation – everybody! The whole family ripped to shreds. They'll all go down with you.

'Are you strong enough to cope with that? Because if you're not, Dawn, and you're not prepared for that outcome, then think very carefully about going down this road. Because your little boy needs his mother. And if you can't handle the fallout and lose the plot, then I ask you: what happens to him? Hmm? Who's going to take care of him if something happens to you?'

It was a horrifying scenario that she was laying out and I suddenly felt very frightened. She went on and on about how this would affect my son, my parents, Susy, Stuart, everyone I'd ever cared about. It was appalling and I just sat there, stunned into silence.

'But, look, you don't *have* to report him,' Jenny concluded. 'We could keep an eye on him, make sure he knows *we know* and make it clear that he's to stay away from children, at all costs. And then, for you, Dawn, we get the best counselling money can buy. That's your other option.'

Jenny watched my reaction carefully, observing the impact of her words. 'So,' she said brightly, assured her work was done. 'What's it to be? Think very carefully now. Do you want to talk to the police?'

'Erm, no, I guess not,' I stuttered. My head was throbbing and I felt a familiar stabbing pain in my side. My kidney stones had been getting a lot worse recently and now I was desperate to get home so I could take some painkillers.

'You could see a good psychiatrist, couldn't you?' Jenny went on encouragingly.

'Yeah, I suppose,' I said, rubbing at my temples. I just wanted to get out of there. I'd had enough. It was like I'd opened Pandora's box, seen the terrible contents and just wanted to close the lid and put it away again.

'Good girl.' Jenny smiled at me; there was pity in her eyes, but maybe also a certain satisfaction. Then she nodded to my mum, who had stopped crying and was looking at me with something resembling hope.

'Very wise, Dawn,' Jenny added quietly. 'Very wise indeed.'

Chapter 14

The Sadist

It was not long after the discussion with Aunt Jenny that my phone rang one morning. I'd been sorting out some paperwork for the new flats I was buying and, distracted, I answered without really thinking.

'What the fuck did you have to go and bring all this up again for?' hissed a familiar voice in my ear.

It was a shock to hear it again, after all these years.

'John?' It took a while to register that it was him. Despite myself, despite the fact I told myself he couldn't hurt me anymore, I felt my heart start to pound in fear.

'Yeah, it's me. Do you know what's happening here? I've lost my fucking job! That interfering bloody aunt of ours called my boss and told him that I wasn't safe to be around children.'

'In the call centre . . . ?' I was confused. I'd heard through Mum that John was working in a call centre.

'No. Not the fucking call centre. My job as a caretaker in the leisure centre after work and at weekends. I hold two fucking jobs here to make ends meet. So tell me, Dawn, why the fuck did you have to bring this up again and ruin my fucking life? Why couldn't you just let it be?'

Suddenly, I was angry.

'Why should I hide?' I countered bravely. 'I didn't do anything wrong. I'll tell everyone what you did to me, you arsehole. And don't speak to me ever again!'

With that, I slammed the phone down, shaking with rage. How dare he! I was outraged that he put this thing back onto me, and I found my anger gave me strength. I had spoken back to John. He *couldn't* hurt me anymore.

Still trembling, I pushed the paperwork on my desk away from me, unable to concentrate, and took a big gulp of breath, trying to calm myself. *Why can't it all just go away?* I thought wretchedly.

Since that conversation with Aunt Jenny, I'd felt so confused about everything. Now my 'secret' was out, the whole family knew. My sister Susy had called from London to sympathize with me. She said she was shocked to learn what John had done – and had confronted him about it. Apparently, he told her he felt awful about it, really guilty, but – I thought testily – I didn't hear any sign of remorse in his phone call to me.

Susy and I had been close as young girls, but living at opposite ends of the country, leading very different lives, meant we didn't see or even speak to each other that often. Nonetheless, my kind-hearted sister wanted to know how she could help but, frankly, I didn't want to talk about it anymore. I couldn't even bring myself to call the psychiatrist that Mum had found for me. My aunt had convinced me that going to the police would definitely be a bad idea and, since then, I'd just been too embarrassed to talk about it. So I thanked Susy for her concern but I told her I was fine. Like I did with everyone, I pushed her away, on the other side of the wall I'd built to protect myself.

As for my so-called partner, Stuart was appalled the subject of me 'dobbing' on John had even come up. 'Go to the fucking pigs?' he railed at me, beer bottle in hand. 'Are you fucking kidding me?' It was against everything he believed in.

My family and my boyfriend had made themselves quite clear. So there was nothing else for it – I had to put up and shut up. All I wanted to do now was forget about the abuse and get on with my life – bury the memories, try to put it behind me.

The one thing I didn't expect was that my mum would find it so easy to forget too. Within a couple of weeks, she was talking to John on the phone just like she did before. I overheard her one afternoon when I arrived with Callum, though she quickly put down the receiver when she realized I was there. Had she forgiven him so easily? Did his rape of me mean nothing to her?

'Mum, how can you do that? Talk to him as if nothing's happened?' I asked her, shocked.

'Because he's my son,' she said simply, as if that explained everything.

'I don't understand,' I replied.

'Well, you *won't* understand,' she snapped and left it at that.

By now my kidney stones were flaring up almost daily; maybe prompted by all the emotional trauma I was enduring at this time. The doctor had given me pethidine to cope with the worst attacks, when the stones moved, and I kept the painkillers in my bag at all times so that when I felt an attack come on, I could deal with the pain.

It was late July when I accompanied Stuart to a photo-shoot with a local rugby team his property company, Mayfair Holdings, had sponsored. He enjoyed it when I came with him on official engagements, especially if I drove, which meant he could drink. But it was still early today so Stuart decided he would drive us in his Bentley. It meant I wasn't driving us for a change – and thank goodness because, on the way back, I felt a twinge in my side and winced involuntarily, doubling up in pain. *Thank God I'm on the waiting list for an operation,* I thought, as I braced myself against the agony. It was absolutely unbearable.

'How bad is it?' Stuart asked, seemingly concerned.

'It's really bad. Worse than childbirth,' I said. 'If I didn't have these pills, I'd be vomiting and shivering uncontrollably right now.'

Stuart nodded, taking in that information. 'How often do you get the attacks?' he asked, probing me. 'I mean often, like once an hour, once a day, what?'

'Well, about every hour the pain comes and lasts about fifteen minutes, then it becomes a slow ache around my back and side. The pethidine keeps the worst of it at bay for around four hours, until I can take more.'

'Can I see the pills the doctor gave you?' he asked, casting me a gentle look as he drove.

So I reached into my bag and pulled out the heavy box of pills. I handed them to Stuart, who promptly wound down the window and threw them out of the car.

'What the hell . . . ? Why did you do that?' I shouted at him, tears pricking my eyes at his cruelty. I expected him to brake and turn around so we could get them, the 'hilarious' joke over, but we didn't slow down. Not one bit. 'Stop the car, Stuart!' I shrieked at him, clutching my side. 'Stop driving!'

But Stuart just laughed and kept motoring on.

'You don't need those,' he said dismissively, in a tone that brooked no argument. 'You just need rest. It's all in your mind, ken?'

I had lived with Stuart for six years now; I knew my partner well. I had a terrible feeling that he was planning something awful, but I didn't dare disobey him when we got home and he told me to go to bed.

I don't know, maybe he just wants to show me a way to cope with the pain? Give me an alternative to taking the pills? I thought hopefully as I fell awkwardly into bed, spared for a moment the excruciating pains in my side. Hannah was out with Callum for the day so it was just the two of us at home. *Or maybe*, I thought, feeling a bit brighter, *he'll get me something else from the doctor, something more effective.* I knew better than anyone that Stuart could pull strings when he wanted to. I felt myself drifting off. Once the pain had gone, I was always exhausted afterwards. It really took it out of me.

'Just lay there and rest,' Stuart shouted as he uncorked a bottle of cabernet sauvignon and switched on the TV. 'Call me when the pain starts.'

He sounded like any concerned husband would do.

I did as I was told. I quickly fell asleep but, inevitably, some time later I was woken by a wave of pain that flooded my body.

'It's started!' I shouted out to Stuart, hoping he would come through with some kind of relief. God knows, I needed it! The pain was stronger than ever, leaving me doubled up and breathless. I closed my eyes as it overtook me completely and my whole body just became a sharp shard of pain, vibrating at a high frequency.

When I opened my eyes again, Stuart was standing in front of me, naked and masturbating.

'Ha – I'm not going to stick this in your mouth, with you writhing in pain, you might bite it off!' he laughed.

Is this a joke to him? What is he doing? I couldn't believe it – was he really getting off on watching me suffer? A sob escaped me now; I couldn't bear it any longer. I needed my pills. But Stuart had other ideas. Once hard, he pinned me to the bed and started to fuck me. I screwed my eyes shut against the awfulness of it all.

'Look into my eyes,' he grunted. 'Look at me, Dawn! I want to see your eyes!'

But I couldn't look at him; I couldn't focus at all. I felt I had been cut adrift on a sea of pain and I barely registered what he was doing to me. All I wanted was to bring my knees into my chest, to give myself a little relief, but he pushed against me hard, using all his strength to pin me down.

'Yeah, that's right,' he breathed hard as he thrust into me.

Then he reached down and, using his fingers, he jabbed me in my right side so hard I screamed out.

'It's here, isn't it?' he murmured sadistically. 'Go on! Scream. Cry. Let me see you in pain. That's it, keep fighting, let the pain take over, make me fight you. C'mon . . . is that the best you can do?'

All I wanted was to make him stop but the strength fled

my body now and I collapsed under him, tears streaming down my face.

'Please, please . . . please stop, Stuart,' I whispered. 'Please.'

But when had any man listened when I'd asked them to stop?

He kept on going, kept on and on, getting off on the expression on my face, on the tension in my body, as I endured spasms of pain that he timed to his unforgiving thrusts. Eventually, he came and rolled off me, then walked through to the lounge again. He picked up his red wine and took a long swig.

Him closing the bedroom door was the last thing I saw before I passed out.

The next day, I woke to the sound of Stuart showering next door. I hated him right then, hated him for what he had done to me and how he had used my pain against me. I fantasized about taking a knife from the kitchen and plunging it into his back while he was in the shower, just like in that scene from *Psycho*. I wanted to hurt him, but more than that I wanted him punished. But how? Who was I going to tell? Who would help me?

I knew the answer to that one: nobody.

No, I knew I couldn't confront Stuart about this. I knew that by the time he came out of the shower, I would have to try and put it to the back of my mind. I had a lot of practice at that, at least.

I didn't always take Stuart's sadistic sex and hurtful treatment of me in my stride. But whenever I had challenged him in the past about something awful he had done to me, he'd told me it was normal. That it was how relationships between men and women worked. And I didn't know any different; he was the only man I'd ever been with, ever since I was fifteen years old.

With the benefit of hindsight, I can see now that he duped me just as my brother had once duped me with his lies about what he did to me being 'normal'. Stuart said the same. He said that since I was his woman, I was to do whatever he wanted and when. If I didn't, he would get it elsewhere. And I knew *that* was true. After all, he had been unfaithful to Maria with me.

'If you stay with me, I won't hurt you,' he'd said on several occasions. 'You are inside the circle of protection.'

He then grabbed my jaw and tilted my head to look at what he was doing with his other hand.

'Look, do you get it?'

He drew circles in the air . . . once, twice . . . before releasing me and gently slapping the side of my face.

'If you leave then you are outside the circle and I can no longer protect you or be responsible for what might happen to you . . .'

So, lying in bed that morning, I buried it. I buried the memories of what he had done the night before, just like I had buried the memories of John's abuse. I thought I could forget, I thought that if I chose not to think about it, it would all go away.

But although I got up and carried on with Stuart like nothing had happened, I did take some action. That morning, I called my doctor and told him I wanted to get the kidney stones removed privately. It would cost me a couple of grand, but that was a small price to pay. For I knew now that I couldn't afford to show Stuart any kind of weakness – or he would exploit it.

Just four days later I went under the knife. In my own small way, I was trying to fight back.

Chapter 15

Elvis on Astroturf

Meanwhile, I had some spare cash so I took a few months off and allowed myself to enjoy life. For the first time in years I had some free time on my hands, so Stuart and I booked a long holiday to the States with Callum and Hannah. I didn't really want Hannah to come – it was an expense we didn't need – but Stuart had insisted, since we would be out every night and Callum needed a babysitter. Stuart told me that after this holiday Hannah would continue to be employed, as he would find me something to do straightaway and he needed her to take care of Callum. 'The hours you work, I would need three Hannahs!' he said. 'And then how would I get my cut if all that money was on other staff? Hannah's staying.'

I couldn't wait to go away. The night before we caught our plane, Hannah took me aside.

'I think Stuart's going to ask you to marry him while you're in Las Vegas,' she whispered.

'What makes you say that?' I asked, astonished.

'Hmm? Just a feeling, that's all. Would you do it?'

'I don't know . . .' I was still very young, after all, and the idea of getting married filled me with dread. It seemed so permanent. I would be officially tying myself to the man who constantly threatened and belittled me, who always took and gave nothing in return. Then again, it wasn't as if I was thinking of leaving Stuart. I couldn't imagine leaving the 'circle of protection' or trying to bring up our little boy on my own.

The following day I looked at him, as he downed tiny bottles of red wine on the flight, mulling over what Hannah had said. As much as I disliked many aspects of his character, in other ways I admired him – for the way he took what he wanted from life, the way he trampled over the rules (even if that did involve trampling over people). I had been brought up to adhere strictly to society's perceptions of what was 'acceptable'; my mother had been obsessed with how things looked on the outside, as if nothing else mattered except what other people thought of you. But Stuart didn't give a toss what other people thought of him and that was strangely refreshing. He was fearless – and I wanted to be the same.

No, I thought to myself, *I don't love him, but I respect him.* No wonder I did; he was always banging on about 'respect' and demanding it from me. But it went beyond that: he had built a successful business empire and, even though he seemed pretty lazy to me now that he'd 'made it', the fact that he had done so at all showed he had something about him. *There's still a lot I could learn from him.* On the other side of me, I kept Callum busy with colouring books throughout the flight; we both looked up as Stuart let out a loud belch after his latest bottle of vino. It was hardly what a prospective groom might do to romance his potential bride! *Nah*, I told myself. *Hannah's wrong. Stuart wouldn't want to get hitched again. After all, he's only just come out of a bad marriage. Why would he want to do all that again?*

With that, I put the ridiculous idea to the back of my mind. The holiday was great fun – we visited Los Angeles, San Diego, San Francisco and finally, on the third week, we had five nights booked at the Caesar's Palace in Las Vegas. For Stuart, it was the ideal way to end the holiday – he liked nothing better than spending all day gambling and drinking. This was like his very own paradise!

As for me, I didn't really drink and I wasn't interested in gambling either. Besides, I had to take care of Callum, so the two of us wandered in and out of the most luxurious hotels, admiring all the fountains and crazy architecture, while Stuart spent his days at the tables. Callum and I played crazy golf, went swimming and in the afternoons we saw a couple of shows on the Strip.

Two days before the end of the holiday, we were all downstairs in the dining room, having breakfast, when Stuart turned to me and said: 'Let's get married today!'

'What?' I nearly choked on my croissant. *Hannah was right . . .*

'I said – let's get married. Today!' He grinned. This was clearly his idea of a romantic proposal and I could see that he was completely serious.

'But how can we get married?' I smiled back, bemused. 'Don't you need documents? Erm, birth certificates and stuff?'

'Yep, I got all that,' he said.

'Really? You planned this?'

For a minute we just stared at each other while Callum shovelled Cheerios into his mouth. Then Stuart took a sip of his tea. When he put the cup down, there was a change in his demeanour – the playfulness had disappeared and now he spoke with a certain cool detachment: 'You know, if someone asks you to marry them and you say no, that's effectively the end of the relationship. Did you know that?'

He was staring into the distance as he spoke but I knew it was a threat. This was now or never. My mind was running at a hundred miles an hour. If I said no, then that was the end of us: I would be a single mum on the scrapheap and he would take everything. I couldn't see a future without Stuart – where would I go? Back to my parents'? Urgh, the thought of returning to their house, where I had been abused so badly, was appalling.

'Listen,' he went on. 'Why don't you go to the hotel salon and get your hair done? Make yourself look nice. I'll take Callum to the shops to get him something to wear. We'll make a day of it. What do you say?'

I just nodded. There was nothing else to say.

Sat in the hairdresser's chair that morning, I must have seemed like I was a million miles away as the customers and staff buzzed around me.

'You getting married today, sweet pea?' my hairdresser drawled as she clacked a piece of gum against the roof of her mouth. Her name tag read 'Cindy' and she had bright-orange fingernails and long hair extensions which reached right down to her bum.

'Hmm . . . yeah. How did you know?'

'Oh, everyone who comes in here is getting married, honey,' Cindy laughed. Did my nervousness give me away? Or my quiet detachment? But something prompted her to say: 'You know, it's not too late to change your mind, sweet pea. We've heard it all in here. You know, the strippers who marry the men they've just met. Jilted brides who turn up to the church, only to find their men have gone and married their best friends! You name it, we've heard it. Nothing to be ashamed of, changing your mind. Because, you gotta know this, sweet pea, once it's done in Vegas, it is D.O.N.E. Done!'

She went on like that for a while as she styled my long blonde hair into loose, tumbling curls around my face and the other members of staff in the salon each contributed their own horror stories of weddings gone wrong. Eventually – I couldn't help myself – I started laughing. I was glad they had cheered me up, if only for a short time. I had needed someone to take my mind off my predicament. Gratefully, I left them a big tip and went up to the room to change into my cream Whistles skirt and pale-blue blouse – they were the smartest clothes I had with me. Then I went to the front lobby, where Stuart had instructed me to meet him.

I was astonished when, ten minutes later, he jumped out of a giant stretch limo, Callum at his side wearing a white-and-blue sailor suit.

'Well, what do you think?' He gestured to the giant white car. It was a monstrosity but I daren't criticize him so I just gave him a big smile as he opened the door for me. I was happy to see that Callum, at least, loved it and bounced around the seats excitedly as Stuart instructed the driver to take us to the Graceland Wedding Chapel.

There's no backing out of it now, I thought nervously, as I stepped out of the limo and surveyed the large gaudy billboard outside the Graceland Wedding Chapel. Inside, there was a colourful explosion of fake flowers and the floor was covered in Astroturf. *Hmm . . . just what you expect to find in the desert.* The place was busy, with various couples milling about the gift shop, having their pictures taken under the floral arch or waiting in the pews to be married.

While Stuart dealt with the arrangements, I took a stroll around the gift shop with Callum at my side, surveying the mugs, keyrings, T-shirts and champagne on offer, all at sky-high prices. This didn't feel quirky or fun – it felt cheap and naff, just like those plastic keyrings. We took our places at the back and waited our turn.

In front of us was a large group of African-Americans in shiny white suits and red bow ties, who were shouting in a loud and good-natured way over each other. *They seem so happy*, I noted sadly to myself. I couldn't help comparing their joyful, noisy group to our own sad little gathering. *The whole thing is crazy. Crazy!* Even inside the air-conditioned room, it was baking hot and I could feel myself sweating through my blouse so I tried fanning the material at my armpits.

'Callum.' I bent down and whispered to my son. 'Callum, I'm really nervous.'

'Don't worry, Mummy,' he whispered back. 'I'll hold your hand.'

All too soon, it was our turn and we approached the main chapel font, where a strange-looking man who called himself 'the minister' beckoned us forward. He was short and slim with slicked-back hair and wore a white Seventies-style suit, like the type Elvis wore at the end of his career. The whole bizarre ensemble was topped off with a thin leather tie and slippers.

'So, who's your best man?' He spoke with a relaxed southern twang.

Callum's hand shot up in the air.

'Me, me, me!' he shouted.

'Now then, this little fella can be your witness,' said the minister. 'Just the three of you, is it? Okey dokey then! No need for a best man.'

There was very little preamble – just a quick confirmation of our names, then the minister started on the vows.

'Do you, Stuart Michael Kelly, take Dawn Jean McConnell to be your lawfully wedded wife . . .' I started to zone out. *Is this really happening?* That morning I'd woken expecting a day of sunbathing and sightseeing and now I was getting married! It was madness and I couldn't take it seriously. I felt a quivering in the pit of my stomach and I started to giggle uncontrollably, until I heard Stuart say: 'I do.'

Then the minister turned to me.

'And do you, Dawn Jean McConnell, take Stuart Michael Kelly to be your lawfully wedded husband? To look after him in sickness and in health? To love, honour and obey him all the days of your life?'

Stuart was looking at me levelly now, his head bobbing up and down and his eyes signalling to me silently: 'say yes, say yes – or else . . .'

Oh Christ . . .

'Yes, I do,' I said. I felt I didn't have a choice.

The minister smiled and then asked Stuart for the rings. There was a moment's hesitation and then Stuart said: 'What do you mean? We don't have any rings.'

'You need a ring,' the minister explained. 'To seal the marriage.'

'Right, Dawn, take off your earring.' Stuart pointed at the hooped earring on my right ear.

He can't be serious? He hasn't even bought a ring?

211

I just wanted it all to be over as quickly as possible now so I didn't object, I just slipped the earring out of my ear and handed it to Stuart, who gave it to the minister.

'With this ring, I thee wed,' he intoned. 'I now pronounce you man and wife. You may kiss the bride!'

It was all so bizarre, so utterly unreal. I could hardly believe it when the minister finished and handed us a goody bag. This was to start our married life together. I took a quick peek: washing powder, one condom, bleach, paracetamol, a White Chapel keyring and some soap.

'Smile!' The photographer grinned cheesily as we stood underneath the arch of fake white lilies and the bulb flashed, once. Instantly the image was printed and we were offered a range of products upon which to memorialize this magical moment forever. We turned down the T-shirts and opted for a normal framed picture and a mug.

The mug broke on the flight on the way home, which seemed pretty apt. As for the photograph, I hid it away as soon as we got in the house, unable to bring myself to look at it.

Many years later, I came across the picture again and, for the first time, I properly examined our wedding photo. There I was, a small woman aged just twenty-two, clutching the arm of a man who was more than two decades older and starting to go to seed. I looked so frightened, so utterly terrified, that even while my mouth was smiling, my eyes were screaming.

Screaming for help.

'Oh, I'm so pleased!' Mum exclaimed when I told her our good news on our return. 'That's so good for Callum because he's starting school at the end of the month and it would have been terrible for him to start school with unmarried parents. Can you imagine? Poor boy would have stuck out like a sore thumb.'

Really? Is that all she cares about? Mum's snobbishness never ceased to amaze me. Dad, meanwhile, was polite and shook Stuart's hand but he didn't seem all that bothered. Neither of them offered warm congratulations to us. *Fine*, I thought to myself. *That suits me just fine.* I wanted as little fuss made as possible. To me, it didn't feel like something to celebrate.

The fact was, I couldn't get used to the idea that I was now married to Stuart. There was no engagement, no run-up to the ceremony; it's not even as if we had talked about the idea generally before the big day. No, it was just sprung on me and I was told I had to accept his decision or else. Or else I would be thrown out of that 'circle of protection' to who knew what wolves. I couldn't let that happen to me and Callum.

Stuart and I didn't even buy a ring together once we got back, he just handed me £400 and told me to 'get something nice'. So I chose a simple gold band and, for the most part, I kept it in my drawer at home. Stuart didn't notice that my wedding finger was naked much of the time, nor seem to mind that I kept my own name. I wanted to remain a McConnell. The world was already full of too many Mrs Kellys to my mind.

Apparently, Maria had cried when she found out we were married. Now working in a fish and chip shop, she didn't have a penny to her name. Stuart liked to pop in there every now and then. He didn't even order anything, he just wanted to rub her nose in it. He had to see for himself that he had 'won'. For he hadn't just left her, he'd taken it *all* from her: the money, the lifestyle, even her self-respect. And he'd laughed about it with me when he told me how she had cried.

I think he expected me to laugh too – but I wasn't a love-struck teenager anymore, in competition with Maria and desperate to hang on to Stuart at all costs. When I'd been caught up in my obsession for my much-older lover, swept away by his words and by his promises to keep me safe, I hadn't cared one bit that we were hurting her, but things were different now. Unlike my new husband, the pain of others wasn't something in which I found my entertainment.

In fact, for the first time, I felt a pang of sympathy for my ex-rival. *Oh, just leave her alone,* I thought angrily.

Thought, but didn't say – I wasn't brave enough for that.

We've all moved on since those days, I told myself. Now our son was old enough to start school himself, I knew that I'd left the young, innocent schoolgirl I'd once been far behind me.

But funnily enough, the man who had led her astray was still yanking at that invisible lead he had tied firmly around her neck.

Chapter 16

Hotel from Hell

About a month after we got back from the States, Stuart made a new investment in a hotel with Adam, and installed his friend Kevin as the manager. The Cavendish had eighty-two rooms, two bars and two nightclubs on the premises. It had once been a grand Victorian building but, in the last decade, it had been run into the ground. Several previous owners had failed to make the capital investments needed for the upkeep so the place had become an eyesore. Crumbling and much unloved, it was run as a doss house for council tenants. And this, Stuart felt, was a perfect money-spinner.

But almost immediately alarm bells started ringing. For just six weeks after Kevin had been installed as the manager Stuart came to talk to me, needing my help.

'We've got a problem,' he said grimly. 'It's Kevin. I think he's stealing.' He wanted me to look at the books.

It didn't take long for me to figure out what was going on. After spending just one week at The Cavendish, I saw how it all worked. This wasn't a hotel for tourists, it was more like the hotel from hell – peeling wallpaper, tatty carpets, broken windows and battered furniture. For £20 a night anyone could

215

get a roof over their head – and I mean *anyone* – so it was here that the very dregs of society washed up. In The Cavendish the council housed its very worst tenants, the people they couldn't put anywhere else. There were heroin addicts, shoplifters, murderers, rapists and sex offenders. But I wasn't worried about this – to my mind, people were just people underneath and I had run pubs before where hard Glasgow men drank nightly. I had dealt with flashers and the criminal underworld and I knew I could cope. The council was happy to pay £140 a week for each resident on a bed-and-breakfast basis – though many weren't up in time for breakfast – as long as the hotel could ensure the residents stayed in one place and didn't skip town. There was even a weekly register for the council tenants to sign, just to ensure we kept tabs on our guests.

From looking at the books, I saw that Stuart was right: Kevin was stealing on a grand scale and he was doing it so openly, so brazenly, it was shocking. The hotel had its fair share of permanent council residents, which brought in a lot of money, but it also took in business off the street: customers who paid cash. The bars and clubs were also cash businesses. But there was no cash in the safe – no cash anywhere at all! I estimated that in the past few weeks, £40,000 had gone missing from the business. Stuart had installed his pal to run his hotel but Kevin had had his grubby little hands in the till the whole time.

'Right, he's out,' Stuart told me decisively after I went through all the figures with him. 'He doesn't get away with this. I'll sack him tomorrow. You think you can step in?'

I nodded. I didn't really have much choice and with Callum at school now, I suppose I was ready for my next challenge. This was a big one – a hotel, two bars and two clubs – but already I could see the potential. With the right management, and good practices, this place could be a gold mine!

The following morning Stuart confronted Kevin at the hotel and the pair had a massive row. I was taking Callum to school at the time so I didn't see what happened and, when I got to work to find Stuart had a busted, bloody nose, he didn't want to tell me either.

'He's gone,' he said, shaking his head. 'That's all you need to know.'

Now I took over running The Cavendish and for a while I just sat back and took notes, watching how the business worked.

Our residents weren't the average type of person. On the first floor we kept the shoplifters and elderly people, the ones who had spent their lives in and out of prison. These old folk were institutionalized. They didn't like to leave the hotel for any reason, eating their meals in their rooms in front of the TV and sending out the younger shoplifters to get their booze and fags. On the second floor were the junkies, the heroin addicts who stayed in their rooms unless they went out to collect their methadone prescriptions, which they frequently sold to each other to buy bags of heroin. On the third and fourth floors there was a mixture of standard housing-benefit tenants, who smoked weed all day or had a drink problem. They were constantly thinking of ways to make a quick buck, usually by stealing.

These residents brought in a steady revenue stream from their rooms but it was clear that we had the chance to make some big money from our bars and clubs, which I was surprised to find were mostly empty during the week. *How is this possible?*

I wondered. We had over eighty people in the hotel at any one time, people who didn't work and had nothing to do all day. *Where are they going? More to the point, where are they spending their money?* I knew if I could persuade them to stay and spend money in the hotel, we'd be onto something good.

So the first thing I did was to simplify our drink and food prices. Everything was a pound – a cheese toastie was a pound, a shot of vodka cost a pound. A soft drink, pint, bag of chips – it was all £1. The only thing that was not a pound was the pool table, which I set at the below-average price of 20p a game. This encouraged people to play pool at our hotel rather than go to the pool halls, which charged 50p a time. So now we had cheap entertainment and the pool table was busy from eleven in the morning until twelve at night. That pool table made £700 a week; money that went straight into Stuart's pocket.

But this was just the first step. Since most of the residents were on benefits and got £90 every fortnight each from their giro, we started up a 'giro scheme'. I put a spreadsheet up on the wall with each resident's name, followed by ninety spaces indicating 90 credits from the bars and hotel. At the start of every fortnight, they handed over their giro money to the bar and that would give them ninety credits. Every time they had something to drink or eat, a box was scored off. This way they could make their giro last longer, enjoy a social life in the hotel and know their money was safe. They could even earn extra credits by doing little jobs for us like taking out the rubbish or restocking the bars. The Cavendish was now a place where our guests could spend their days in the company of others instead of hiding out in their rooms alone.

So we became very popular with our residents and also

attracted punters from outside – and they came from first thing in the morning till last thing at night. Because The Cavendish wasn't for people who drank occasionally, after work or sociably, it was for people who drank *all the time*, which meant the money started rolling in. And this pleased Stuart no end. If there was one thing my husband liked more than anything else, it was money. As long as I could guarantee the cash flow, then I knew he was a happy man.

To be honest, though, it even surprised me how successful we became so quickly! We could earn £30,000 from one weekend in one bar alone. Once we'd paid all our bills and settled the staff wages, this meant we walked away with thousands each week. I worked out that after our first year, Stuart and I took nearly half a million from The Cavendish, and most of that was cash.

Of course, The Cavendish wasn't a pleasant place to work; I banned Callum from coming to visit because I was afraid for his safety. Violence frequently broke out for little or no reason and we had to break up fights all the time. But I never felt scared for my own safety – I was The Boss, the one who kept the hotel open and under control, so I knew that most of my residents felt loyal towards me and would never threaten my safety. If anything, they wanted to protect me. With my new regime, I gave them a home, a place where they felt welcome; something many of them hadn't had in years.

There were only a few rules at The Cavendish. No subs – if you didn't have the money, we couldn't serve you. And there were strictly no drugs in the bars and clubs. Of course, I couldn't stop anybody shooting up in the privacy of their own room but in the public spaces we came down hard. The toilet lids were smeared with Vaseline to prevent them snorting cocaine from them, and anyone caught dealing drugs in front of the staff was banned for life. I'm sure it went on all the time – I couldn't change these people – but I warned them not to let me see it or I would call the police. So they hid from me, down the back stairs, in one of the many toilets on the landings, or in the fire escape. They huddled together in pairs, striking deals for dope, weed, coke, heroin, dihydrocodeine, methamphetamines, barbiturates, crack or valium – anything they could get their hands on. The junkies hid their wraps behind their backs when anyone passed by, and the men waited until the corridors were clear before visiting the hookers. In many ways, the debauchery was as bad as that of The Schoolhouse. It was hard to believe that I was actually running and condoning everything I was against at The Schoolhouse.

At The Cavendish we quickly came to an understanding with the police. They left us alone as long as we cooperated fully with their investigations. Frankly, they saw the advantage of putting all the criminals in one place so that they always knew where to find them. Often, they would call to ask when certain tenants were likely to be in, then they'd come to collect a key at reception and either take them in for questioning, or arrest them.

One time, six police cars screamed up to the front of the hotel and out jumped a dozen armed police, followed by several important-looking detectives. The chief detective said he'd come from London to arrest a man who was on the run from down south. To my horror, I learned that this new resident of ours was wanted for the rape and murder of a young woman in London. When he'd signed in with us a week before, he'd applied for full housing benefit. That's what had alerted the authorities and they had swooped in to arrest him and make him pay for his crimes.

Coming into contact with dangerous individuals was only part of the hazard of working in my hotel. In fact the biggest danger at The Cavendish was fire. Whether it was by accident or arson, the number of fires at The Cavendish was frightening – and worrying about the threat of fire kept me awake at night. Frequently, there would be rows between residents and some stupid bugger would throw a lit cigarette into his neighbour's room, hoping to burn him to death. Then he'd actually fall asleep in his own room, not thinking for a moment that the fire might engulf him too. Or burn the whole bloody building down for that matter!

Our fire extinguishers were used on a daily basis. All the staff got used to running up the stairs to put out fires, either set deliberately or caused accidentally by drunks falling asleep with lit fags, or by the Bunsen burner of a heroin addict catching fire to the curtains. Even the residents got used to putting out each other's fires.

Thankfully, I employed a brilliant team of sixteen staff members who all knew the kind of people we were dealing with and, together, we became like a little family. The things we saw in our daily work, the difficult situations we had to handle, made us all very close. Stuart was hardly there at all – only at the weekends when he came in to skim the tills. He certainly never showed any concern for me or the environment I was working in.

And, as sad as it sounds, death became a daily occurrence – either from heroin overdoses, old age or asphyxiation from solvent abuse. During the daily handover, from one shift to the next, we had a series of questions to run through with the person taking over. One of those questions was: 'Any deaths?' It was that common, I once counted six deaths in a week.

One day, about six months after I took over, a resident's girlfriend came running to reception when I was on shift.

'Help! Please help – ma wee lad is dead!' she wailed.

Bolting up the stairs, I arrived at their room. All the walls were painted purple and there were no belongings at all, just a bed in one corner and a Bunsen burner in the middle of the floor with tinfoil smouldering away. It was a typical junkie's room. They sold anything that they could get their hands on, even their own clothes, so junkies never had any possessions. The man's body was on the bed, naked save for the needle sticking out of his groin.

'Help him,' the girl shrieked. 'Please help him. He's gonnae die! Gi' him mouth to mouth. Please!'

I stared at his naked, limp, skinny pale body – he couldn't have been more than twenty-five years old – and all I could see was his massive erection. He was dead, that was for sure, for his eyes were open unblinkingly and fresh vomit had collected in his mouth and over his torso. No doubt he'd overdosed from a lethal cocktail of heroin and prescription methadone.

'I'm sorry, love, I can't do anything for him,' I said gently. 'He's gone now. He's gone.'

Then I left her crying over her dead boyfriend to phone the ambulance. Sadly, this was all too often the way we found our heroin-addicted residents. For the most part they were zombies, harmless individuals too stoned to threaten anyone, only ever looking for their next hit, unaware that every hit could be their last.

Another time, the cleaner reported a terrible smell coming from what she thought was a blocked toilet on the second floor, and that a large amount of flies had gathered outside Room 73.

I exchanged a fearful look with Laura, the other girl on reception with me that day. We both knew who occupied Room 73. The tenant was a young man called Ted who had fallen from an oil rig whilst up working in Aberdeen and had epilepsy to add to all his other physical injuries. Now Ted's face was also disfigured from banging into the rig on the way down and he struggled to walk with all the pins in his hips, dragging his left leg behind him. He didn't like people to see his disfigurement so he generally kept himself to himself. He had no family, no friends, no one who cared for him or his existence. Even so, we liked Ted, he was a dignified soul, a true young gentleman, and he had become part of our little community. We exchanged 'good mornings' with him every day when he hobbled downstairs for breakfast. I checked with the other staff – nobody had seen Ted for four days.

So on this hot day in July Laura and I went up to Room 73, full of fear and dread. When we got to the room, there were flies crawling out from under the door, up the door and over the carpet. After knocking a couple of times we unlocked the door and entered the south-facing room. The heat and stench hit us both at the same time. I could taste death in the air, it was that strong.

Ted was propped up in the corner of the room against a radiator that was on full blast, facing a closed window. The July sun beat down on him, as it had probably done for the past four days straight. It was baking hot and the flies were everywhere so we quickly covered our mouths with our sleeves and opened the window. Now, up close, we took a good look at Ted.

Oh my God, there is nothing left of his face!

His face and body were completely infested with thousands upon thousands of maggots. Bodily fluid seeped out through his clothes and his eyes were now just hollow spaces with maggots feasting inside. His whole rotting body seemed to be visibly moving as the maggots writhed and crawled over each other. When Laura touched his head, it fell forward revealing his skull, maggots gorging on his brain with half his flesh still stuck to the radiator. We both screamed and ran as fast as we could out the room and down the stairs. After calling the authorities, Laura and I both took a stiff drink of whisky. We agreed: it was the most horrifying and gory sight we'd ever encountered.

But, incredibly, despite the deaths, the violence, the fires, the arrests and the unmanageable clients, The Cavendish was actually a terrific success. The social community we'd fostered within the hotel made our guests fiercely loyal and many stayed with us for years.

The wealth that it generated, meanwhile, significantly affected the lifestyle of us so-called newlyweds. Within a year, Stuart and I had traded in our old house for a new six-bedroom pile in a posh part of town with electric gates and a beautiful big garden. For cash! In fact, we bought everything with cash – top-of-the-range cars, expensive holidays, artwork and investment flats to rent out. By now we had built up our joint property portfolio to thirty flats, bringing in around £12,000 every month.

Money definitely made my home life easier. Stuart still controlled all my movements with threats and coercion, but now he had 'secured' me with the marriage and the cash was free-flowing, my husband was generally a contented man. The more I brought home, the happier he was, and he liked to flash the cash and show Glasgow that he was still a force to be reckoned with. Don't get me wrong, I was still scared of him, still cowed by his nasty temper and sadistic threats. I was warned over and over that if I stepped out of line or disobeyed him, he would 'destroy me', and not just financially. He would cut all my hair off while I slept and throw acid in my face so that nobody else would ever want me, but as long as I could make money for him, the actual violence simmered below the surface. So cash became my friend too. It cemented us together in appearance and security and, looking back, I can honestly say these days were the best in our marriage. I was out to prove to everyone that I was a great big success and not a loser like everyone had assumed, and showing the world that we had succeeded financially was important to me.

One weekend in 1994, we took the train down to London and I picked out a new, top-of-the-range Ferrari for £76k, paying for it in £50 notes, sourced from two weeks' work at the hotel.

'Can you give us a day to complete this transaction?' asked the very posh salesman. I agreed and that weekend Stuart and I stayed in one of the best hotels in Mayfair. The following day, I picked up my car.

'What did you need the extra time for?' I asked innocently.

'Well, to be perfectly honest with you, Miss McConnell, we had to check the serial numbers on the bank notes. There was a . . . ah . . . ahem . . . bank robbery two days ago in Cirencester and of course we were obliged to ensure that the money was not obtained illegally. So sorry for the delay!'

When I told Stuart later that day, we both laughed about it. I certainly didn't have any qualms about how we were

225

making our money. I worked hard to earn an honest living. Certainly, I was at the hotel almost every day and worked from first thing in the morning till midnight most nights, which meant the only time I got to see Callum was when I took him to school in the mornings. Stuart was the house-husband, the man of leisure; a position he felt he had earned now that he was in his late forties. He took Callum to school and tennis and in his eyes that made him a good father. But Callum wanted more from him and often used to ask him to do activities with him, which he refused.

'Callum, I am not the type of father who does stuff with their kids,' he scoffed. 'If you think kicking a football around makes someone a good father you are wrong.'

I bitterly regret now that I didn't get to spend more time with my son when he was growing up – he was always asking to see me more and I felt constantly guilty. But in my mind I had to give him the best of everything. I was the breadwinner and he depended on me financially, and I couldn't be a home mum too. Hannah was still helping us out and I just hoped that he was getting the attention he deserved from his dad.

I knew Stuart was cheating the taxman but in that regard, I didn't have any influence. I knew enough by now to know he wouldn't appreciate any interference from me in his affairs. I was just the workhorse and that's the way Stuart liked it. I was never the licensee of the bars, I was just an employee and Stuart set up lots of different companies within the hotel so that they fell under the tax threshold for everything. Besides that, the rest of it was cash, which of course wasn't declared. So when Her Majesty's Revenues and Customs (HMRC) came knocking, which they did several times, I was well versed in how to respond. Stuart had put the fear of God into me, saying he would destroy me if I came between him and his cash.

'I only work here,' I told them each time. 'You'll have to write to the director of the company.'

They would write to Stuart at one of his many companies, he would ignore their letters and eventually he would liquidate the company, taking all its debts with it. Then a new company would spring up to take over the business. It was a corporate maze and none of the authorities managed to solve it. The only asset was the hotel and since Adam owned that in an offshore Panamanian company and rented it to Stuart's 'shell' companies, there was no way of pinning either of the Kelly cousins down. No company accounts were ever done, no government agency paid. It was a labyrinth.

Of course, Stuart knew this was a complicated operation to explain and that this left him vulnerable. It was bound to unravel one day. I mean, how could he live such a lavish lifestyle and pay no tax? We flew first class all over the world, we sent our son to private school, we owned a big house, for God's sake! It didn't make sense.

So he told me on several occasions: 'If anything ever happens to me, there are bearer shares in the safe. That's your inheritance. That's the key to realizing my assets.'

The money he had squirrelled away from both the taxman and his ex-wife had been put into a company called Mayfair Holdings, managed by his cousin. Mayfair owned tons of property, apparently, including several blocks of flats and offices and Stuart estimated that he and Adam had a joint wealth of over £7 million. This, he told me breezily, gave him a private income of around £1,000 a month. Mayfair was where he'd hidden his wealth, but it was all under Adam's control and if I needed access to the money after he was gone, I was to go to Adam.

But as he boasted of the set-up, there was something that didn't quite add up in my mind. If Stuart jointly owned £7 million of assets, why did he only get £1,000 a month from the rents? We now owned a tenth of that jointly and we were bringing in £12,000 a month from around £850,000 worth of investment. Something stunk. I had watched Adam at work before and I knew he wouldn't think twice about screwing Stuart over, but questioning Stuart on this was taboo – he wouldn't hear a word against his cousin.

If it all went wrong tomorrow, there were the bearer shares: that's all I had to know. Other than that, Stuart hoarded large amounts of cash in our home just in case he had to make a quick getaway. It all sounded very dramatic, very far-fetched to me, but Stuart was dead serious.

'If you have to get out of town, never use a credit card,' he warned. 'Fly under the radar.' Stuart had secret panels all around the house where he hid rolls of £50 notes. If anything happened, Stuart said he could get to the airport, get on a flight and lay low abroad for a year on his savings. The respectable middle class had savings accounts in banks, insurance policies and investments. Not us – we had wads of cash hidden in our wardrobe and in our curtains.

My parents finally sold their hotel in 1996. They got a much smaller sum than they had anticipated but the money didn't matter – not now I was so wealthy. I bought my parents a lovely flat nearby and they were grateful when I told them they could stay rent-free so they could enjoy their retirement. Given that Stuart and I were doing so well, I felt I owed it to them to give them some measure of comfort in their old age, especially now that Dad was in a bad way physically. He was constantly out of breath, and instead of booze, he was now sustained by a cocktail of different pills. But instead of staying at home to rest or put his feet up, Dad came to The Cavendish every day.

Each morning at around 10.30 a.m., a motley collection of shoplifters, junkies and drunks bustled past my dad on the hotel steps as he slowly hauled himself up with the bannister, stopping every two or three steps to catch his breath and rest. Now twenty-seven, I'd watch this scene unfold from the CCTV behind the reception desk and then, unable to bear it any longer, I'd run out of the hotel lobby to help him up the last few steps.

'Dad, it's okay,' I'd say, taking his arm. 'Here, let me help you.'

All day long he'd sit there in reception, silently reading the paper and drinking tea. I was always rushed off my feet so I often didn't have time to stop and chat. *Why is he here?* I always wondered. He came every single day and stayed for hours. *Why? What does he get out of it?*

I might have been smart when it came to business, but I was still a poor student of human behaviour. By the time I worked it out, it was far too late.

Chapter 17

Last Fight

'Bloody hell, Dad, what's wrong with your toe?' I exclaimed when I saw Dad's foot one Thursday morning in early October 1997. I was due to start work at the hotel in an hour and I'd popped into their flat to offer my mum a lift into town for her weekly trip to the hairdresser's. But when I came into their kitchen, I was met by the sight of my dad, still in his pyjamas, with his left foot propped up on a stool in front of him. His big toe was completely black.

'I don't know,' he sighed. 'It's really sore. It's been like this for a couple of days now.'

'Well, you're going to have to go to the doctor,' I said.

Mum, who had been fussing around us, getting her hat and coat from the hallway, suddenly interrupted: 'When?'

'Well, we'll have to take him now,' I replied, flicking through their phone book to find the number for their doctor, an old family friend.

'But what about my hair appointment?' Mum said irritably. 'I'm going to miss my hair appointment.'

'You go if you want, Mum, but I'm phoning the doctor.'

I could tell at once this was serious. Dad was a sick man

and he'd lost so much weight in the last few months, his face was gaunt and his oversize clothes hung off him. More recently, he'd been diagnosed with diabetes. The doctor was there within half an hour and the moment he saw Dad's toe, he called an ambulance.

'Don't worry, Dad!' I smiled at my father, who seemed shrunken in his six-foot-one-inch frame. There was real fear in his eyes now; something I had never seen before.

'Well, bloody well thank you, Dawn!' Mum muttered to herself, shaking her head, angry at having to cancel her hair appointment. 'Thank you very much!'

I followed behind the ambulance in my car and then met Mum and Dad in A & E where we were shown through to a bed. It didn't take long before a young doctor came round. He examined the toe, asked my dad a few questions then went away to check his files.

When he returned a few minutes later, it wasn't with good news.

'Okay, Mr McConnell. I'm afraid this is gangrenous. You've nicked your nail here – you see? – and it's become infected. Now because of the diabetes, the veins in your toe have collapsed and the infection has spread. In other words, the toe died because the blood flow stopped.'

Dad looked at me with wild-eyed alarm. Gangrene was a common problem for diabetics because their veins collapsed, which meant they couldn't heal after small infections. That was why so many lost arms and legs. I tried to put on a brave face but, inside, I was scared for my father.

'We need to take the toe off really quickly because it's blood poisoning and we can't let it spread,' the doctor went on. 'I've booked you in for surgery early this afternoon.'

231

Dad didn't say a word; Mum covered her mouth with her hand and looked away, as if she couldn't bear to face my father.

'It's going to be fine, Dad,' I said reassuringly, squeezing his hand. His eyes were full of fear, it was too much for him to take in. *Is this why he hadn't gone to the doctor sooner?* I wondered. *Had he suspected his toe was dead?* Instinctively, I looked at the clock – it was nearly midday and I needed to get to the hotel.

'Look, I've got to go to work right now,' I told Mum. 'But I'll arrange some cover and I'll be back later on. It'll be fine. I promise. It will all be okay.'

For the rest of the day, I was busy with the hotel and hardly had time to think about my dad's operation. It was only when I returned to the hospital at 5 p.m. that I recalled the scared look in his eyes. *He'll be fine,* I told myself. My dad was such a strong man, a war veteran and a warrior! He could survive anything.

But when I arrived on the ward, I discovered Mum weeping in the corridor.

'Mum, what's wrong? Is Dad okay?'

'They've taken his whole leg off. His whole leg, Dawn! He's going to be crippled for the rest of his life!'

'What? Why?'

'They had to keep going back to the first vein that hadn't collapsed. All his veins in his foot were gone and then they couldn't find a vein until they got right up to his groin. He went under the knife thinking he was losing a bloody toe and here he is waking up without his leg, Dawn!'

Oh Christ. I felt terrible. 'Where is he? Can I see him?'

'No, he's still in recovery. He's sleeping. They said to come back in first thing in the morning.'

I drove Mum home that night, trying to come to terms with Dad's altered state. He was going to have to learn how to walk with a prosthetic limb – that wasn't going to be an easy task for a man his age.

'Do you have any idea how this is going to change our lives? My life?' Mum spoke with horror. 'I'm going to be a carer for him for the rest of my life. He won't be able to do anything for himself – I mean how is he going to bath himself or get around?'

'Mum. Mum, it's okay, it's going to be fine,' I replied automatically. I couldn't bear her relentless negativity; somebody had to stay positive. 'They'll send him to rehab,' I said. 'He'll learn how to use a prosthesis and he'll be up and about sooner than you think. We can make alterations to the flat to make things easier for him – we'll put in a disabled bath. We'll get carers for him. He'll be okay. You'll be okay.'

'He's a big man.' Mum shook her head, unconvinced. 'I don't know how we're going to cope with this.'

'You know, this isn't the end of the world. He'll be fine. Honestly.'

And he was – once he got over the initial, dreadful shock, which at first left him very low. My family and I spent the next two weeks in and out of hospital – me, Mum, Callum and Stuart, all of us trying our best to cheer Dad up. Gradually, the antidepressants kicked in and after a couple of days he was asking for a copy of the *Telegraph*. A few days later, he was back to his usual self, talking about politics and the problems with 'New Labour', asking for Mum's home-cooked food and gossiping about the other patients on the ward. He was resigned to the fact that his leg was gone but he said he was determined to use a prosthetic limb.

'I'm not going to spend the rest of my life sitting down all the time in a bloody chair,' he said determinedly and I was relieved to see the fire back in his eyes. With his fighting spirit so evident, I felt we were probably over the worst of the crisis.

It was a good thing, too, since I was due to fly to Goa with Stuart and Callum for two weeks. Susy had offered to come up to help Mum out while Dad was still recovering in hospital and I was looking forward to a break. The last few weeks had been gruelling and we all needed some time out. Dad had given me a long list of spices and condiments to bring back from India for his famous curries and he promised to be up and about by the time we got back. It felt like everything was going in the right direction and Dad would make a strong recovery.

Then, the night before we were due to leave: a setback.

'Gangrene,' Dad announced when I walked onto the ward that evening. 'In the right leg. They're going to have to take that too.'

He spoke in a flat monotone but behind the words I could sense the intensity of his emotions. He was utterly devastated and the black cloud of depression that had fogged him when they first took his leg had returned.

'Oh Dad. I'm so sorry.'

'Hmm.' Dad nodded. He looked away, didn't trust himself to speak.

'Look, it will be okay, Dad,' I started, but then he fixed me with a baleful look and I fell silent. He didn't think it would be okay and he wasn't ready to hear me say it.

'A wheelchair, Dawn,' he said at last, his voice shaking. 'I'll be in a wheelchair.' And that was the last thing he said to me before I left. No matter how much I tried to cajole and encourage him, he refused to say another word.

'I'll bring back all your spices,' I whispered as I hugged him goodbye; Dad had insisted we should still go away. 'I love you.'

Afterwards, I stepped out into the corridor to speak to Mum, who was beside herself despite my reassurances that we'd do everything we could to help out. 'I don't know how much more of this I can take!' she declared dramatically.

And then, just as we were about to leave, we heard my father's voice calling for Callum. My eleven-year-old son had been sitting in the corridor the whole time, silently absorbing the news. Alone, he went onto the ward to see his grandpa.

'Well, that was weird,' my son said later as we drove home.

'What was?'

'Grandpa,' he said thoughtfully. 'He told me he loved me and said "I'll see you soon."'

What an odd thing to say, I thought. We were due to set off first thing in the morning so Dad wouldn't see us again until we came home in the New Year. I thought about Dad the whole thirteen-hour flight, wondering how the operation was going. As soon as we landed, I called Mum to find out how it had gone.

'Mum – it's me. How did the operation go?'

'Your father's dead,' Mum said dully.

'What?' Tears sprang to my eyes. '*How?*'

'He had a complication in the night,' she went on. Her voice was thick and strangely flat. 'They did the operation but then he got an infection afterwards and his heart gave out and he died.'

There was a long silence. I couldn't be optimistic anymore; I couldn't tell her everything would be fine. It wasn't.

'Oh Mum, I'm sorry.' And then: 'We'll be here for you,' I said, immediately. My brain was already ticking over what had to happen. *What's next? Should we turn around and go home again? There's the funeral to organize; Mum will need help with all of that . . .*

But her next words stunned me.

'I've called John,' she went on, barely acknowledging what I'd said. 'He's coming up tonight.'

'Oh . . . er . . . okay,' I replied, shaken. I suddenly felt sick. 'Okay, erm . . . Listen, I'm just at the airport. Let me call you back in a minute.'

I had to put the phone down in a hurry before I burst into tears. I don't know why, but Mum mentioning John like that, coming on top of the news about my dad, just sent me over the edge. I slumped forward in my chair and started to weep. Callum held me close as I cried like a baby.

Stuart had guessed what had happened by my reaction on the phone and shook his head. 'What a shame. Poor old fella.' Then his mind turned to practical matters. 'So what do you want to do, Dawn?' he went on. 'You want to go home?'

I thought of Mum. I thought of Dad. And, then, I thought of John. His pale face. His guiltless eyes. Returning to the bosom of the family in Mum's hour of need, like a prodigal son. And in that second, I knew I didn't want to go back. I couldn't face John and I didn't know how on earth I'd get through a funeral with him there. Dad was gone now – there was nothing more I could do for him. He had said goodbye to my son, his only grandson, because he had guessed he wouldn't make it through another operation. It was over.

'No,' I said resolutely. 'Let's stick with the plans. We'll say goodbye to Dad in our own way.'

I was angry with Mum that she hadn't called a doctor about it before it was too late, angry that she hadn't done something sooner. And I was even angrier with myself. I'd known he wouldn't make it, I had seen the sadness and fear in his eyes when I'd left him for the last time. *I should have stayed*, I berated myself. *I should never have left him.* If nothing else, I would have seen him one more time before he died.

My failure to return did not go down well with my family. 'What are you doing in Goa?' Susy called a few hours after I'd spoken to Mum. She was furious with me. 'Don't you think you better come back? Mum's falling to pieces here. They've put her on tranquillizers. We've got a funeral to organize. Don't tell me you're not going to be here for the funeral.'

'Susy, is John there?' I asked coolly.

'Yes, of course he's here,' she said. 'You know he is.'

'Well, then I think Mum has ample support so, no, I don't think we're going to come back for the funeral. Remember, we've been there for Dad throughout all of this. I've been there for both of them, in fact. You're in London and that's fine but I'm the one who's taken on the responsibility of caring for our parents. And trust me, when you go home again, I'll be there for Mum. But I don't need to be at Dad's funeral – I visited him every single day in hospital when he was alive. So *my* conscience is clear. *You* help Mum. *You* help organize the funeral.'

'But how will it look if . . .'

'I don't care how it looks to anyone!' I suddenly exploded. I couldn't bear this obsession with public appearances. It all came from Mum, of course. Yes, it looked bad me not coming home; but it would look a whole lot worse if I'd gone to the police about John's behaviour. *She should think about* that, I thought angrily. And it strengthened my resolve. I wasn't the youngest child any more, biddable by her older siblings. I was a grown woman and I was sick of putting on a show for everyone else's sake. I wasn't coming home.

But I didn't say any of this. After all, it wasn't Susy's fault. Right now, she was just the one trying to keep everyone together. So I apologized.

'Look, I'm sorry, Su. Really, I don't mean to take it out on you. It's just that I think I'm better off away from things right now. Dad's dead and whether I come back home or not, nothing's going to change that.'

It wasn't a particularly great holiday, but I have to admit that it was what I needed after spending so many weeks running back and forth to the hospital, and it was a hell of a lot better than making small talk with my childhood abuser over a funeral buffet. I hadn't appreciated just how upsetting it had all been.

We stayed at a beautiful beach resort for two weeks and, on the second-to-last day, Callum and I visited a stunning waterfall a few hours inland from our hotel. Once we reached the top, we had a little ceremony for my father. We each said our own goodbyes and then threw a handful of long-stemmed tiger lilies into the waterfall. As I watched the white-and-orange striped flowers swirling into the pool below, I spoke to my father:

'You're better off now, Dad. If you'd survived, you wouldn't be a happy man, I know that. You were a warrior – a strong man, so full of pride. My hero. You chose to let go. I accept that, Dad, and I'm sorry, I'm really sorry you left us, but I know it was probably for the best. Mum wouldn't have coped well. You did the right thing by her. You let her go. I'm sorry, Dad. I love you and I'll miss you so much.'

It was a relief not to go to the funeral, not to have to face my abuser brother or all the drama I knew my mother would create around herself. And there was worse. Talking to my sister about the arrangements, I learned that John was due to give the eulogy – how repellant! He'd had a terrible relationship with my father all his life – he would talk a load of rubbish and I knew I didn't want to hear it.

It irritated me so much that John was in Glasgow, staying with my mother in what was still my property! The fact was, he'd got away with the abuse for all these years and he was still getting away with it now. Several times that holiday, I found myself returning to a moment when I had finally plucked up the courage to ask Dad about John.

One drizzly afternoon in March 1997, we were alone in reception at The Cavendish when it suddenly occurred to me that I had never talked to Dad about the abuse. I was curious so I decided just to ask him, out of the blue.

'Dad, did you know about John?' I asked him.

'Know about what?' He squinted up at me from his regular seat in the lounge area. He had his *Telegraph* open on the table in front of him, next to an empty cup of tea.

'Did you know he abused me? Did you know at the time, Dad?'

Dad put a hand out to signal for me to stop and with his other hand he fished out a large white handkerchief from his trouser pocket.

'Oh. Oh . . .' He seemed in distress.

'Dad?'

He put the hanky to his nose and started to weep then. I

couldn't bear it – he was then seventy-two years old and a frail, infirm old man. Watching him cry like that was possibly the saddest thing I had ever seen. He looked at me with his bloodshot eyes and shook his head. Eventually he spoke: 'Can I have another cup of tea please, Dawn?'

What did it mean? I wondered on that Indian holiday after his death, as I stared out to sea. *Did it mean he knew or he didn't know? Why the tears? Why was he there at the hotel so much?*

I listened to the waves gently lapping at the sand and in those few seconds, it was as if the answer to the question I had sent out to sea had washed up onto the shore. A thought struck me like a bolt of electricity. *Dad was there to protect me!* Whether or not he had known about John when we were children, he certainly became aware of what he had done to me after I spoke to Mum aged twenty-two. And he came to The Cavendish because he thought it was a dangerous place. He came to give me the protection he had failed to give me as a child. That was why he had cried!

I shook my head at my own foolishness and short-sightedness. *Why hadn't I given him the time he deserved? Why hadn't I just sat and talked with him?* Now it was all too late and I was filled with regret at all those missed opportunities. *How shallow and silly I have been,* I reflected sadly, *so caught up in my day-to-day problems, I didn't make the time for my own father.*

By the time we returned to Glasgow the funeral was over and my siblings had returned to London. If Mum was angry with me for staying away she certainly didn't show it, but then Mum so rarely showed her emotions. After forty years of marriage, she was now on her own and though she was far from a sobbing wreck, neither was she quite herself either. For the first few weeks she spent a lot of time alone in the flat, quiet and withdrawn. Eventually, we managed to coax her round to our house and she found small moments of joy in the domestic life we shared. She loved to cook Callum's favourite dishes for him – steak pie and pancakes – and the pair became close as they spent more time together. I encouraged her to help me sort out the garden and as winter turned to spring and we saw the fruits of our labours, we both started to enjoy the time we spent together outside, weeding, planting and pruning. Gradually, the four of us learned to be a family together, going to movies, visiting historic gardens and supporting my sporty son Callum in his tennis and rugby matches.

Then, just as my home life settled down, the business took a fatal blow. After so much upheaval – the regular deaths, fires, violence, health-and-safety demands, police raids and drug busts – I thought we could survive anything. I was wrong.

The fire certificate at The Cavendish was due for renewal in the next twelve months – and the legislation had changed massively since our last certificate was issued. To bring the hotel up to compliance with the new regulations, we needed to invest in hard-wired smoke alarms and a sprinkler system at a cost of £300,000. But the owner of the building, Adam, decided he didn't want to put in the capital. We didn't have the money either – after all, Stuart's wealth was tied up in the cousins' jointly owned Mayfair Holdings company – so, in the end, we simply closed the doors. That was it.

Adam was about as hard-nosed as you could get. There were never any favours from him when it came to business. He took what he could get, and woe betide anyone who stood in his way. There were many evenings when I would sit silently as he regaled Stuart and me with boastful tales about how he had screwed people over and ran circles round the authorities. Nobody could catch him, he laughed. Nobody knew his devious, deceitful tricks because he always stayed one step ahead. Stuart lapped it up while I looked on distastefully at this poor excuse for a human being. Contractors were never paid, partners were dumped and the taxman was sent away empty-handed. He was a millionaire many times over but he was the meanest man I'd ever met. He'd steal the coins from a beggar's hat if he thought he could get away with it. Often the people he hurt weren't even business associates, but were just innocent bystanders who had the bad luck to cross his path. In the early days he had even tried to bed me – so much for family ties! Of course I had turned him down flat. I knew he only wanted to have sex with me so that he would have power over me, and I was never going to let that happen. One controlling husband was bad enough without being blackmailed by Adam too. No, Adam was a nasty piece of work – he would do anything to get what he wanted, and I knew that of the two cousins he was the one with the real money, brains and power. But I couldn't say a thing against him. In Stuart's eyes, he could do no wrong.

And so, like so much of my life with Stuart, I didn't have any choice in the matter. In a way, however, although it broke my heart to say goodbye to the staff I'd worked alongside for so long, and to the many residents who had become like my own family, I couldn't help breathing a sigh of relief. For after seven years of worrying about residents killing themselves, each other or burning my hotel down, I didn't have the burden of responsibility any more. I hadn't touched alcohol for seven years because of the worry that I might have to dash to the hotel at a moment's notice.

And yet, and yet . . . if Adam *had* made the investment, we could have gone for years, extremely successfully, providing that warm community for society's cast-offs – and raking in the money ourselves. It annoyed me that Adam had rejected the idea of carrying out the works without a moment's thought. It was so short-sighted, so selfish! He had the money, I knew that. He had tons of cash.

But it wasn't a surprise. I'd been involved in the cousins' business dealings for ten years by now; I'd seen for myself the way he and Stuart operated – and it was purely for themselves. They never invested or created anything, just plundered and pillaged a business till there was nothing left to take. If only he *had* invested, then he and Stuart could have been taking carrier bags of cash out of The Cavendish every week for years to come. But no, Adam decided to close it and sell it instead; give someone else the headache and the expense of overseeing the works.

I knew by now: if it wasn't an easy win, a quick buck, then the Kelly cousins just weren't interested.

Chapter 18

A Change of Perspective

I hate you, I thought, staring blankly at my husband as he went off on one of his usual rants. *I hate you and I wish I'd never married you.*

Stuart, face flushed from booze, the purple veins throbbing in his temples, his grey hair receding into a widow's peak and his little pot belly poking out through his dressing gown, was pacing our living room, working himself up to full-on apoplexy. For years I had put up with these rants of his, his violent temper and his constant drinking. And, frankly, I was tired of pretending that it was all okay. All the lies, the abuse, the control and the torture he'd put me through had built up like a brick wall in my head, just waiting to topple over and bring down the whole edifice of our marriage. I never contradicted him, never showed him my true feelings or fought back against his outrageous demands, but I couldn't help how I felt inside. As the years had gone on my hatred for my husband had grown in my heart. There was no love from this man, no care and no respect, just endless abuse and manipulation. He only cared about the money and I had accepted that a long time ago. I didn't have to like it, though.

'How am I going to live now?' he railed, practically frothing at the mouth as he considered life without The Cavendish's cash. If only he got up off his backside and did some work occasionally, he wouldn't be so heavily reliant on me and my labours! He'd been at the booze since midday and now it was gone 4 p.m. His eyes were bloodshot and his mouth was stained red from the wine.

'What am I going to do for cash?'

'Well, you could always ask your cousin to let you have a couple of properties from your so-called property empire,' I responded drily from the sofa. 'This supposed empire which gives you a grand total of £12,000 a year. I can't quite believe that it exists, frankly. I mean, how could it? We get that much every month from our flats. And you get £1,000 a month from £7 million? Why don't you try selling a couple of flats? I'm sure that will tide you over for a while at least.'

'Don't speak about me or my cousin in that tone,' Stuart snarled. 'I made you and I can quickly destroy you. You think all this is yours? Think again. If you like your face the way it is you'd better shut your fucking mouth.'

I shot him a surly look. I was like a rebellious teenager, enjoying the challenge of verbally sparring with Stuart yet too scared to really stand up to him properly. After all these years, I knew my boundaries. I knew by his demeanour if he would be violent or verbal; I knew if he would hit me or if he would just rant. Today I guessed it was probably just a rant. He might throw a pot at me if I carried on giving him cheek, but nothing more. Although I was growing up, I didn't yet feel strong enough to stand up to Stuart, and I believed him when he said he would do those horrible things to me. As much as I yearned for freedom from Stuart's control, I also clung to the life I had created with him because it was all I knew – and all Callum knew too.

'You need to work so that we have cash flow,' he went on. 'Don't think for a minute you're not going to be doing anything, you need to work!'

'I *could* always get a job . . .' I mused, setting up the idea of me working for someone else rather than running one of his businesses. I rather fancied the idea of going to work in the real world, but I knew the idea was out of the question to Stuart.

'You will not get a fucking job, Dawn! You will not get a fucking job because I need to know where you are at all times. You are not going into business with anybody but me. Got it?'

I decided to change tack: 'Well, I suppose there's a business in town I've been thinking about – a cafe.'

'Yeah, that's more like it . . . Go on . . .'

'Well, I think I can make it work but, you know, it won't be like before, Stuart. The hotel made a lot of money for us. It won't be anything like that.'

'Humph. Better than nothing, I suppose.' Stuart poured himself another large glass of wine.

'Honestly, Stu, what about this money you've got invested with Adam? I just don't see why *he* should decide where to invest *your* money when you're clearly smarter in business. A grand a month is peanuts! Surely it makes more sense for you to make your own money?'

Now I was buttering him up – it couldn't have been further from the truth. I'd seen from the way he had plundered the bars and hotel that he had no clue about how to keep a business profitable. All he knew was how to get his grubby hands in the till and run when the business collapsed. But I had a long-term plan and that basically was 'don't get screwed'! If I had learned anything from watching the way Stuart and Adam treated their former partners, it was that they would stop at nothing to leave them penniless. I wouldn't let that happen to me. If I was going to leave one day, I would walk out with what I had earned for myself. But if this plan was going to work, I needed Stuart to get his cash back from Adam. I needed to kill the Panama connection.

The only way I could do that was to make Stuart see that Adam was screwing him over. It was clear to *me* that Adam wasn't giving him a proper return on his money; if I could make *Stuart* see that, we could take those millions and re-invest the money together in the property market.

The money and the property would then be part of our matrimonial pot – and not a separate side pot for him. I'd seen what he'd done to Maria and I was determined that I wouldn't get trampled the way she had. At one time, I might even have been worried that Stuart might find himself another, younger version of me – another schoolgirl who didn't know better, another innocent ripe for his demands – and consequently send me packing. But Stuart didn't seem to be actively looking for another woman at all. No, he seemed pretty happy just to sit back and let old age come to him.

After all, I was a nice little earner.

Now, as I carefully flattered his ego, my husband preened himself. A more intelligent man might have noticed I was giving him a load of old flannel but then Stuart was hardly an acute observer of human behaviour at the best of times, let alone after three bottles of Pinot Noir.

'It's true,' he sighed between swigs. 'It's true – I could make that money really work for me, but you know Adam. Adam would never let me dissolve the partnership.'

'Not let you? *Let* you? Well, it's nothing to do with me, of course, but it does seem that he's controlling all your cash. As I said, £1,000 a month is a very poor return on your investment. I'm sure you could do better than that.'

'Of course I could do better!' he snapped, then he went back to his study to watch TV and brood. *Aha!* I thought. *The seed has finally landed in fertile ground.*

It was just one of many conversations we had in the weeks between the end of the hotel and the start of my new business: the cafe.

It was on a recent trip to London that I'd had the idea; I'd seen some new-style cafes in Shoreditch with large sofas, soft music and free USB terminals to plug into which were doing a roaring trade. Cafes were turning into hang-out destinations and coffee was the new beer. In the course of a few conversations with owners, I'd discovered that the profits were massive. There was a 600 per cent mark-up on a coffee and, best of all, you didn't need a licence to sell the stuff. I'd visited some brilliant new cafes in London, which sold food all day, and I realized that if I could bring this idea to Glasgow, I could be one of the first to create a destination coffee shop in the area. So I'd been scouring the trendy parts of town for suitable premises and eventually settled on a tatty, run-down greasy spoon in an up-and-coming area. Now, using the money I'd saved over the years, I completely redesigned the place, preparing for my grand opening.

First I put in a solid glass front, then I installed USB sockets and stripped back the walls to the old brick behind. We regrouted so that it looked quite industrial and I put in an assortment of comfy sofas and chairs. The look was half-industrial and half-shabby chic and by the time we finished, I knew we had pulled off something quite special. This was a place I would want to come and hang out!

The next thing I had to do was work out my core business – I reckoned this would be coffee and soup. Both cost a small amount to produce and yet I knew we could sell them for a premium if we used the best quality ingredients. Two hundred cups of soups and four hundred coffees a day would net me £7,000 a week. This was my foundation and everything else would be extra. We had lovely display cabinets with home-made cakes, pastries, biscuits, traybakes, fresh sandwiches, paninis and a selection of soft drinks. Catering was about making things look good – I had learned this from my previous businesses – so as long as we had full fridges and our displays looked attractive, people would buy from us. I bought the best quality coffee I could find, hired two members of staff and named our cafe Terminal Two – now I was ready to open the doors for business.

At first, we just had a few curious stragglers coming to look at the distinctive new decor but it didn't take much to persuade them to stay for a coffee and a slice of cake. Then the lunch-time market wandered in and started ordering our home-made soups with a slice of chunky wholemeal bread. And then, at around 4ish, people started to come in for a coffee and a panini. This wasn't like a normal restaurant or cafe – the idea wasn't to serve people and turn them out, it was to encourage them to stay as long as possible, to keep ordering coffees, to bring their friends and use Terminal Two (or TT as we became known) as a meeting place. I started selling magazines at the counter and we had a rack of daily papers people could read for free.

The paninis were a cut above the usual fare: we had roast chicken with stuffing, roast pepper with courgette and Stilton, curried potato and wilted spinach, buffalo mozzarella and sun-blushed tomato. It was all a bit different to the boring cheese-and-ham, tuna or egg mayonnaise fillings that you'd get in a standard cafe. Word got round and gradually, the idea caught on. Within a few months we had a strong business bringing in £22k a month, though of course it wasn't easy. I had to be in at 5 a.m. every morning to put on three pots of soup and produce one hundred sandwiches before the morning rush. Fortunately the hours were more sociable than at The Cavendish and I was able to finish work at 4 p.m. so that I could have all of the evening with Callum – ultimately what I wanted and what he wanted too. He was growing up but he still needed his mum around.

We were open 364 days a year which meant there was very little let-up for me or the staff but there was no denying it was a good cash business. In the course of a year, TT became a favourite hot spot with the young, upwardly mobile set, who all came to us for their morning coffees and croissants. At lunchtime we had office workers and the buggy brigade and throughout the day there was an assortment of freelance 'creative' types who brought their laptops and drank coffee like it was going out of fashion. I felt so proud that, for the third time in my career, I had built a successful business from scratch. *Not bad for a school–dropout teenage mum with no qualifications.*

As for the man who had got that teenage girl pregnant, well, as usual, Stuart made his contribution – which was to wander in every other day and empty my till. It drove me mad. It was so selfish and destructive and, worst of all, it took advantage of all my hard work. But I'd learnt not to confront Stuart about things that bothered me – that never worked with him, for he would threaten and lash out, and I'd had enough of enduring his vile temper – instead, I found a way to thwart his greed.

I had a regular customer called Pam who became my eyes in the shop front. She'd sit on one of the large chesterfield armchairs in the glass window, smoking her Benson & Hedges, and when she saw Stuart coming down the road she'd roar: 'He's coming, Dawn! Action stations!' At that, I would pull out every large note from the till and hand it to her. She would put it all in her bag and then sit there, calm as you like, smoking her fags and reading the *Racing Post* while he ranted and raved at me.

'What do you mean there's no bloody money?'

'We've just paid the cash-and-carry, Stu,' I'd say. 'What do you want me to do?'

'Find some more!'

'I haven't got any. See for yourself. Nothing!'

Then he'd storm out, puce with rage, just as Pam prepared to hand me back the contents of the till.

'Disgusting, that's what he is.' Pam shook her head disapprovingly. 'Leaching off you like that. He's nae a real man.'

It wasn't just resentment that made me employ this subterfuge, though: there was a point to denying Stuart the cash from my till. I wanted to make him desperate for money. I wanted to make him see there was another avenue for cash apart from me.

'Just think of the life you could have if you had your half of the £7 million at your disposal . . .' I'd say at night, uncorking another bottle of red wine for him. I rarely drank but I liked to keep him nicely sozzled because I knew that if he were drunk enough, he wouldn't pester me for sex.

Over the years, I'd come to realize that sex with Stuart was quite simply bad. I'd never realized before because I had nothing to compare him to but, in time, I started to read magazines and watch films and I came to see that sex with Stuart was only ever about his pleasure and he never once took the trouble to make me happy in bed. He said that it was my duty to give him oral sex, but that giving a woman oral sex was disgusting and insisted he would never do it. Neither did he bother to try and arouse me with his hands. He just grabbed at my tits when he was trying to get himself hard. I was no more than a blow-up doll to him, an inanimate object there for his pleasure. To me, sex with Stuart was passionless and predictable, a dismal duty I had to carry out if he wanted it. He had never once given me an orgasm, or even tried to, so what was the point? I hated the look of him, the smell of him and the touch of him too.

Now thirty-one years old, I'd begun to feel that life was passing me by. I had worked solidly since the age of eighteen and now I wanted more from life than working to keep Stuart happy.

'We could buy a nice place in Portugal,' I suggested one day. 'If we had our £3.5 million we could enjoy our lives. You know, we would have plenty of income coming in. Don't you want to enjoy your money before you die? What's the point of having it all tied up with Adam? I mean, is he really giving you the best return for your money?' This was a slow-burner, this project of mine, but gradually, very gradually, it began to gain ground.

Meanwhile, our son Callum had decided on a new direction for his life and I did my best to encourage him. He wanted to train to be a professional tennis player and he had his heart set on a school in the US which specialized in turning out the next generation of Grand Slam title winners. At first neither Stuart nor my mum understood my eagerness to send my son abroad at the youthful age of fourteen. He was still so young!

But I kept insisting how important it was to follow his dreams. After all, I hadn't had the chance to follow mine and I wanted to give him everything I wished I had done myself. Fourteen – it had been such a critical age for me. I looked back and saw how weak I had been, how impressionable. I was there for the taking and Stuart had seen that. He had plucked me so easily . . .

I knew, too, that if I let Callum stay in Glasgow, there was every chance he would get sucked into Stuart's world. I didn't want that. I wanted more for him and if sending him to the other side of the world was the personal sacrifice I had to make to give him a fighting chance of a good life, then it was a small price to pay.

There was no question that now, at the age of thirty-one, I was starting to change. I had shrugged off my youthful insecurities and I was now a woman of the world. Confident in both my abilities and instincts as a businesswoman, I was realizing my own power now. I could challenge Stuart's views occasionally because, ultimately, I thought that one day I would leave him. I earned the money, I cooked the meals and I washed his clothes – and for what? This fifty-three year-old drunk gave nothing in return except threats and intimidation. Don't get me wrong, he could still scare the hell out of me when he wanted to, but nothing could stop me growing up. Not even him.

One day, after two years at the helm of Terminal Two, I looked in the mirror and I realized that I'd let myself go. *Too many cakes, too many Danish pastries* . . . I sighed, grabbing hold of a large portion of flesh where my waist should have been. *Dawn, you have to get your figure back!*

That's when I started training. Now, instead of going home every night, I went to the gym for a session with a personal trainer. At first I found it exhausting and annoying but within a couple of weeks I started to see the results. For the first time in years, my arms looked toned, my stomach was flat and I'd dropped a dress size.

'Who are you getting yourself all buffed up for?' Stuart demanded to know, suspicious of this sudden transformation. 'Thinking of having an affair? There's no point, you know. Nobody would have a fat bitch like you!'

But I didn't need his approval anymore. I was beginning to find my inner confidence.

'Don't you want me to look good for you?' I asked slyly. 'Don't you want to impress your mates with a young, slim wife? You're always telling me I look like an elephant. Well, I'm doing something about it for a change.'

But this only wound him up more.

'You are nothing, Dawn. Nothing! I own you! I made you and I could take it all away tomorrow. Never forget that!'

His words were no longer true. The house was in my name, the cafe was in my name, we had twelve flats in our joint names and all the money I made was mine. So how could he own me? He couldn't threaten to take it away anymore because *he* was the kept man!

For three years I ran Terminal Two with my brilliant staff. It was a wrench to send Callum off to America and for the entire month after he left I slept in his bed, refusing to change the sheets because I couldn't bear to wash out the smell of him. But I knew that he was following his dream and I didn't want to hold him back.

With our son gone, the house seemed empty, and it forced me to look at my relationship with Stuart anew. My husband spent his time either drinking with his pals or taking tea at the cafe; he liked to keep an eye on me, especially now that my hard work in the gym was paying off. After months of regular exercise, I became a trim size eight again, so I stopped wearing shapeless trousers and started to enjoy buying nice clothes to suit my figure. I even dared to wear dresses again, something Stuart had forbidden years before.

And Stuart hated it; his jealousy and possessiveness got worse by the day. Now he took my phone when I was in the shower and read all my text messages. I was never allowed to go out and meet friends on my own. He timed me from all my meetings and errands and if he thought I had been at the gym or Waitrose longer than was necessary I would feel his wrath. He would take my car keys away, take my wallet, take my house keys and leave the house, locking me in. I was literally a prisoner in my own home.

I never confided in anyone or asked anyone for help. Partly it was because I was embarrassed about his behaviour and my inability to stop him. But there was another side to it too. He would remind me over and over again that I belonged to him. If I dared to think about leaving him he would do horrific things to me – not kill me, but disfigure me, disable me, leave me in a pitiful state so no one would want me. That was chilling. So, despite myself, I stayed. I stayed because leaving felt like suicide.

Eventually, in 2001, when I was thirty-two, I received an offer for the lease of the coffee shop.

'I'm shutting the cafe,' I told Stuart that night when I got home. 'I've had a good offer on the lease and I'm going to take it. I can't bear the early mornings anymore and I'm tired. I'm really bloody tired.'

'What? You can't do that!' Stuart's face fell. I noticed that his wrinkles were now so deep they looked like permanent folds in his face. He had aged badly over the years.

'I need £1,000 a week to live and I need you to work,' he went on. 'I'm certainly not going back to work. Do you know who I am? What I represent?'

Finally, I snapped.

'Yes, you are right, I will work,' I said quietly. 'I will work and I will have money but you will have none, so again I suggest you go cap in hand to that cousin of yours and have this conversation with him. I have no idea what you own, all I have is words. You do not contribute and I do not need to keep you. I have one dependent, not two.'

'You think that all this is yours? The house, the cars, the properties? You have nothing, Dawn. I'll make sure you never work in this town again. The cars – I'll smash them up. I'll take the house and the properties so fast you won't know what's hit you. I'll cut your hair when you're asleep and I'll throw acid in your face so no other man will look at you. Don't think for a minute you can get away with this, Dawn, because you know what I'm capable of. You saw what happened to Maria.'

I sighed. Conflict wasn't the right strategy to use with Stuart – he always went on the attack, like a vicious dog. No,

I needed to be smart, to bide my time. What I needed above all was his trust. Quickly, I changed tack.

'Look, Stuart, I love you,' I said in a soft, conciliatory voice. 'And I want to spend the rest of my life with you. But we don't want to slave away till we're old – and we don't have to! I've had a good offer on the cafe and, if you go to see Adam, we'll have that money too. Together, we'll reinvest all that capital and make some *proper* money. I'm talking big money, Stuart. You deserve this, Stuart. We both do!'

He looked at me hopefully then, and I could see he wanted to believe me. This was it – I knew I had him!

'Look, we're on the same side,' I went on, stroking his arm. 'It's silly being at war with each other. We can do this together. You know what I can do with property, you know I've got the acumen to make us a fortune.'

For my plan wasn't just to buy the properties and rent them out as they were. That would never have been enough for me – it might have been how Adam and Stuart had always worked, but I was far more creative. I genuinely enjoyed the challenge of refurbishing old flats and selling them on for a profit and not just because there was good money to be made this way. It was more the transformation I enjoyed: taking something shabby and unloved and turning it into a beautiful home. I loved the creative and practical challenges of making something lovely out of a wreck. I guess you could say I'd had enough practice in my own life of doing that.

Stuart, of course, only ever focused on the bottom line – and that's what I focused on now too.

'Just think of it – all that money in your hands again!' I said persuasively. Stuart was a man who liked to see things before him: wads of cash, little girls in their school uniforms. The paper fortune of Mayfair Holdings really wasn't his thing. I saw his eyes light up and pressed home my advantage.

'So . . . what do you think of this plan: I drive you round town tomorrow and you can point out all the property you own with Adam. Then we'll sit down and work out the values and we'll see about a sensible split so that when we go to Adam, we'll already have our own proposal.'

Stuart was nodding enthusiastically.

'You're cousins, you're the best of friends,' I reminded him. 'And I'm sure if you tell him what you want he'll let you take your money.

'After all, why would he want to stand in your way?'

Chapter 19

Uncovering a Betrayal

I hit the 'return' button and the page on the Land Registry website refreshed. For a moment I just stared at the computer screen, letting the information sink in. It seemed unbelievable – but here it was in black and white. The facts were undeniable. Stuart and Adam's company – Mayfair Holdings – no longer owned the commercial building in Margate Street which Stuart had shown me that morning. It had been sold to another company called Salisbury Alliance in 1992.

My heart raced as I realized the implications of what I had discovered. Adam had sold the building from under Stuart's nose without telling him. He had betrayed him.

'Stuart!' I called out to my husband, who was busy watching *CSI* in the living room. 'Stuart, I think you better come and see this.'

Earlier that morning, in August 2001, I had driven Stuart around Glasgow so he could find all the blocks of flats and commercial buildings that he owned with his cousin in order to make a proper inventory of their joint assets. He had nothing in writing himself because Adam looked after all the paperwork. That afternoon, he handed me the list we'd compiled from our sortie. It was 100 per cent correct, he assured me, since he had personally overseen building work in all of them.

I had agreed that I would research property values for the ten commercial buildings and twenty blocks of flats in order to make an accurate estimate of the total worth. But, first, I thought I had better make sure that he had got the right buildings, so I did a quick title search on the Land Registry. To my amazement, I found that Stuart had indeed got the right building on Margate Street, but it was no longer his.

'Look at this.' I pointed to the computer when he came into the room. 'This is the Land Registry website which lists the titles of all property in the UK. That commercial block on Margate Street isn't owned by Mayfair Holdings any longer. It was sold to a company called Salisbury Alliance in 1992. Nine years ago!'

'What?' Stuart was baffled, uncomprehending. 'No, that can't be right. Are you sure you've got the right building?'

'Yes, positive,' I said, seriously. 'Stu, do you know who owns Salisbury Alliance?'

'No idea. Never heard of them. Look, are you sure that thing's right? I can't believe it.'

'Yeah, I'm sure. But let me do a few more searches. I think we better get to the bottom of this.'

I did searches on all the properties in the end and found that four of the largest commercial buildings previously owned by Mayfair Holdings had been sold to Salisbury Alliance. Just on instinct, I then did a title search on Adam's house – *bingo!* As I suspected, it was owned by Salisbury Alliance. *You sneaky little bastard*, I thought to myself, as I realized what was going on. Adam had been transferring the properties to himself – in other words, putting all the assets under his control and not telling his so-called business partner anything about it. I had known he was up to something all this time. The fact that he received a pittance from a business allegedly worth millions was enough to arouse my suspicions, but I had no idea he would simply be stealing the property from his cousin. *Well, that's the nature of the beast*, I thought. *Adam is a first-class bastard and here is the ultimate proof.* Sighing, having completed my investigations I called Stuart back in. This was not going to be easy.

'I'm sorry, Stuart, but you don't own the blocks on Princess Street, Daimler Avenue or Grove Road either. Adam transferred them to Salisbury Alliance. Salisbury Alliance is another offshore company, Panamanian-based, and it owns your cousin's house too. So it must be Adam's company. I'm really sorry, Stuart.'

'What are you talking about?' He was angry now. 'Show me! Show me the proof!'

I had printed out all the pages from the internet and I handed them to Stuart. One by one, he went through the documents, hardly able to believe what he was reading.

'It can't be,' he kept saying to himself. 'It can't be right. This block is still in our company accounts. We're getting rents from it. I saw it in our accounts this year.'

I didn't want to state the blindingly obvious but it seemed I needed to.

'It's a trick, Stuart,' I said patiently, as if explaining to a child. 'He's putting them into the accounts to stop you getting suspicious. The deeds prove you don't own them.'

'He's . . . he's betrayed me?' Stuart gasped. The full horror of what his cousin had done to him was now beginning to sink in. 'He's just stolen the fucking buildings from under me?'

'Did you sign stuff, Stuart? I mean, did you ever sign things which you didn't read?'

'ALL THE FUCKING TIME! You know I did! I trusted him!'

I just sat and shook my head. It was all an act, of course. I wasn't terribly surprised that Adam had double-crossed Stuart. Stuart had been a buffoon to trust him with his money. I had suspected for years that his cousin was screwing him for rents, but then, Stuart was never that smart. It was his cousin who had been the brains behind their success; he had simply carried Stuart with him. Well, at some point he'd clearly got sick of carrying him and he started to take it back. But now this devastating act of deceit had played right into my hands. Stuart was definitely going to confront his cousin now – and it would be two against one as we fought for the assets.

'I've worked out there's about £3 million missing,' I said quietly. 'It's true that your portfolio would be worth about £7 or even £8 million today if it was made up of all the properties on the list. But with the biggest four gone, it's probably only worth about £4 million.'

'What – £3 million? He's stolen £3 million from me?' Stuart was in a state of shock and he couldn't stop the stunned tears now openly rolling down his face. Inside, I felt a strangely satisfying sense of justice. Money was all Stuart ever cared about and now the one person he'd trusted most in the world had stolen the thing he loved best.

Though I wasn't proud of myself for feeling it, it was a treat to watch *him* suffer for a change. Finally, after all the hurtful things he had done to me, I couldn't help taking some pleasure from his pain. He was finally getting what he deserved. And I realized something: if I ever wanted to hurt Stuart, *really hurt him*, I saw that this was the only way. He cared nothing for people or even family ties – money was his Achilles heel. Money was his world. Cash was Stuart's first and truest love.

'Dawn! Dawn, you've got to help me,' he sobbed, a wreck of a man. 'Dawn, will you help me get my money back?'

Now I poured him a large glass of wine. I was the one he trusted now, the only one, and I had to use that new power to my advantage.

'Of course I will, darling,' I soothed. 'You know I will.'

That first night Stuart grieved. He grieved for the cousin who he'd thought had loved him and he grieved for his missing millions. He didn't even think about the rents going back years, it was the fact that the properties weren't even owned by his company any longer that cut him up.

The following day, he had switched – now he was angry and he wanted revenge. Adam had stabbed him in the back and he wanted justice but he didn't want to confront his cousin directly, he said, or he wouldn't get anywhere. So he rang him up and put the call on speakerphone so I could listen too. They had a very brief chat first, about a car they were buying through a friend, before Stuart asked casually: 'By the way, Adam, have you heard of a company called Salisbury Alliance?'

There was a moment's silence before he answered: 'Who?'

'Salisbury Alliance. The name's cropped up recently and I wondered if you knew who owned it.'

'Salisbury Alliance,' Adam muttered carefully. 'Yeah, I've heard of them. Why? What have you heard?'

'Oh, not much. I just wanted to know who the owners were.'

'Yeah, well, I can't really talk now, Stu. Erm . . . are you around later? I'll pop round.'

'Yeah, I'm in. I'll see you later.'

The phone went dead and Stuart looked at me, his eyes blazing with rage.

'He didn't know what to say, did he?' he said. 'He knows he's been caught.'

'Look, Stuart, I think you've got to get your money back. Today.'

'Too fucking right. I'll tell him when he comes round – I want my money out. And then we'll see what he says. I'd like to fucking hear what he says about that.'

At around 4 p.m. Adam's Jaguar rolled up to our gates and we buzzed him in. We'd agreed that Stuart would do the talking but I wanted to be in the room, just as a backup. We were most definitely in this fight together now.

Adam came cockily into the lounge, a large fake smile covering his discomfort. He wore a white shirt, denim jeans and a dazzling mouthful of veneers which had cost him a small fortune. He was clearly rattled from the conversation earlier but he didn't want to show it, prattling on for a minute or so about what a busy day he'd had while Stuart just stood at the French doors, staring out onto our garden. Stuart, casual in a pair of grey jogging bottoms, didn't even turn around to welcome his cousin and felt no need for any small talk.

Suddenly, Stuart interrupted Adam in mid-flow: 'Adam, I want my money out of Mayfair.'

'Excuse me?' Adam looked down at me where I sat on the sofa, flicking through a magazine. He gave me a quizzical half-smile, as if to say – *what's going on?* I smiled sweetly back at him. *We've got you, you little rat. Now let's see you squirm.*

Stuart didn't answer him – instead he turned round and stared at his cousin and for the first time Adam saw the fury in Stuart's eyes. Still, he tried to play dumb: 'Stu, why do you want to split the company up after all these years? I don't understand.' He was asking Stuart, but his eyes were firmly on me. 'Remember, this is the safe card, Stuart,' he went on, still glaring at me, his voice dripping with insinuation. 'Mayfair is our safety net, for a lot of reasons. Not least, to stop *people* –' another pointed look at me '– taking our money from us.'

'I want my money out, Adam.'

'Why? What do you need the money for, Stuart?'

Stuart, stupidly, replied: 'I want to buy a house in Portugal and I want to buy a car for Callum.'

'Okay, okay. Show me this house in Portugal, I'll tell you if it's any good.'

At that point, I had to intervene.

'Hang on a minute.' I put my hands up in the air, like a referee halting a football match. 'Stop, Adam. You are not in this marriage. This is my life. And if Stuart wants his money, for any reason whatsoever, just give it to him.'

'Okay. Okay . . .' Now Adam pulled out a cigarette and clamped it between his teeth as he fished around in his pockets for his silver lighter. He looked mad as hell. I exchanged a look with Stuart – *what will he do now?* we both wondered. Adam lit his cigarette and took a long pull on it, then started pacing up and down the living room. He was thinking about his next move. But Stuart didn't give him time to think.

'So I've done a calculation of all the blocks,' Stuart began. 'And I've worked out that it's worth £7 million. We can either split the company down the middle, splitting up the properties, or you can give me cash.'

Adam was pacing anxiously now, murmuring to himself: 'Seven million. Right.'

'I mean, I don't know if cash is an attractive option for you, Adam, so it might just be best if we each take half the properties . . .'

'Yeah . . . I see. Well, I'll have to go away and think about this . . .' Adam was stalling for time. He knew he was in trouble.

'Tell you what, I'll come down to the office tomorrow and we'll hammer it out.' Stuart pushed home his advantage. He was clearly sick of taking instructions from his cousin and he wasn't going to give him any more time than he had to.

The next day, I drove Stuart to the office at 9.30 a.m., by which time Adam had changed all the locks and instructed his security not to let him in. I knew instantly why he'd done that – there was obviously a whole stash of paperwork that he didn't want Stuart to see.

'I'm really sorry,' said the burly security guard in the black bomber jacket. 'We can't let you in. I suggest you speak to Adam about it.'

'Get out the fucking way!' Stuart was in no mood to argue. I could see the red mist was down and he was ready for a real fight. 'I SAID "MOVE", YOU FUCKING GOON! IF YOU DON'T LET ME IN THE FUCKING OFFICE I'LL KICK THE FUCKING DOOR DOWN!'

It had been a while since I'd seen Stuart in full flow. His reputation was such that most people had long since learned to play by his rules and he didn't have to resort to the violence that came so naturally to him. It was a chilling reminder for me to see how quickly he could flip.

By now, the second security guard was on his mobile to the boss.

'Adam's coming down!' he shouted as he hung up. Then he tried to reason with my husband. 'Stuart, come on. Come away from the door. Adam's on his way.'

Two minutes later, Adam's silver Jaguar screeched to a stop in the car park and Adam jumped out, all fired up.

'Alright. You want a fucking fight? Let's fight!'

Stuart ran to our car and took out the crowbar he kept there. *Oh shit! He's going to kill him*, I thought. I knew from experience that nothing stopped Stuart when his mind was set on something. But, just then, a police car pulled up behind Adam's car, lights flashing and siren blaring. Two coppers ran out and, quickly sizing up the situation, they each faced off against the raging men, who looked like they were about to start taking lumps out of each other.

'Sir – what are you doing with that crowbar?' one shouted at Stuart.

'Sir, return to your vehicle, please,' the other instructed Adam. 'You've been caught speeding. Please return to your vehicle.'

Stuart let the crowbar drop to his feet at the sight of the coppers but he yelled over their heads at his cousin: 'You fucking betrayed me, you bastard! You've stolen from me!'

Adam shouted back: 'I'm not going to speak to you while you're in this mood. We'll talk another time.'

Then he turned to the coppers: 'Officers, was I really speeding? Are you sure about that? I had no idea you were chasing me. I thought you were after the fella in front of me . . .'

Wasting no time, Stuart got into the passenger seat of my Ferrari.

'Just go. Drive,' he ordered. 'To the airport. I've got to get to Guernsey, get to Mum's house before he does.'

So we drove straight to the airport and Stuart caught the first flight over to Guernsey. The next morning he was back at home with the boxes of files he had taken out of her loft. For the first time in years, he stopped drinking in the middle of the afternoon and set his mind to unravelling the complicated web of deceit his cousin had woven for the past nine years. For weeks, he went through all those documents in the boxes and even hired someone to translate the Panamanian scrolls written in Spanish.

Finally we found the paperwork Stuart had signed in 1992, transferring all his shares in Mayfair Holdings over to Salisbury Alliance. With all the property now in his own name, Adam had taken the lion's share of the rents to fund an increasingly extravagant lifestyle, as well as borrowing against the capital to invest in other properties. Judging by the papers, it looked like Adam had built up a vast, global property portfolio behind Stuart's back and was now worth tens of millions of pounds.

But we had the smoking gun – we had the proof that Adam had deliberately deceived and stolen from Stuart and after each cousin had instructed lawyers, Adam agreed to repay Stuart the original capital investment.

'Why do you think he agreed to give it back?' Stuart asked me when we got the news.

'I don't know.' I was equally baffled. 'He didn't have to. I'm guessing he's already made so much money from screwing you over for the past decade, he worked out it's the very least he owes you.'

So the companies were split and Stuart walked away with

a property portfolio under Mayfair Holdings worth £2.5 million with no tax implications. In actual fact, it went into my name, since Stuart had been declared bankrupt for unpaid tax revenue. We created a new company called Hexagon Properties, another Panamanian company, which owned Mayfair Holdings and this contained seventy-four properties and instantly gave us £400,000 a year in annual rents. Now I had what I wanted all along – steady income and property, all of it in the matrimonial pot.

The one thing I wasn't comfortable with was keeping up the Panamanian connection. To my mind, it was crooked to the core and I worried that somehow it was all still connected to Adam.

'I just don't understand how it works,' I complained to our accountant, Melvin, one day. I'd been kept ignorant of all this for too long now and I wanted some answers. 'How can my company be owned in Panama if there are no actual owners? Who is in charge of this company?'

'Okay, let's take this one step at a time,' Melvin said patiently. 'All the assets belong to a company registered in the UK, but the UK-based company is in turn owned by a parent company registered in Panama. That company has Panamanian citizens as the directors and shareholders who are issued with something called 'bearer shares'. The share certificates belong to the 'bearer only', which means they have no names on them, but they are numbered as to how many are issued. The person who physically has these in his or her possession is technically the owner of the company. The benefit of this is you pay no tax on assets because no one can prove you own them.'

'But isn't tax evasion a crime?' I asked innocently.

'Not in Panama,' laughed Melvin. 'Under Panamanian law a corporation can be owned by the physical holder of the bearer share certificates, with no recorded owner in any database or public registry. The corporation records and bearer share certificates can be kept anywhere in the world and the location need not be disclosed to anyone.'

So this was how Maria had lost the fortune she thought she had worked so hard to help her husband build up over eighteen years of marriage. The rents which she helped to collect were from properties that didn't technically belong to her or her husband. Maria had been told over the years the reason for the Panamanian connection was to save the family tax. She had signed any papers she had to, relinquishing ownership in the process and unknowingly sealing her own fate. The cousins had her well and truly stitched up, meaning she was only entitled to half what her husband had in his name, or what they had in joint names, which was very little. At the time of her divorce, her solicitors had no idea how to unravel this corporate maze the two cousins had created. They didn't even know where to start.

The poor woman, I thought now. *She didn't stand a chance.* In the end, she had been offered a pitiful settlement – it's this or nothing, they said, so she took it.

Now it was all clear to me, I thought about Maria a lot, and I regretted how unkindly I had treated her. All these years later, I finally realized the terrible position she had been in. A very astute older lady once told me that there was only one way to judge a divorced man and that was to see how he treated his last wife in the divorce. If he had been cruel, then he would be cruel to you too. Finally, I was getting wise.

As my life shifted into a whole new gear, I resolved never

to let myself become another Maria. Nobody was going to pull the rug from under *me*. I was going to be smarter than that.

After all, Stuart wasn't the powerful man he once was. His power had waned, both over me and over the world he had once ruled with an iron fist. Two decades of living off me like a parasite had made him flabby and lazy, his mind not as sharp as twenty years before. And I was determined not to be his victim anymore.

No, if anyone was going to lose this game, it would be him. I just had to stay one step ahead of him . . .

PART IV
ESCAPE

Chapter 20

Changing Places

I lay in bed and grinned to myself. Outside, the early dawn chorus started up and already I could see the bright sun glinting through the curtains. Things were definitely looking up. In the past year there had been a complete shift in my relationship with Stuart. It had taken me nearly twenty years but I had finally managed to tip the balance in my favour. In addition – and crucially, given the role Adam had played in Stuart's divorce with Maria – the Kelly cousins were no longer thick as thieves; though that, of course, was really Adam's own doing. If he hadn't betrayed Stuart, it would not have been as easy to separate them. 'Divide and conquer', wasn't that the phrase?

On paper at least, on that bright summer day in 2003 I definitely looked like a conqueror – and to the victor, the spoils. Thanks to Stuart's tax avoidance and subsequent bankruptcy, everything was in my name.

It was a peculiar role reversal. For so long I had put up with my husband's threats, violence and intimidation because that was the price I thought I had to pay to be in a relationship. But now, now that our son had left home and I had secured the finances in my name, it felt like a new beginning. And something else, too. It felt like my leaving Stuart was only a matter of time. After all, I was a woman in my prime now – I was thirty-four years old – and I was sick of being dragged down by his controlling behaviour. He no longer owned me: I wanted to own my *own* destiny.

I hopped out of bed and turned on the rain shower in our wet room, mulling over my meetings for the day. Now that we had a steady and significant income from our property, there was no more backbreaking shift work for me. I chose my own hours for the time I spent running our property business and, apart from meetings with contractors on site, I usually had my work meetings over lunch or dinner.

Stuart was happy to leave me to it, knowing that I had the skills and acumen to keep the money flowing; when had he ever contributed to our businesses anyway, apart from to demand his petty cash? But really there was no magic involved. It was a fairly straightforward formula – we bought flats cheaply, refurbished them and then either sold them or mortgaged them for 50 per cent at their higher valuation. This gave us enough funds to buy the next project and keep the flats, as well as meaning we were never exposed to the banks, in case the market changed. We had a dedicated team of carpenters, joiners, electricians, plumbers and painters who worked for us on a freelance basis. I handled everything: met with the banks, the planners, the agents, the tradespeople and the other dealmakers. As long as Stuart had cash and wine, he was satisfied.

I dried myself off and slipped into my red-and-white silk kimono, wandering through to my walk-in wardrobe, still towelling off my newly highlighted hair. Now that we had a very good income and I had the time to take care of myself, I was investing in the new me. I had already lost three stone through my regular trips to the gym and now I was also getting my hair done in the best salon in Glasgow, as well as having my nails done and legs waxed. In fact, as I confided in my old friend Hannah, it was more out of necessity than anything else. Now that I was known in the business world, the banks were falling over themselves for my business and I was invited out to several networking events a month, such as charity balls, black-tie events, galas and large functions. This was where the real business happened – not in an office but over the dinner table – and I had to look my best in order to negotiate the best deals.

I flicked through my rail of designer dresses – what to wear today? The Gucci, Dolce & Gabbana, Alexander McQueen or Yves Saint Laurent? I picked out a rather simple but elegant black dress by my favourite designer, Roland Mouret, and teamed it with a pair of delicious six-inch Louboutins.

Three years earlier, I would never have dreamed of spending hundreds of pounds on a dress or a pair of shoes. Slender, toned, well-groomed and immaculately turned out, I felt every inch the successful businesswoman and I couldn't help but enjoy the compliments I now attracted from the young, well-educated men I met in the course of my work. Architects, engineers, investors, solicitors and surveyors – these were the people I met day in, day out. It was all a far cry from the days when I saw no one but murderers, junkies and thieves. These days, I was a person of influence and being one of only a handful of young women at this level of business, I always stood out a mile.

And now, for the first time, I felt a yearning for somebody

to give me satisfaction – I wanted love, happiness ... not to mention good sex. After all, I had never, ever had it.

It was in Hannah I confided all this. Over the years she had settled down and married a lovely man called Bill and together they had had three children of their own. Now I employed her again, but this time to run my office, organize my diary and manage the 130 flats we owned.

'You could have anybody you want!' she told me whenever I moaned at her about my lack of a fulfilling sex life. 'Just pick one of those hot young bankers who always have their tongues lolling out of their mouths when they see you!'

I giggled at the mental image. Hannah always made me laugh and after all this time, the two of us were still extremely close. Like sisters. There was nothing I couldn't talk to Hannah about. She was close to my son too – after all, she had practically brought him up and she had cried when he had gone to study in the States.

Thankfully, it had been one of the best decisions we'd ever made. Callum was a handsome, confident young man of eighteen these days and his strictly disciplined athletics school had given him impeccable manners. Sure, he'd come back with an irritating American accent, but he stood up whenever you came into the room and he took his cap off indoors. He tidied up after himself and he always said 'please' and 'thank you'. I was so proud of him; he was a true gentleman. So unlike his father!

It was wonderful to spend time together whenever he came home in the holidays and he always made sure to spend time with his 'other mother', Hannah, too.

In many ways, Hannah was the only person on the planet in whom I could confide about my longing to meet someone who would treat me right. She knew that Stuart had never been a good husband to me. She'd seen and heard his violent, threatening rampages for herself. For so many years she'd been my rock and my confidante: picking up the pieces when Stuart had broken me apart, helping me to face another day. Meanwhile, at work, I relied on her heavily to manage the flats and keep my diary. As a friend and employee, Hannah was invaluable.

'I don't want just *anybody*,' I'd daydream to her about my fantasy man. 'Firstly, I need someone really discreet. *Totally* discreet. But, also, I want someone really special.'

'Well, who is that then?'

'Oh, I don't know,' I'd sigh. 'I haven't met him yet but, trust me, I'll know when I do.'

I shook my head as I finished dressing, slipping on a pair of silk Wolford tights and selecting a pair of simple Marc Jacobs stud earrings. It was the stuff of fantasy, surely.

It was still only 6 a.m. but I had a breakfast meeting at a boutique hotel at 7.30 a.m. and I was planning on dropping into the office first to catch up on my emails. I walked out onto the landing and down the stairs. From the sound of the TV blaring in his study, I guessed that my husband had once again fallen asleep in his La-Z-Boy reclining chair.

Gently, I pushed open the door. Yes, as predicted, there he was, dressed still in his grey tracksuit from the day before, eyes closed, head back, snoring loudly, his wine glass still tilted in his hand, unconscious to the world. It was a huge relief to find him sleeping off his drunken stupor, for I was in no mood to face one of our now-constant arguments about what I was wearing.

'What have you put that dress on for?' he'd sneer whenever

he was up early enough to watch me getting dressed. 'You look like a man in drag.'

Though his insults no longer touched me, he'd always do his best to try and undermine my confidence.

'Seriously? That outfit makes your legs look enormous. You look like the Honey Monster! Why would you want to embarrass yourself like this? I mean, I'm only telling you because I care and I don't want you to go out thinking you look good when you don't. I'm only saying what other people will be thinking.'

Ha! If only he knew what other people thought of me, he probably would have locked the doors! But he didn't do that anymore, keeping me prisoner in my own home, because he knew that I was wheeling and dealing big time now, pulling in over £50k a month sometimes. I brought home the bacon and my pig of a husband wanted that to carry on.

But knowing I was out there in the world, dolled up to the nines, pushed his insecurities way out of control. He'd wait anxiously for me to get home from the office every day, eager for me to return and fill his belly full of good home-cooked food. Stuart couldn't cook. He didn't even know where the frying pan was. He relied on me 100 per cent and if I wasn't home when I said I would be, he'd call my mobile every ten minutes to check up on me. He even joined my gym so that he could keep tabs on me. It was ironic: there he was in the gym, horribly out of shape, but he did nothing except sit in reception, drinking tea and keeping me under surveillance. He never took a class or lifted a weight. It was beyond him.

And God help me if I didn't pick up my phone or if a meeting ran over and I was home late. Then there would be hell to pay – bottles of wine would be smashed against the walls, he'd destroy expensive pieces of art on our walls or smash beautiful vases against the floor. It could be terrifying. The same old speech was trotted out, but it was now tired and ineffective from years of overuse: 'Did I want to be single? Did I know who he was? He could destroy me . . . *yadda yadda yadda* . . .' It was all so much rubbish and, these days, it bored the hell out of me. I'd just look at him and think: *You're pathetic.*

But out loud I would just say: 'Pick it up yourself. I'm not tidying up after you.'

He ranted and raved, but it no longer meant anything to me. Instead, I'd try to find ways to avoid his constant surveillance. I'd 'accidentally' leave my mobile phone at home. But he would bring it into the office. Then I left it in the office. That day, he spent the whole day looking for me, following me from one meeting to the next, to make sure I wasn't having an affair. Yes, that's what he feared the most. He feared that I would find another man and leave him.

One morning, I'd decided enough was enough and I'd stopped taking his calls. Predictably, he'd turned up at the office half an hour later.

'Why didn't you answer the phone?' he'd demanded.

'I didn't answer because I'm working and I have nothing to say to you,' I'd said calmly. 'You are becoming pathetic, Stuart. These constant calls! I won't take your calls in the day anymore. I'll see you in the morning and when I come home at 6ish. Other than that, you won't be hearing from me.'

For a minute, Stuart had just stood there, open-mouthed, too outraged to speak. But I'd just ignored him and, finally, when he'd realized I was serious, he stormed out. I was standing up to him more and more as we both realized the truth:

he didn't have any hold on me whatsoever. We had changed places. I was the strong one and though he still had his violent temper and sick, sadistic threats, I was learning, little by little, that I could push back too.

Now, finally ready to leave for the day, I got into my car and drove up to the gates. While I waited for them to open automatically, I checked my make-up in my mirror. At thirty-four, I looked good – all the soft edges of my youth had gone and now my high cheekbones accentuated my blue eyes. I even sported a year-round tan thanks to the house we had bought in Portugal the year before. The villa in the Iberian hills was the love of my life and every time we visited, I felt my heart soar with happiness.

It was a lovely white house with pale blue shutters high up in the Serra de Monchique mountains, surrounded by olive groves, orangeries and lemon trees. I'd drive up to the large wooden door surrounded by bright purple bougainvillea and always feel a sense of coming home. Then I would pour myself a large gin and tonic and sit by the large stone table on the terrace, looking out over the hills towards the sea. Sitting there, absorbing the peace of the mountains and breathing in the fresh, fragrant air filled with the scent of almond blossoms and wild rosemary, I'd feel held, comforted, as the hours passed.

Stuart still found his moments to control me, of course. That time he locked me out on the balcony was awful. And when he was drunk, he could lose control completely. Despite all the changes of the past few years, his temper still frightened the life out of me. During one trip to Portugal, I got a massage at a local hotel while Stuart decided to watch the

Manchester United game on the TV. I told him where I was going and that I'd be one hour.

I was thirty-five minutes into the massage, just relaxing, when I heard Stuart shouting my name repeatedly in the main reception. How embarrassing! The masseur carried on, assuming there was a drunk outside, which there was, but it was *my* drunk! When I didn't appear, Stuart stormed into the room, threw the masseur to the ground and grabbed me by the arm. He started pulling me towards the door. Grabbing my clothes as I went, I tried to resist him but he dragged my half-naked body into the street, like I was a dog on a lead who doesn't want to go out in the rain. It was a horrible scene and I eventually broke myself free, slipped on my dress and paid the girl behind the desk, apologizing like mad. I left with Stuart bawling and shouting indecencies behind me as I hurried up the large hill.

I hailed a taxi and went back to the villa. Stuart arrived back six hours later, too drunk to know who I was. He fell into bed and I ignored him for the rest of the holiday. Stuart muttered his daily threats on how he knew people who could make people disappear. The more I ignored him the more he drank.

In fact Stuart had soon found himself a group of alcoholic expats to drink with daily, and that meant that, other than the occasional outburst, I was allowed off the leash more. Generally, in Portugal, I had space and freedom like never before, only ever seeing Stuart at mealtimes. As long as I checked in when I was supposed to, Stuart wasn't bothered. He liked to think that by giving me times to report in he was still in control. As long as I showed up when he told me to, he was calm.

So in Portugal I'd started socializing with a young, cosmopolitan crowd. And, among these young people who showed me nothing but respect, I found myself exposed to a different way of living. I saw men behaving well towards women, opening doors for them, listening to their opinions and laughing at their jokes. Freed from mixing with Stuart's older group of friends, who always treated their wives and girlfriends like second-class citizens, I'd begun to yearn for a new life for myself. A new way of being. The path of my life was evolving and, as the gates opened and I zoomed off down the road in my Ferrari, I could feel that change was now inevitable.

To the outside world, Stuart and I shared the perfect life – the thriving property business, a home abroad, expensive sports cars, a beautiful house with all mod cons and wonderful holidays. But success only served to paper over the cracks in our marriage; cracks that were getting bigger every day. The more confident I became, the more independence I craved and the more it fed my husband's insecurities. He was convinced I was having an affair and it drove him mad now that he couldn't control me.

It was bound to come to a head one day. Two weeks ago, it had finally happened.

It was a true turning point for me. Until then, I had only had the vaguest feeling that one day I would leave Stuart. I could sense a change in the air, but it seemed like the stuff of dreams: insubstantial and shifting, like walking on sand. But, two weeks ago, one violent and vengeful act had convinced me that I would have to cut ties with him, once and for all.

It had happened in the morning, after I'd left for the gym. In the past few months, I'd taken membership with a second gym on the other side of town, just to throw Stuart off my trail. I knew he sometimes checked up on me in the mornings but now he never knew which gym I went to and that way I could avoid him. On this particular morning, I had decided to stop at the office first to attend to some pressing business. Two hours later, I got a call from my trainer.

'Dawn, we have a situation,' he said, very seriously. 'Your husband has just smashed the hell out of one of my clients' cars by repeatedly reversing into it with his truck. We've got him on CCTV doing it. I would appreciate it if you could come and sort this out please, as soon as possible, as my client is threatening to call the police.'

'Oh shit, Mike, I'm so sorry. Don't let him leave. I'm coming now.'

It took almost £20,000, a lot of grovelling and some very creative lies to convince the man in question not to call the police on Stuart. 'My husband was having a breakdown,' I'd told him with tears in my eyes. 'He has just been betrayed by his cousin in the worst way possible and he thought yours was his cousin's car.' I'd gone on and on: he drank all day and night; he was on pills for depression . . . I threw everything I could at this bloke and, at last, the man, very reasonably, relented and accepted my offer of cash to fix his car. But it was a close thing.

'What happened?' I'd asked Stuart when I'd got home later that day. I was calm on the outside, but inside I was raging. Stuart had been slumped in front of the TV as usual, a glass of red wine in his hand.

'I fucking destroyed your gym instructor's car,' he'd spat, eyes still fixed on the TV. 'The one you're having an affair with.'

'Idiot,' I'd whispered under my breath. Then, loudly, so he could hear me clearly above the TV, I'd said: 'Well, the first thing is I'm *not* having an affair. And the second thing is that *wasn't* my instructor's car. That car belonged to one of his clients – and you're very lucky he's decided not to press charges. That little jealous fit of yours cost us seventeen grand. Happy? Was it worth it?'

'Fuck off,' he'd said. And *I'd* walked out.

That night, I'd sat in my kitchen, staring out onto our beautiful garden, nursing a glass of wine. *This is the beginning of the end of our marriage*, I'd thought, swirling the honey-coloured liquid around the glass. *He's out of control and I have to get away from this man, whatever the cost.*

Now, as I drove to the office, mentally preparing myself for another busy day ahead, I gave a deep sigh. I had meetings scheduled back to back with the last one at 6 p.m. this evening. It was a late one, but Hannah had been trying to set up a meeting for me with this landlord, Bryce Loweth, for weeks now. It seemed he was so busy he rarely answered his emails. Finally, she had called his office and his secretary had offered her the 6 p.m. slot in his office downtown.

It irritated me that he couldn't meet me sooner, or at a more convenient time, but his secretary had assured Hannah it was the earliest time he could possibly fit me in. Mr Loweth was the senior partner in a well-known firm and he was constantly on the go, she'd told her.

Typical! I thought now, as I pulled into the parking space outside my office. *Another self-important man! Well, we're all busy these days.*

What makes him so special?

Chapter 21

Bryce

'Come in!' a deep voice answered my knock that evening as I banged on Bruce Loweth's door. *A lovely voice,* I noted as I pushed it open, *smooth like melted chocolate.* It had been a very busy day and I felt exhausted.

But when I walked into that basement office, to be met by a handsome, distinguished-looking man who was sat behind a large desk, it suddenly felt like all my senses came alive.

Jesus! I couldn't breathe. *Who is this man?* For a moment, I lost my cool completely and I didn't know what to say or do. My mouth went dry, I started to sweat and my ears burned hot with embarrassment.

I'm holding my breath. Why am I holding my breath? God Almighty, Dawn, I rebuked myself. *What's the matter with you? Pull yourself together!*

At the same time, the man at the desk, who I reckoned to be in his mid-forties, looked up from where he had been writing and I felt my insides flip over. As we locked eyes, I knew in that instant I had fallen in love.

'Hi, I'm Dawn,' I managed to squeak, as the man fixed me with a warm but intense look.

287

'Yes, of course. Nice to meet you, Dawn. Please, grab a seat. Sorry I couldn't see you any earlier. Bit under the cosh here.' He spoke quickly and politely as he waved at the seat in front of him.

There's that amazing voice again! Oh, I could listen to it all day!

It was so rich in tone, it really did something to me. Now, as I sat myself in the chair opposite his desk, it felt like every sinew in my body was on fire. I *wanted* this man. I wanted him more than I had ever wanted anyone in my life before. And it was terrifying!

'So, what can I do for you, Dawn?' he said brusquely, with a quick downward glance at his watch. It was abundantly clear that whatever I was feeling at that moment, Bryce Loweth was not feeling it too.

'Erm, right . . .' I tried to compose myself, but at the same time I couldn't help clocking this man's thick black hair, fine-boned cheeks, his immaculately tailored suit and strong Roman nose. He was slim, I could see that – he probably worked out. Broad chest, slim hips . . .

'You wanted to see me?' he prompted.

Oh God, I'd stopped talking! How embarrassing. Got. To. Stop. Staring. Quickly, look away . . . !

'Yes, sorry. It's been a long day,' I spluttered. 'Look, I'm selling a flat in the first block on Dean Street and we have to paint the communal entrance and fix the entry door system to ensure the sale goes through. Just as a courtesy I'm contacting all the landlords in the block to let them know. Yourself included.'

'I see – and are you looking for a contribution?'

'No, not at all. We're happy to do the work ourselves. Like I said, it's a courtesy call.'

Bryce sat back now and looked at me with smiling but confused eyes.

I wonder what he'd do if I reached over the desk and kissed him right now? My mind played out this erotic scenario as he stared at me. I could have grabbed him right then and there. I had never known such an intense, electric feeling before. It was overpowering.

'Would you like a cup of tea?' he offered.

'Yes, that would be lovely,' I replied, equally polite. *If only he knew what I am thinking!*

'That's really good of you, Dawn,' Bryce said as he got up and filled the kettle in the sink behind him. 'So, I hear you're in property. Is that right? How many properties have you got?'

'Erm, currently around one hundred and thirty,' I replied, undressing him in my mind. I had never done this before, never felt like this before. *How am I going to see this man again?* At that moment, nothing else mattered in the world.

'And are you looking for more?' he went on sweetly.

'Always.'

'What about managers?'

'Oh, we manage our own properties.'

'It's a great time to be in this business, isn't it? Prices are rocketing at the moment. We've got some great properties on our books.'

'Really? Anything for me to look at?'

'Maybe. I mean, you know that we manage rentals, don't you?'

'Hmm.' I did know that. In fact, I could see where he was going with this. He wanted our managing business, but I didn't want to give it to him. No, *I* wanted something else entirely . . .

But, as he passed a cup of tea to me across the desk, I couldn't help noticing the ring on his finger. My heart sank. He belonged to someone else! For the next hour we talked business, only, though afterwards I couldn't for the life of me remember what was said. All I knew was that I had to have this man.

Suddenly it was 7.30 p.m., which meant I had to get home or risk Stuart's wrath. After his stunt two weeks before at the gym, I'd been walking on eggshells and didn't want to set him off.

'Look, I've got to go but it was really nice to meet you,' I said.

'Dawn,' he said formally as he got up, grinning, and shook my hand, placing the other over the top. My hand was encased now and I didn't want to let go. It felt safe, somehow, like he was protecting me.

'Look, we really appreciate your work on Dean Street,' he said as he showed me out. 'It's very good of you and I'm sure my partners would be interested in meeting you. My firm has a table at the Macmillan charity gala in a couple of weeks. I'd be delighted if you would join us?'

'Yeah, that sounds good,' I said solemnly. *Stay calm, stay calm, Dawn!* I shouted at myself inside.

'Great – I'll get my secretary to email yours with the details.'

And, with that, I turned around and left, my heart thumping like crazy. Outside, I walked quickly to my car and then, finally, when I got inside, I let out a massive sigh and my face broke into a large, stupid grin. Oh my God. Oh my God. OH MY

GOD! I was in love! For the first time in my life, I was in love! I couldn't stop myself smiling and laughing all the way home. I refused to let myself think about Bryce being married. Not because I didn't care about his wife, but because it was just a fantasy to be with him, and that was all. I thought that after all this time with Stuart, I deserved a little daydream. And Bryce was certainly an unforgettable mystery man. I couldn't wait to see him again to fuel my fantasies further. I couldn't believe I had to wait two weeks. It was an eternity!

That night I lay in bed, tossing and turning, unable to get this man out of my head. Over and over I replayed our meeting in his office, examining every detail, searching for signs that he fancied me too. From the moment I had heard his voice and laid eyes on Bryce Loweth, I was a woman possessed. I'd never felt this way before – it was incredible.

I barely slept a wink that night and I was surprised that Stuart didn't notice the change in me the next day. Wasn't I transformed? Didn't my face give me away? But no, he didn't pick up on anything.

That morning, I dressed in a hurry, eager to leave the house. I had to confide in someone or I would burst.

'Hannah! Hannah, it's happened!' I blurted out as I strode into the office that morning. With the phone crooked between her neck and shoulder, Hannah was typing on the computer in front of her.

'Hmm? What's happened?' she said distractedly.

'*It*! Love! I've met him! I've met *the one*!'

Hannah immediately slammed down the phone and swivelled to face me in her chair, her whole body tense with anticipation.

'Who? Who is it? Oh my God – tell me everything!'

Now that I had her attention, I filled her in on what happened the night before and she shrieked and laughed with me all the way.

'You've got to see him again!' she said finally.

'I know and I will. He's invited me to a business dinner in two weeks,' I said. 'But he's married!'

'So what? So are you!'

The next two weeks were hell, waiting for the next chance to lay eyes on Bryce again. In the meantime, I worked out every day, trying to exhaust myself so I didn't lie in bed every night, thinking of him till the early hours. Bryce Loweth consumed my every waking thought. I wanted him so much but, at the same time, I had no idea how to get him; even if I should try.

The night before the charity do, I went through my wardrobe with a fine toothcomb, trying to nail the perfect outfit. *Nothing too sexy*, I told myself. I didn't want to arouse Stuart's suspicions, plus this was a work do so, obviously, I had to be smart enough for everyone to take me seriously. In the end, I opted for a black Armani tuxedo.

Simple but elegant, I told myself, as I turned to admire the trouser suit in the mirror. With a white silk blouse underneath, it definitely stood out from the average ballgown. Now sporting a sleek blonde bob and with blood-red nails and lipstick, I knew the whole ensemble exuded power and confidence. I wanted to look good, but I wanted to meet this man as an equal.

Funnily enough, Stuart offered to drive me to the event. He did this more and more these days – I knew it was his way of keeping an eye on me, but it meant I had to be extra careful not to give myself away.

'Sorry, no partners invited,' I told him when he asked if he could join the table.

'Fine, I'll just stay at the bar and wait for you,' he said, with a stern look in his eye. I had a curfew, and he didn't want me to forget it.

The ball was held in a swanky hotel half an hour out of town and, when we arrived, the large hotel was awash with the great and the good from our local business community. It was an upmarket, moneyed crowd, the type of people I was now used to mixing with. Even so, they all seemed to disappear the moment Bryce walked towards me, his hands extended in greeting and a great big smile on his face.

'Dawn, you look amazing! Let me take you through to the table – I want you to meet the other partners in my firm.'

With that, he put his hand on the small of my back – my body thrilled to his touch – and led me through the crowds. He wore his black tie and kilt with real panache and he fitted in so well with this well-heeled set. He was smooth, elegant and charming – everything Stuart was not. At the table, he introduced me to a handful of middle-aged men; there was a real ripple of excitement when they realized I was joining them. Even so, I didn't let the attention go to my head – I stuck to sipping mineral water so that I kept my wits about me and tried to sneak little sideways glances at Bryce. Meanwhile, Stuart stayed in the bar with the other chauffeurs.

For the best part of three hours, I talked business with all the men around the table. Bryce was three seats away from me so we couldn't speak one on one. It was agony being so close to him, having longed to see him again, and yet be unable to hear his voice or exchange views.

Finally, as it approached 11 p.m., I was painfully conscious of Stuart waiting in the bar so I excused myself from the table. Frustratingly, Bryce and I hadn't had a chance to chat the whole night. He stood up as I approached his seat to say my goodbyes. *Like a gentleman,* I thought.

'I'm afraid I've got to go.' I smiled apologetically. 'But it's been a lovely evening and it was great to meet your partners. Thank you for inviting me.'

'So soon? Cinderella, home before midnight, eh?'

I looked down and blushed.

'Ah, what a shame,' he went on, saving my embarrassment. 'I so wanted to sit down and talk to you but, ah well, never mind, I'll see you again soon.'

Then he kissed me full on the lips. I felt a thrill of sensual pleasure like nothing I had ever experienced before. It was easily the most arousing moment of my life. My heart was doing somersaults and I could sense my whole body tingling with excitement. Did he do this to everyone? Did he fancy me? Or was he just drunk? If only I knew what that kiss meant!

More. I want more!

Forget Cinderella, I was more like Sleeping Beauty, being awoken from a very long, deep sleep by the kiss of a prince. I was *alive*. For the first time in my life, I felt alive. Every cell in my body screamed out for more but I knew it couldn't be. Not here.

Quickly, I looked around. Thank God Stuart hadn't seen the kiss or he would have hit the roof! But, as it turned out, I had nothing to worry about on the Stuart front . . .

'Who's that bloke that invited you, then?' My husband quizzed me on the way home.

'Bryce Loweth,' I replied, as casually as possible. 'He's the

CEO of an asset management firm. Says he's got some property we might be interested in.'

'Short black hair? The one with the kilt?'

'Yes, that's him.'

'He's gay.'

'Do you think so?'

'Definitely.'

'Hmmm. You're probably right.'

No, I thought to myself, as my lips still tingled with the pleasure of Bryce's kiss, *you're most definitely wrong*.

Chapter 22

Awakenings

The very next day, I emailed Bryce, thanking him for the invite and asking if he had any property he wanted me to look at – an excuse to get to see him again.

But I didn't get a reply for six weeks. *Six whole weeks*. In that time, I drove myself mad, wondering what I'd done to offend him or make him think badly of me, but it turned out – as Hannah had experienced before me when she'd tried to set up our initial meeting – that Bryce Loweth was just a very busy man. For finally, after six weeks of hell, I got an email inviting me for a Christmas drink at an upmarket wine bar in town. *Yes!*

This time, I wasn't going to mess around. I'd been far too bloody subtle last time in my androgynous tuxedo. For our lunchtime drink, I poured myself into a red Roland Mouret dress that clung dangerously to my curves and squeezed my feet into a pair of killer Louboutins. I didn't like to wear heels most of the time – I was far happier in trainers – but after six weeks of waiting, it was time to get my man. After all, I had endured years in a loveless marriage, sealed with vows I had made only in fear. My feelings for Bryce were overwhelming and I wanted to feel special – the way he had made me feel even on the two brief occasions we had previously met; the way Stuart never, ever had.

But that didn't mean I was going to be easy pickings. *I am an ice queen, I am an ice queen,* I repeated to myself – advice from Hannah, who was the only person I had taken into my confidence about my feelings for Bryce – as I pulled open the heavy glass doors of the bar that afternoon in late December. Bryce stood up and waved to me from a booth at the back and my heart seemed to somersault right out of my chest.

'Wow!' he said admiringly as he greeted me with a kiss on each cheek. 'Great dress. Please, take a seat.' And he held my hand as I slid into the booth. His manners were so beautiful, I immediately felt good in his presence. *Nobody has ever made me feel like this before, like a lady, like a woman of worth,* I thought. *I could get used to this . . .*

'Champagne?' Bryce poured me a large glass from a bottle of Laurent-Perrier on ice. I accepted graciously; I needed some Dutch courage.

'So you said you had some properties for me?' I asked; I wasn't very good at small talk. He opened his briefcase and handed me a sheaf of papers. For a while, I leafed through the property details. There were three which had promise and I told him I would take these – they were worth about £400,000. *Expensive drink,* I thought, as Bryce topped me up.

Gradually, Bryce got me talking; I found I relaxed in his presence, let my guard down in a way I hadn't for decades. I told him about how I came into the property business and a bit about my background with the bars and hotels. In turn, he regaled me with stories about his work as the CEO of an asset management firm and how he had helped to build up his company's portfolio.

But while our work was the main topic of conversation, there was another form of communication that was going on all at the same time. *The way he's looking at me, the way his eyes keep sliding down my body towards my legs*, I thought, *I can tell there is something between us*.

He wants this too, I realized.

Finally, on the third glass of bubbles, I screwed up all my courage and quizzed him on the elephant in the room.

'So, you're married?' I asked, my heart in my mouth as I waited for his response.

'Hmmm . . .' He nodded, twirling the stem of his champagne flute. Then he cleared his throat and added: 'Not happily though.'

I let out the breath I'd been holding. *That makes two of us.*

'Well, what you need, then, is a mistress who is discreet,' I said slowly, deliberately, barely able to believe my brazenness. 'Someone with just as much to lose as you.'

'And where do I find one of them?'

'*I'm* one of them,' I replied steadily. My heart was in my mouth again. Here it was, finally: *I want him and now he knows it*. Bryce's eyebrows shot up and he broke into a massive grin while I looked at him demurely, then I tipped back my head and downed the rest of my drink.

'You're married too?' he asked.

'I'd say ours is a more platonic relationship,' I said, and burst into nervous giggles. The truth was that as Stuart neared sixty, he went off sex. It was probably the years of heavy drinking, but these days he much preferred to knock back a bottle of Merlot in front of *CSI* than try to have sex with me.

Sex was an effort for him, one that I did nothing to encourage.

Bryce and I were both laughing now and I yearned to feel his arms holding me, to feel his soft lips on mine again.

'Hey, I got you a present!' He suddenly whipped out an envelope from his briefcase. 'A Christmas gift.'

It was a full day's worth of pampering and treatments at the best spa in Glasgow.

'That's such a lovely gift,' I said gratefully. 'Thank you.'

It was one of the only presents I had ever been given by a man – and Bryce barely knew me! Stuart had never bothered before, always insisting that presents were a sentimental waste of money. If I wanted something, he said I should just go and buy it myself. Bryce was clearly of a different mindset and when we left he insisted on paying for our drinks too.

'I wouldn't dream of it,' he objected, when I tried to get my money out. *Such a gentleman*, I thought again, as he held open the glass doors for me on our way out. *Where have you been all my life?*

'So do I get a Christmas kiss?' he asked as we stood outside.

'Of course.' I smiled – and that's when he took my face in both his hands and brought his soft lips to mine. It was the best kiss I had ever experienced: tender, gentle, sweet and sexy. He smelled so nice, so clean, and his lips tasted almost sugary, like candy floss. Warmth spread throughout my body. It felt like we were locked together forever . . . but in another second he pulled back and we both stared at each other.

'Would you like to come back to my office?' he whispered.

Yes! Yes, I really did but, at that moment, I knew I was playing with fire. We were outside on the pavement, in full view of the whole world, and if this ever got back to Stuart my life would not be worth living. I couldn't go back to his office now. Already I'd been out too long and I was worried about Stuart.

'Another time,' I said.

'Promise?'

I nodded. Now I knew what he wanted, but I was frightened of letting him down.

'Just go for it!' Hannah said the next day when I told her about the lunch. 'He's not going to tell anyone.'

'So what do we do?' I felt very insecure about sex and relationships. After all, I'd been with Stuart since the age of fourteen. I had no clue about how to behave or what to do.

'Is it just sex at his office and then we go home?' I asked. I knew I sounded foolish but I honestly had no idea what I was getting into.

'Yes, that's about right,' Hannah said with a smirk, clearly amused by my naivety. I should have been ecstatic – after all, this was what I'd wanted all along – but the Bryce situation had screwed me up. I couldn't eat, sleep or think about anything else. He consumed me completely.

'Just get it over with,' Hannah urged. 'Have sex with him. Don't worry about Stuart – I'll cover for you.'

I wanted Bryce so much. Even so, he was a hard man to pin down. I'd expected that he would contact me soon after our Christmas drink but it was another three months before I heard from him again. Hannah made me swear I wouldn't contact him so I just had to wait for his call. Meanwhile, the sale of his flats was going ahead. I didn't care about the cost – I would have spent a million just to see him again. Finally, he called and invited me for a drink at a museum bar I'd never heard of. *It's out of the way*, I thought as I checked the address, *so we don't get seen by anyone.*

Once again, I dressed to kill; this time in a scarlet Victoria Beckham dress and beige heels. Bryce was waiting for me when I sauntered into the bar, swaying my hips with far more confidence than I felt, and he had a bottle of pink champagne on ice. He seemed really pleased to see me and we talked and drank and laughed for an hour. And then, just as we were leaving, he grabbed my arm and gave me a passionate kiss. I pulled away, terrified of getting caught.

'Not here,' I whispered.

'Come back to my office,' he urged, and this time I didn't resist.

We caught a taxi to his basement office, where he had more champagne waiting. The rest of the partners had offices on higher floors so there was literally nobody else there. Even so, Bryce locked the door. My heart pounded harder in my chest as I heard the key turn. *What happens next?* I wondered. All I'd ever known was Stuart – I didn't allow myself to think of John – and my body seemed all at odds to be with this man I so desperately *wanted*. Never had I felt like this before about any man.

Bryce came towards me then and kissed me passionately. With a touch so erotic I nearly collapsed in his arms, he took my dress off and caressed me, gently easing me out of my silk La Perla lingerie. He lay me back on his large couch and slipped off my knickers and then, for the first time in my life, he gave me oral sex. It was *incredible* and I actually had an orgasm – something that Stuart had never even attempted. For the first time I had amazing sex and I loved every minute.

With Stuart it had all been about him; now, with Bryce, it was about me, and that was fantastic.

Afterwards, I tried to get to the bottom of what was going on with him at home but he deflected my questioning with good-natured ripostes. And so, despite what I told myself about me deserving someone who treated me nicely for once, I felt sick with guilt about our infidelity that night – but also desperate to see him again.

And it seemed he felt the same way. In time, it became a regular thing: we would meet up for drinks once a week or so and then go back to his office or a hotel for sex. He never asked me about my home life and I didn't ask about his either now. Instead, we lived out our fantasies like a pair of lovers in a movie. There were hotels, bars, restaurants and long, highly charged bouts of lovemaking. Everything he did to me, with me and for me made me fall so much more in love with him, but I just couldn't tell him. I wanted to shout from the rooftops how much in love I was, but I had no one to tell. Hannah had to cover for me regularly with Stuart as he often popped into the office when I was meeting Bryce. She'd say I was at a viewing or in a meeting. But eventually, after nearly a year of this clandestine relationship, she confided in me that she was worried.

'You're not actually falling for this guy, are you?' she asked one day, after I floated back into the office following another energetic hour with Bryce.

'Oh, I don't know,' I sighed.

'Because if you fall for him, Stuart will kill you. You know that, don't you?'

'Yeah, I know,' I snapped. *Why is she trying to bring me down? Can't she see I'm happy for the first time?*

'Well, I'm just saying. I'm just warning you, for your own good, Dawn. I can't cover for you for ever, he's going to figure it out sooner or later.'

She was right, I knew: it couldn't last forever. Besides the danger of Stuart catching us, I was beginning to turn into a demented woman. Inevitably, after each wonderful, illicit encounter, I would return home miserable, knowing that I would not see Bryce again for another week or so. Even Mum noticed I'd been out of sorts recently and asked whether something was troubling me. I couldn't tell her, of course. I knew that she was now a fan of Stuart thanks to the help he had given her since Dad died. She was also a firm believer that if you were married, that was it for life. Divorce was a dirty word in her book.

Despite my passion for Bryce, I was still playing 'the ice queen'. I never called him; I never told him my true feelings, scared in case it ruined everything. *You don't marry the man you have an affair with*, I told myself. *It's just supposed to be sex.* But I couldn't help myself – I wanted so much more. After we made love he would wrap his strong arms around me, kiss the top of my head and stroke my hair. But he never said a word, never showed any emotion. I had no idea what was in his head and I was afraid to ask.

Meanwhile, Stuart noticed I was pulling away from him. If I wasn't meeting Bryce I would go out with business friends, giving me a social life I hadn't previously enjoyed. My husband tried to demand that I stop going out – but I refused. So then he started turning up unexpectedly in the restaurant or bar where I was meeting friends, just to check up on me. It was highly embarrassing.

Exasperated, I sat him down one day and said: 'Stuart, I

need my own time. My own space. Why don't you see your friends anymore? There was once a time I didn't see you from one day to the next. How about you go out with your friends again?'

'I'll do what I fucking want,' he'd snarled before storming off upstairs. There was no reasoning with him.

The truth was, he didn't really have friends anymore. Some had died, others had retired to the Costa del Sol and the rest were simply old men who didn't enjoy hanging around in loud bars anymore. Just like Stuart, they preferred to be at home in a pair of slippers with their feet up. He was old now; there was no getting away from that. But at thirty-six I was still young: I wasn't ready for old age. I'd missed out on my teens and twenties and now it was my time to have some fun. In my opinion, I'd bloody earned it and I was angry at the way he refused to give me my freedom after all these years. So the more he pushed, the more I pulled away from him. It was getting to the point where our marriage ties were strung so taut, they were bound to snap.

Two years after our first meeting and eighteen months into our grand, dizzying affair, Bryce invited me to his fiftieth birthday party. This was a big deal, I realized. He wanted me to meet all his friends and family. *Are we finally getting serious?* The thought made my heart soar. *Maybe he feels the same way I do?*

I wore an elegant navy Dolce & Gabbana dress to the restaurant he'd hired for the evening, determined to make a good first impression when I met his nearest and dearest. The moment I walked in, Bryce came up to greet me with a big smile. I handed over the silver cufflinks I'd bought him as a special birthday gift and he thanked me sincerely, his eyes fixing on mine as though drinking me in.

'I need to talk to you,' he whispered at last, leading me by the elbow to a quiet corner.

'I've left my wife,' he said. My heart felt like it was floating free, untethered by his words. *This is it! He's left his wife for me because he loves me and now he wants to marry me. Yes. Yes! I knew it, I knew it . . .*

'But,' he said, swallowing hard and not meeting my eye, 'I'm seeing someone else.'

What? WHAT! Someone else? How could there be someone else? His words made me feel like I'd been punched in the stomach but I kept the smile fixed to my face, the ice queen to the end, frozen in pain.

'I think you and I should cool it for now,' he went on. His voice seemed strained – but no wonder, I thought, he was breaking up with me. 'This – us – it's been amazing but, Dawn, I need to give this other relationship a chance.'

I nodded and smiled but I couldn't speak. I could barely breathe. *How could I have got it all so wrong? I didn't understand. I just didn't get it.*

I stayed ten minutes longer at the party, weirdly detached from the other guests who all seemed to know one another. I recognized a couple of the businessmen from his office but Bryce didn't introduce me to his friends and family and now I felt foolish and out-of-place. Eventually, I slunk away unnoticed and ran to my car, sobbing all the way home.

That night, I threw caution to the wind. Bryce had seemed so weird when he was telling me it was over, like he wasn't quite himself. If there was any chance I could change his mind, I had to fight for him. His love was too important to me to just throw it all away. So, I sent him an email, saying he had broken my heart and that I loved him.

He didn't reply.

Over the next few weeks, I felt increasingly despondent. *What did you expect?* I told myself. *He is now single but you are still married, it is as simple as that. You have no hold on him – of course he wouldn't be on the market long. A man like that!*

But he knew I was unhappy in my marriage too, some part of me piped up. *He could have asked me out, but he didn't. Why? Didn't he feel the same? I'd always imagined he did and he was just waiting for the right moment to tell me.*

Now I fell into a deep depression, one from which I thought I would never fully recover. For the first time in my life I had glimpsed happiness and it had been cruelly snatched away. *Had I been wrong about Bryce?* I wondered. *Had I misread the situation?*

I should have guessed at the truth but in that moment, wracked by insecurity and misery, I simply blamed myself.

Chapter 23

Behind the Curtain

Empty, bare, pale, lifeless – the snow-covered fields provided a blank backdrop to our journey as we whizzed along the motorway. It was December 2006, over a year since Bryce had finished with me yet from that night on my life had felt lonely and featureless, just like the landscape around us. Stuart and I were on our way to one of Callum's tennis tournaments at an indoor arena an hour out of town. Naturally, since my husband had drunk booze at lunchtime, it was up to me to get us there.

Callum had worked hard to build his career and now, at twenty, he was a professional sportsman. I was so proud of him. He was the shining light of my life and seeing him play always made me happy. Above all, I was pleased he had forged his own path and hadn't been diverted into a life of crime. Of course, I didn't relish attending these events with Stuart. I had nothing but contempt for my husband these days and we rarely went anywhere together. Now he was staring at me in that creepy way he always did while I tried my best to ignore him.

'What are you thinking about?' he asked after a little while.

'Nothing,' I replied automatically.

'You're thinking about *him*, aren't you?'

'Who?'

'That lettings agency bloke – Bryce Loweth. You're having an affair with him, aren't you?'

'No, I'm not,' I sighed. And, sadly, it was the truth.

'Don't lie to me. I know you are. You're fucking him and you're planning to leave me.'

'No,' I said again. It was always the same with him: endless accusations about different men I was screwing from one week to the next. At least this time he'd pinpointed the right one, I noted wryly.

'You know that if you ever tried to leave me I'd kill you,' he said.

At that, I lost it. I was so tired of his threats.

'Oh shut up!' I snapped. 'You always say you're going to kill everyone. This speech you do, it's boring! Well, you can't keep me prisoner all my life. I'm not a little girl anymore, Stuart. I can make my own mind up about where I want to be.'

'If you leave me, so help me I WILL FUCKING KILL YOU. I MADE YOU AND I CAN DESTROY YOU TOO!' Now Stuart was shouting over me at the top of his voice.

'Just shut up!' I repeated.

'You're not leaving me. We'll both die before you leave me . . .' And with that he grabbed the steering wheel and gave it a hard right spin so that our car swerved into the right-hand lane.

'What the fuck are you doing?' I screamed, terrified. We were doing sixty miles an hour with another car heading straight towards us, beeping and flashing his lights. We were going to collide head on! Stuart, grim-faced and spitting in anger and outrage, gripped the wheel tightly, steering us straight into the car's path.

Panic gave me a strength I didn't know I had. Somehow, I managed to wrest back control of the wheel and steer us back onto the left-hand side of the road – and just in time. Then I took my foot off the accelerator and pulled off the road, bringing the car to a stop in a farm ditch. I jumped out of the car, shaking and panting from the shock. Stuart frequently made threats, but I had long ago thought him incapable of carrying any of them out. *Have I been wrong?* I wondered as my heart slammed fearfully in my chest. *He could have killed us both!*

'You're off your fucking head!' I screamed at him. I was so angry now that I couldn't hold back any longer. 'You fucking moron! How would Callum feel if his mother and father were both killed in a car crash? On the way to his tournament?'

I was so mad at him that I didn't stop there. I had just stared death in the face and it was a hell of a lot scarier than Stuart. 'You want to know the truth?' I spat out. 'Here's the truth: yes, I do want to leave you. I hate you. I've never loved you. I want a fucking divorce and I want to have sex with other men. Because you . . . *you* make my skin crawl. I have never enjoyed sex with you – you are nothing but a controlling demon who preys on young girls. But I'm not a young girl any more, Stuart. I'm thirty-seven, I'm a woman. And I may have lost my teens and my twenties to you but I am *not* going to lose my thirties.'

I stood back, still shaking and breathing hard, and waited for the retaliation. I braced myself for the verbal onslaught that I knew would now be unleashed. Despite myself, I couldn't quite believe I'd been so brave as to tell him the whole and unvarnished truth. *What will Stuart do now?* I felt tense and tired, trying to anticipate his next deadly move.

But Stuart, who had also got out of the car, took me by surprise. He said nothing. He just leaned against the roof, staring at me with sadness in his eyes, like an old man who had been beaten. His whole body slumped forward, his shoulders sagged. He looked like he'd just gone ten rounds with Tyson. *What's happened? Why isn't he saying anything?*

To my utter shock, Stuart then fell to his knees and started to weep.

'I'm sorry,' he sobbed. 'I'm so sorry, Dawn. I'm just so scared of you leaving. I can't live without you and if you leave me I'll kill myself.'

It was like the curtain had been pulled back and instead of a wizard there, I had just found a weak, pathetic old man. Now he was exposed and vulnerable and I was the strong one.

'Fine,' I seethed. 'You kill yourself – but you're not taking me with you!'

I called Hannah from my mobile, who was also due to watch the tournament with us. Of course she was horrified when I told her what Stuart had done.

'I'm not getting in the car with him again,' I told her. 'You'll have to come and collect me.'

Really, I should have called the police, but I suppose a lifetime of being warned that the police were my enemy had embedded itself into my character. Never invite the authorities, that was Stuart's mantra, so I simply got into Hannah's car and refused to let him get in with us.

'How am I supposed to get there?' he whined.

'I don't care. Just stay away from me,' I spat. 'He tried to kill us both, Hannah! He's a madman!' I wasn't ashamed of his behaviour anymore. Once upon a time his power to embarrass or scare me had imprisoned me in silence but not anymore. I was bubbling over with rage, and I wanted everyone to know what an utter bastard he was. Let *him* take the shame. I was done.

As we drove off, Hannah tried her best to calm me down but she could see that the situation had become very serious.

'He'll never let you go, you know,' she said as she drove.

'So I've got to put up with him all my life?' I raved. 'Is that what you think I should do, Hannah?' I was furious at her, too. Of all the people in the world, she knew best how miserable he had made me. Whose side was she on?

'I'm just saying, Dawn, you've got to be careful. I'm trying to look out for you.'

'Aye, well, the best thing for me would be to stay as far away as possible from that monster!'

From that day onwards, Stuart and I lived entirely separate lives in the same house, though strangely Stuart now decided to try and win me back. He surprised me with flowers, bought me gifts and even tried to take me away on a romantic weekend to Brussels.

'Are you crazy?' I asked when he presented me with the flight tickets.

'No, I'm just trying to do something nice for you,' he offered lamely.

'Forget it,' I scoffed. 'I'm not going anywhere with you. Never again.'

Stuart, now playing the part of the spurned husband, even enlisted Hannah and my mother to his lost cause.

'Darling, it's your *marriage*,' Mum implored. 'You can't just throw it all away like it doesn't mean anything.'

'Mum, why don't you mind your own business? I don't see how this has got anything to do with you.'

'It's got everything to do with me.' She frowned. 'You're my daughter, he's my son-in-law and you are both parents of my grandson. When you commit to marriage, that's it, for life. Whatever he may have done to upset you, you have to stay with your husband. God knows, your father wasn't the easiest man to live with but I put up with all his drinking and . . .'

'That's enough,' I said. 'I've heard your opinion. Now please just keep it to yourself. You are not welcome to interfere in this matter.'

'Well, if you don't care to listen to me, perhaps I'll go back to the flat then . . .' Mum loved to play the wounded martyr and of course I refused to rise to her theatrics.

'Aye, you do that, Mum,' I said flippantly. 'See ya!'

But Hannah, too, was keen to maintain the status quo, offering Stuart advice on how to win me back while at the same time telling me how much he wanted to try and fix our marriage.

'There's nothing left to fix,' I snapped at her one day. 'Can't you understand, Hannah? It's over and it has been over for a very long time. He has to get used to the idea. He has to let me go.'

'Honestly, Dawn, I think he's changed. He's really trying hard, he loves you! I mean, isn't it worth giving him a second chance? It's not like there's anyone else around. You had your fling with Bryce. That's over now.'

'Don't remind me,' I said quietly. 'But you know what? I

would rather be alone for the rest of my life than with Stuart for another day. The man is poison.'

My words weren't strictly true. In fact, I was devastated about losing Bryce and still, a year after our split, it hurt me to think about him and my heart yearned to be with him. The worst part of our break-up was that I realized I'd never been truly honest with him: I'd never shown him the real me. It was all tight dresses, pink champagne, sexy underwear and secret trysts. He must have thought I was a high-maintenance, hard-nosed businesswoman who strutted around in heels all day, but it wasn't true. I was far happier in my onesie and Uggs with a cup of tea, watching *EastEnders*. *No wonder*, I thought, *he chose to be with another woman*; someone I imagined to be more down-to-earth. I had pretended to be an ice queen and he'd found that terrifying.

Well, I didn't blame him. I'd found it exhausting too, playing the part of the heartless seductress. I had been so obsessed with being a sex goddess that I had presented a completely false image of myself and that broke me up inside. To my horror, I had the worst of all worlds: a desperate pensioner trying to rekindle a romance that never existed and an absent lover who didn't want to know.

It was a few months later, in March 2007 on my way to a session with my personal trainer, that I saw Bryce in town, parking his car. At first, I pretended not to see him, still ashamed at the false woman I'd professed to be and still hurt by his leaving me, but the moment he caught sight of me, he called out my name. I put up my hoodie and took out a pair of sunglasses to hide my eyes. I really didn't want to bump into my ex!

'Dawn!' he called out again as he got out of his car. I kept walking, ignoring him.

'Dawn!' He was now running across the road to meet me so finally I looked up and acknowledged him.

'Oh, hi Bryce.'

'Hi. Dawn. You look really good.' He smiled down at me. Oh, it was so painful to hear that smooth, deep voice once again. 'Hey, do you want to go for a coffee?' he went on.

'No, I don't. I'm in a hurry.' *What does he want?* I thought impatiently. *Does he think we can be friends? Does he want to tell me how well it's all going with his new woman?* I just wanted to get away from there as quickly as possible – before my emotions got the better of me.

'That's a shame,' he said, his eyes searching mine. 'I . . . er . . . I've really missed you, Dawn.'

'Really?' Suddenly my heart leapt.

'Yeah . . . I can't stop thinking about you,' he confessed.

I wanted to cry. I'd dreamt of this moment but never thought it would come true.

'Do you want to kiss me?' I asked hesitantly.

'Of course I want to kiss you . . .' he laughed. And then he pushed me into a doorway and for a moment our lips locked in a long and deeply passionate kiss. *Oh, how I've missed his kiss!* I'd forgotten how good this felt. For a moment, I felt like I was floating away . . . but then I snapped back to reality.

'No, not here. Not like this.' I pulled away. I looked at Bryce, sizing him up. He hadn't mentioned the other woman, and that kiss had not been the kiss of a man who was into someone else. *What's going on?* I wondered. I felt horribly confused – but I also knew my love for Bryce was as strong and sure as it had ever been. 'Look,' I continued, 'Stuart's

314

away this weekend. Why don't you come over tonight? I'll cook you a meal. I think . . . I think we better talk.'

I was so excited that night, I could barely contain myself, but I was also wary. There was so much I needed to tell him and I had no idea how he would react. After my gym session I'd changed into a pair of combats, trainers and a loose-fitting T-shirt – my usual weekend gear. No more ice goddess for me: Bryce was going to meet the real Dawn McConnell for a change.

Now I opened the oven door and took out the slow-cooked Moroccan lamb that had been roasting most of the afternoon. Carefully, I turned the meat over and basted it with the gravy. The smell was so rich and aromatic, and I hoped Bryce would love this dish as much as I did.

After a year apart, I had done a lot of thinking and I knew that if I wanted Bryce in my future, he needed to know about my past. I felt nervous about revealing the real me to him, but at the same time I was done playing games. Honesty had to be the best policy.

Bang on 7 p.m. the doorbell rang. I met Bryce at the door in my baggy combats, apron and no make-up.

'Hello you,' he said with a smile. 'Long time no see!'

I was awkward at first, being so open with Bryce, but this time I had nothing to lose. We kissed then I told him dinner would be ready in half an hour.

'You cooked for me?' he asked, eyes wide with amazement.

'Don't look so surprised,' I laughed. 'I'm quite domesticated, you know. I enjoy cooking.'

'Smells great,' he said appreciatively. We opened a bottle of wine and at first we made small talk, mostly about the house. Then, over dinner, we talked about the past year and I admitted that I had been very miserable without him. I also told him that my marriage to Stuart was over and I wanted to leave him, I just didn't know how.

'He says he'll kill me if I leave,' I said. 'And I believe him.' After my husband's stunt in the car, I knew he was quite prepared to make good on the threats he'd delivered through the decades.

There was a moment's silence and then Bryce said quietly: 'I believe him too. That's why I stopped seeing you.'

'What?' I was confused. 'What are you talking about?'

'There was no other woman,' Bryce sighed. 'It was Stuart. He paid me a little visit and threatened to kill us both.'

'Oh Jesus,' I whispered. 'I should have known . . .'

'It was the week before my fiftieth. I got into the office one morning and he was just there, sat in my chair, behind my desk. My secretary said she had asked him to leave but he'd refused, claiming I was expecting him. I knew it was him, of course; I'd seen him before, following me.

'When I walked in he asked me if I knew who he was. I said yes. Then he said I had no real idea who he was or what he was capable of because if I did know I wouldn't be doing what I was doing.

'He said he knew I had feelings for you and he told me to stay away or he'd kill you. He'd kill us both. The way he said it, I was absolutely convinced he was telling the truth.

'So that's when I decided to end things. At that point I didn't really understand where we were going or what my feelings were for you. I had so much going on at home, trying to sort things out with my wife and the kids . . . I just felt this was one thing I could do without. So I told him: "Look, I'm with someone else. Your wife needs to find herself something to do.'"

I sat there, thunderstruck by what he'd just told me. 'You mean, you didn't have another woman?'

'Of course not!' he said. 'I just couldn't take the risk of getting you killed! Your husband is a very convincing man. I had no doubt whatsoever that if we had carried on like before he would have tried to kill you.'

'He did try to kill me,' I said, quietly. 'Even after you finished with me.' So then I told him all about how Stuart had tried to drive our car into oncoming traffic. 'It's over now, he knows it,' I added. 'I told him I want a divorce.'

Bryce took my hand and held it to his cheek. 'I just don't understand, Dawn,' he said. 'How did you end up with this . . . this brute?'

I shook my head. 'It's a long story . . .'

'I'm not going anywhere . . .'

'I want to tell you . . .' I started, but I could feel myself shaking. It was going to take a lot of courage but I knew I had to do this. I took a deep breath and tried again: 'I trust you, Bryce, and I want you to know about my past because . . . well, it's who I am. But it's hard. I . . . er . . .'

'It's okay,' Bryce said gently. 'I'm here to listen, not judge. Why don't we relax a little? Take a bath? Maybe once we're a bit more relaxed, you'll feel like talking . . .'

So we both went upstairs and I filled up the large, whirlpool bath with bubbles. As we undressed, Bryce told me he had had a tough year splitting from his wife and it had been particularly hard on the kids who were just nine and twelve.

'We didn't want it to be too disruptive to their lives, of course,' he said. 'And they're great kids – they really are – but

317

it's a big adjustment to make and they're responding to it differently. They live with me in the week and they see their mum on weekends.'

'Does that work?'

'Yeah, well, it's working at the moment. I'm quite domesticated myself!' He laughed. 'You know, I didn't want to end our relationship when I did but, looking back, it was probably the right thing for my family at the time. I needed to give the kids all my focus and attention.'

He's so caring, I thought, as I slipped under the bubbles. *I like him so much.*

'Now, why don't you tell me about you,' he said as he got in beside me. 'I want to know everything about you. I feel like we're still strangers. Start with your childhood ... tell me about that.'

That made me want to cry straight away. Bryce seemed so gentle, so loving, I knew that it was safe to tell him. So I went right back and I told him about my brother's abuse, about how I had tried to stop it but I couldn't. And how this had skewed my view of men and sex. So when Stuart came along, I thought that sex was the way to make him happy. I told Bryce about his false promises, his flattery, the way he had seduced me and, eventually, trapped me with pregnancy. I told him everything, about the years of cruelty, control and mental torture Stuart had put me through; about how years of embarrassment and shame had silenced me; about how I had felt imprisoned by my husband, unable to live a normal life. Bryce held me the whole time and wiped the tears away.

'I just can't believe it ...' he whispered. 'It's terrible. So terrible, Dawn.' I could see he was completely distraught, struggling to hold back his own emotions.

'You don't have to be scared anymore.' He spoke resolutely. 'Because I'm going to take care of you. I'm going to look after you for the rest of your life. I love you Dawn and I'm going to marry you.'

That night, after we got out of the bath, we went through to the bedroom and for the first time in our whole affair, we didn't have sex. We just held each other. I felt weightless, like I was floating. It was as if someone had cut the chains that had been holding me down all my life and now I was free. I didn't have to be scared anymore because I had a true friend by my side. An ally. Someone who loved me without ulterior motives; someone who loved me, no matter what.

'You're not alone anymore,' Bryce whispered in the darkness, and I knew it was true. I had someone by my side to love and protect me forever.

From that moment, we were inseparable. Bryce knew the real me now, and he knew the risks involved in being together. But he was willing to face it all. This was not some superficial infatuation anymore, it was deep love and Bryce showed me how a real man treats a woman. He cooked me special meals and, if Stuart was away for any time at all, he whisked me away for a romantic getaway in the country. We would sit cuddled up on the sofa together and he would rub my feet, massage my shoulders or run me candlelit baths. Once we drove up to the countryside and there, in the middle of the forest, was a table laid out with champagne and a delicious meal. In the middle of nowhere! He bought me cards and gifts and never let me pay for anything. I had never met a man like this; I never knew they even existed! He was so loving and caring, it blew my mind.

But every day we were getting more and more wrapped up in each other; my excuses to my husband were wearing thin. Once, I got back from meeting Bryce to find Stuart waiting for me in the office. He was still following me, turning up unexpectedly when I was meeting friends, trying to keep me in my place. I spun him a lie on the spot about getting an emergency callout from a tenant. But how long could this last? How long before we were caught? Surely, it was only a matter of time. And it wasn't only Stuart whose fuse was growing short: Bryce and I, too, were impatient for things to come to breaking point.

'I can't live like this anymore,' Bryce said one day, six months after we'd rekindled our romance. 'We have to be together properly . . . No more sneaking around.'

'But how? He's going to kill me.'

'No, he won't.'

'He'll do something terrible. He will. It's the nature of the man; he won't be able to stop himself.'

'So we have to be smarter than him. We make a plan and it starts today . . .'

Chapter 24

The End

Smoothing down the creases in my beige linen dress, I checked my make-up in the mirror, threw my keys into my handbag and called upstairs to my husband: 'Bye! See you later!'

Then I walked out of my house for the very last time.

It was 22 June 2008 the day Bryce and I had been planning for months, the day I was finally leaving Stuart – only he didn't know that. Not yet, anyway.

Despite the hammering in my chest and my shaky hands, I walked towards my car at my usual brisk pace, not too fast, not too slow, trying not to give anything away. Everything about this day had to be as normal as possible to ensure my safety, which was why I was leaving the house with just my handbag and nothing more. I couldn't do anything to arouse Stuart's suspicions.

Behind the wheel, I glided through the early-morning traffic to my office, where I met the man who was due to take my car. His name was Brian and he was a friend of Bryce's who owned a farm just outside of Glasgow. Brian's job was to hide my car in one of his outhouses while I was away. It was too risky to leave the Ferrari where Stuart could find it. He would almost certainly smash it up when he found out I was gone, so the idea was to hide it until the heat had died down.

Right, part one complete, I told myself, as I watched my Ferrari disappear down the road. Inside the office, I met a very nervous-looking Hannah, who jumped up the moment she saw me.

'You're still going ahead with it?' she asked uncertainly. Of course I'd had to take Hannah into my confidence about the plan; I needed her to keep the business ticking over while I was gone. She was the only one who knew the significance of today and she was sworn to secrecy.

'You know I am, Hannah,' I said sternly. 'There's no alternative.'

After all, it was nearly a year and a half since Stuart had tried to kill us in the car and I'd told him I wanted a divorce. Almost eighteen months on, we weren't a single step further forward along that path thanks to Stuart's obstinacy and insistence that I was his. I had to take drastic action to prove to him that I *wasn't* – and drastic action to ensure that my new life without him wasn't a murderously short one.

I looked at the clock on the wall – it was 9. 15 a.m. and my flight took off at 2 p.m. I'd be in the office for the next three hours and then the plan was to get a taxi to the airport. Bryce was due to meet me in Cyprus. *Tick, tick, tick* . . . I was acutely aware of the sound of the second hand on the wall clock as I worked through the emails that had landed in my inbox overnight.

After a while, Hannah stopped working and leaned towards me conspiratorially.

'Okay, so you'll leave and then what happens?' she asked.

'What do you mean?'

'Well, what happens next? He has to be told or he'll go crazy wondering where you are. Who's going to tell him that you've left?'

'I don't know.'

'Do you mind if I tell him? I just think it would be best coming from me.'

'Okay, but wait till the flight's taken off.'

We spent the next hour tip-tapping away in complete silence, each of us lost in our own thoughts. It had been a strange few weeks, during which time I had gradually emptied my wardrobe of all my most expensive clothes. Each day, I stuffed a couple of dresses and a pair of shoes into my gym bag then I met Bryce on the top floor of various high-rise car parks across town to hand them over. Meanwhile, I was careful to leave the suit carriers and shoeboxes in place, just in case Stuart decided to check my wardrobe. If he opened the door, he would see all the carriers and boxes there as usual and assume they were full. This way, I managed to move my £100,000 wardrobe from my house to Bryce's.

At 10.30 a.m., Stuart arrived at the office.

'You look nice today,' he said as I shot him a questioning look. 'Don't worry, I'm not checking up on you. I just need to collect some post.'

Ever since the incident on the motorway, I had stood up to Stuart and his outrageous behaviour. The way he was always checking up on me – I hated it. In his effort to woo me back, he had promised now to stop making spontaneous visits. Still, old habits die hard and he couldn't help popping in for the most spurious reasons. It didn't stop him from trying to check the messages on my phone either, so I locked both my phone and my sim card. So, despite his promises, it was no surprise to see him in the office that morning, and it hardened my resolve that I was doing the right thing.

Hannah handed him the letters and then glanced at me, guiltily. *Keep it together, woman,* I urged her in my head. Hannah was clearly struggling with this whole situation. *Never mind, just another few hours and I'll be gone.*

Bryce and I planned to stay in Cyprus for two weeks and then I was due to move into his house, deep in the Scottish countryside. Stuart didn't know where Bryce lived and there was no way of finding out since he had given his wife the marital home and was renting a house for himself. What a difference between the way Bryce had treated his wife in his divorce to the way Stuart had walked all over Maria! I just hoped that Stuart wouldn't be able to trace Bryce's new home. I didn't doubt that he was capable of carrying out the threats he had made throughout the years to murder me, cut off my hair or throw acid in my face. He was a cruel and vicious bully and I knew he took real, visceral pleasure from inflicting pain on others, particularly me.

At 12.15 p.m. I closed down my computer and told Hannah I was leaving. I was really nervous now, knowing that Stuart could still be out there, watching the office, just waiting for me to make my move but I didn't let it show. I kept my cool. *What would happen if he knew? Would he stop me getting on the plane? Calm down,* I told myself. *Just keep calm and it will all be fine.*

'Look after yourself,' Hannah whispered as we embraced.

'Thank you. And Hannah, thank you for doing this. I really do appreciate it.'

'Do you have any idea when you'll be back?'

'Not right now. I'll call you, okay?' A small, brave smile flickered over her features but it failed to mask the real fear in her eyes. She had known Stuart and me for decades, she had practically brought up our son, now everything was changing and she had no idea where it would lead.

Once outside, greeted by the warm spring sunshine, I breathed deeply to calm my nerves. I quickly scanned the road to see if Stuart's car was there. *No, nothing.* So I flagged down a black cab to take me to the airport. My stomach was full of butterflies now and I felt sick with apprehension. *Part two complete*, I thought as I slammed the car door closed and gave the driver the address, trying to reassure myself. *Now I just need to get on that flight.*

I checked the contents of my handbag en route to the airport: purse, tickets, passport. Everything I needed. In my purse I had around £5,000 cash and 2,000 euros; enough, I hoped, to sustain me for the next two weeks. I quietly thanked Stuart for his crooked advice throughout the years. 'Fly under the radar, never use a credit card,' he'd said many times. Now that I was doing my own disappearing act, I took his advice. It was cash all the way. I didn't want him tracking me down while I was gone.

'You know he could freeze all our assets,' I'd warned Bryce before he took the ferry across to the continent the previous week. He was driving down to Cyprus and had loaded up his car with all the clothes I needed for our trip.

'Don't worry about money,' he'd soothed. 'I can pay. The moment he does anything like that we go to the lawyer. Whatever he does, we'll face it together.'

At the airport, I managed to get through check-in and security without any problems. Then: *ping!* A text message arrived from Hannah: 'I told him and he collapsed in the office. Can you speak?'

I looked at my watch – it was still only 1.15 p.m. *Why has she told him before the flight has taken off?*

But then I realized: *he was in the office.* That meant he had called in to check up on me *again* and Hannah had cracked. If he was in the office, there was no way I was going to speak to either of them.

I decided not to reply. Instead, I headed to the first-class lounge, where I poured myself a large Scotch on the rocks, which I knocked back in one go. It burned like fire all the way down but it was just what I needed.

Ping! Another text message: 'He's threatening to kill himself. I've called Bill to come and collect him. Can you talk?' Again, I decided to ignore the fact that he had had to call her husband. It was 1.25 p.m. – just another thirty-five minutes to go.

Now I took a seat in one of the plush leather armchairs opposite the runway and flicked through a copy of *Grazia* magazine. The words swam meaninglessly before my eyes; I couldn't take anything in. I was restless and impatient to board the plane. All I wanted now was to get out of the country as quickly as possible. Every time the door to the lounge swung open, I spun round to see if it was Stuart. My heart was doing somersaults every thirty seconds so I got up and poured myself another Scotch. *Come on, come on*: I stared manically at the clock on the wall, willing the time to go quicker. At 1.40 p.m., my phone pinged into life again. This time, it was Stuart.

'You think you're clever? You've got an hour to get back here or one of you will be killed. And I mean it. I was sad when Hannah told me you'd left but now I'm happy because this is just the start! If you leave me I will transfer everything to my name and you will have nothing. Nothing!'

I read the text again – it was what I had come to expect from Stuart but even so, it frightened me. At that moment, the tannoy announced my flight to Larnaca and I got up, still scared but more determined than ever. *You can threaten me all you like, Stuart, but you don't own me. And you can't make me do anything anymore. It's over.* I turned off my phone and went through to take my seat.

It wasn't until the plane had trundled down the runway and lifted into the air that I found myself breathing out properly for the first time that day. Relief flooded my body. *He can't get me now. I've done it. I've escaped!* My phone was switched off for take-off, but as soon as the captain gave us permission, I turned it back on again. *Ping! Ping! Ping! Ping! Ping!* The messages came thick and fast.

'I'll kill you both.'

'Your life isn't worth living.'

'I'll throw acid in your face and disfigure you so badly no man will want you.'

About an hour into the flight, the tone shifted.

'Just come home. Please.'

'If you come back I'll forgive you everything.'

'Please just come home and we'll talk.'

'I love you. Dawn, I can't live without you.'

By the time we started our descent to Larnaca airport, I was relieved to turn off my phone again. I didn't know how much more I could take. It was the same old controlling tactics Stuart had always used, but they had worked for a long, long time – and with good reason. They were scary.

So, once I was off the plane, I practically ran through the arrivals hall and threw myself into Bryce's arms.

'You made it!' He grinned, looking relaxed and tanned from a week of sunshine. 'I knew you would.'

'He's been texting all afternoon,' I garbled. 'Threats, awful threats, threats to kill me, to kill you, begging, pleading, promises. You name it, he's said all sorts of stuff. Come on. Let's go to the car and I'll show you.'

Once in the privacy of his car, I showed Bryce all the texts.

'Hmmm.' He scrolled through them, looking increasingly concerned. 'You know we could go to the police with these? They're threats on our lives.'

'And make him even more angry?'

'Well, maybe we could get a restraining order?'

'From a few angry text messages? I don't think that's going to stick.'

'Well, for now let's just stay in Cyprus until the dust settles a little. We've got all the time in the world so let's just enjoy ourselves. Come on, I want you to meet my family.'

Bryce's sister was holding her fortieth birthday celebrations in a small coastal village about four hours' drive from Larnaca and we were booked into a lovely hotel overlooking the harbour. It was wonderful to meet all of Bryce's family and touching that he was so keen to show me off, but I couldn't fully relax. Stuart was constantly phoning and leaving voice messages and when I spoke to Hannah, she seemed really upset.

'The doctor's been round and he's put Stuart on valium,' she said. 'Callum's here too – he can't believe what you've done. He's furious with you. Right now, he's ready to kill you and Bryce.'

Oh shit. Callum! In all the planning and the plotting, I hadn't thought how this would impact on my son; I'd been too worried about making sure Bryce and I escaped alive. Even though, at twenty-two, Callum now had his own life and flat in Glasgow, I had failed to consider breaking the news of my marriage break-up to him in person and, now, it appeared Stuart had got there first with his own version of events. Poor Callum! And poor Hannah was bearing the brunt of holding up both of them.

'I'm so sorry, Hannah.' I apologized again. 'I'm sorry this has all fallen on your shoulders. Is there anything I can do from here?'

'Well, you could think about coming back maybe and picking up the pieces yourself?' she said tetchily.

'You know I can't do that, Hannah,' I said gently. 'He'd kill me. I've got to give him some time to get used to all this and hope he calms down.'

'Right now he's more likely to kill himself,' she snapped.

As we said goodbye and I put down the phone, I felt sick with worry and guilt. I couldn't live with myself if Callum lost his dad because of me. No matter what Stuart was like as a husband, he was still Callum's father and they shared a close bond. Meanwhile Stuart turned to ever more desperate measures in an attempt to entice me home.

'You can have Bryce for your lover as long as you come back to me,' he wrote in one text. 'I'll do anything to have you back. I know I've been a bad husband – Hannah's explained it all to me – but I can change. I'll be better. I can't live without you. Please come home, Dawn.'

This was the usual way with Stuart – either outright aggression or self-pity, all engineered to get me back under his sway – but nothing in the world could have tempted me to go back to him. This was the end and we both knew it.

It was a strained two weeks in Cyprus. I wanted to enjoy my freedom with Bryce, but at the same time I couldn't help worrying about everyone back home. Callum was refusing to take my calls and Stuart had collapsed one evening at a petrol station after 'overdosing' on valium. It wasn't enough to kill him, of course, not even enough to warrant having his stomach pumped; he'd just swallowed enough pills to get everyone's sympathy and attention.

'Are you made of stone?' Mum texted one night when I said I thought Stuart was overreacting to gain public sympathy. 'The man is distraught.'

Don't be so naive, I thought. He was a master manipulator, my husband, and he knew exactly how to play to the gallery. But I couldn't say that, of course. Frustratingly, I couldn't say anything that would make me seem even more cold-hearted than I already did. Certainly, in the PR battle, Stuart was already gaining ground. It didn't seem to matter how he had controlled me over the years, hit me and hurt me. Everyone was only worried about him.

So I simply wrote: 'I'm sure he'll be fine once he calms down. He knew this was coming. Our marriage has been over for years.'

After two weeks Bryce returned home for some meetings while I took a flight to Portugal. Judging from Stuart's erratic text messages, which still came in at all times of the night and day, ranging from threats to kill me to sweet nothings intended to soften me up, I needed more time to lay low.

By this time I was down to my last few hundred euros so

when I landed at the airport I took out my company credit card to withdraw some money. But I was mortified when it was refused by the ATM. *It's probably just because I'm trying to get cash out from abroad*, I reassured myself. *Thank God I've hidden a few hundred euros in our holiday house!*

With the last of my cash I hired a rental car and drove up to the house. There, I sent an email to my bank manager Sadie Peach – we had known each other for a long time and as two young, high-flying women, we had formed a good rapport over the years.

'Just had my credit card refused,' I wrote. 'What's going on?'

Five minutes later, I got a reply.

'I'm really sorry, Dawn. Stuart and Callum have signed you off as director from your companies. You have no access to the accounts. I'm really sorry – there's nothing I can do.'

Now, for the first time since I'd left home, I broke down. It wasn't so much what Stuart had done, it was the fact that he had managed to convince our son to take his side. Callum had been a director of our companies for years now: it was our life insurance policy. If anything happened to me and Stuart at the same time, Callum could instantly take control of the companies. But now Callum had been convinced to use this corporate set-up against me.

I've been so stupid, I berated myself. *Why didn't I take my son into my confidence?* I had been so worried that he might not understand and would give me away to his father that I had ended up making an enemy of my own child. Now he was exorcising me from his life and from my own businesses too. I cried and cried that day, frightened that I had just gambled with my life and lost it all. Terrified, I called my lawyer.

'It's not legal,' he said when I explained what had happened. 'He can't just steal all the matrimonial assets. Give me a bit of time, I can fix this. Don't worry.'

I stayed just five days in Portugal, enough time to catch up with some of my Portuguese friends, who all congratulated me on my finally leaving Stuart. They knew what my husband was like – over the years, I had confided in them and they had been appalled by what I'd described.

Just hearing their reactions gave me strength. 'It had to be done,' they said, and I knew it was true. If I was going to have a future with Bryce, I needed to break away from Stuart once and for all.

Even so, this certainty didn't prevent my nerves bubbling to the surface as I boarded the plane back to Glasgow. Stuart was so volatile, so unpredictable, that I had no idea what to expect next. Bryce picked me up from the airport and drove us back to his house in the country. It was a beautiful converted barn with amazing glass walls that looked out over rolling countryside. All my clothes were in his wardrobe and my shoes lined up neatly underneath. For a moment, I stared at them. Just seeing my familiar things gave me a tiny bit of hope that maybe one day this would be my familiar, everyday life with no more dramas.

That night, I dialled Callum's mobile number from the house phone and because it came from an unknown Scottish number, he took the call.

'Callum, it's me, I want to talk to you,' I said quickly. 'Please don't hang up.'

'I don't want to talk to you, Mum. Not after what you did.'

'Callum, I'm so sorry. I didn't mean to hurt you.'

There was a long, angry silence. And then:

'You know, Mum, I understand *why* you left him. I really do. I know what Dad is like . . . it's just the *way* you did it. So sneaky, so underhand. You left him for another man. You should have just left him first.'

'I know . . . I know . . . but, look, life's not always that straightforward, it's not always so cut and dried like that. Can I see you? Please, there's so much I need to tell you. I want to explain this all face to face.'

I held my breath as I waited for his response. *Please, Callum, please . . . Give your mum a chance . . .*

'Yeah, okay,' he said slowly. 'But not with *him*. I don't want to meet him. Ever!'

'That's fine. Right now, I don't want you to meet him either because I love him, Callum. And one day I'll marry him so I don't want you to meet him in anger. For now, let's just get you and me back on track.'

'Okay.'

'I've missed you, Callum. A lot.'

'Yeah, I've missed you too.'

With those words ringing in my ears, I put down the phone. I immediately felt 100 per cent better, and stronger. There was hope, after all.

The next day, I stood outside my office at 9.30 a.m., steeling myself to go in. It was a warm July morning, the branches of the trees were heavy with blooms, the air full of promise. It had been three weeks since I'd left but it might as well have been years. In that time, I had taken a giant leap into the unknown and been through every single emotion from elation to despondency as a result. Now I felt like a very different person to the one who had stood here nearly a month before.

My eyes flicked left and right, instinctively checking the road for signs of Stuart's car, fearful of a surprise ambush. *He's not here,* I told myself. *He doesn't even know you're back in the country. Right, time to face the music!*

'Hi,' I greeted Hannah nervously when I got inside. 'How have you been?'

She just stopped and stared at me, the thousand-yard stare of a soldier who'd experienced the worst horrors of war. Finally, she sat back and shook her head ruefully.

'How have I been?' she repeated. 'How have I been? Let's see now. I've been shit, that's how I've been. While you've been swanning around Europe for the best part of a month I've been looking after your family and my own and trying not to let either one fall apart. Oh yes, and I've been keeping the business going at the same time. So I'm fucking tired, fed up and bloody furious with you, Dawn! You've put me under a lot of pressure here and frankly I don't think I deserve it at all.'

'I'm so sorry, Hannah,' I said, truly apologetic. 'I didn't realize just how much Stuart would lean on you during all of this. I know it's been a lot for you to cope with.'

'You could have bloody guessed!' she shouted. I'd never seen her so angry. 'I mean, it was just so selfish of you to go off and leave me in the lurch like that. Who could *I* lean on during all of this? It's been one flipping crisis after another.'

'Is Stuart still at your place?' I asked.

'No, he's gone home now.' She paused. 'He's given me a list.'

'What? What do you mean, "a list"?'

Hannah sighed and opened the top drawer in her desk. She took out a handwritten sheet of A4 and handed it to me.

'He says he doesn't want to involve the lawyers. It's a list of the properties he wants and a few personal possessions from the house. Oh yes, and the house, too. He says if you agree to the list he'll grant the divorce.'

I took the list, absolutely stunned. Stuart would agree to a divorce? My heart soared – this was better than I had hoped for. All those threats over the years and it just came down to this. I'd spent the past three weeks living in fear, but maybe, at the end of the day, my husband wasn't quite as bad as I'd thought him to be. Maybe he did have an ounce of decency in him after all. Maybe, despite all his bluster, he was prepared to let me go.

My eyes scanned the list. Quite reasonably, he was offering me our art collection and the villa in Portugal, plus the properties we had built up over the years together in the company we called Silverbridge. Basically, if he could have the properties in Mayfair Holdings, our Panamanian company, Glasgow and a few personal items like tables and chairs, then I could take the rest.

Yes! I mentally punched the air. *Yes yes yes!* Absolutely. He could have everything he asked for. I mean, how much does a person need to live? I figured I would walk away with nearly £2 million in assets and he would take Mayfair, worth around £2.5 million. It was clean, fair and cost-effective. I couldn't have dared hope for more.

Now I grinned broadly at Hannah.

'It's fine. It's all fine! Really. He can have everything on the list. Tell him that, Hannah. Tell him I agree. This way you can keep running my property business and we'll all be okay.

'Look, I'm sorry I haven't been around,' I went on, 'but you've got to understand I needed to give him time to calm down and think things through. And, look, that's exactly what he's done. He's come up with a reasonable, rational plan.'

I held up the list: vindicated, triumphant, full of self-confidence.

'This, this makes it all worth it, Hannah! He's come to his senses and he doesn't want to fight anymore!'

PART V
THE WARRIOR

Chapter 25

The Enemy Within

Humming softly to myself I turned around in the shower, enjoying the sensual first touch of the scalding water on my body. It had been three months since my return from Cyprus and I was delighted that everything was going so well. I massaged some shampoo into my hair and mentally ran through a list of things I had to do that day. Meeting with the bank, lunch with a prospective buyer . . .

Crash!

What was that? I wondered for a moment. It sounded like Bryce had dropped a plate on the floor. He was always keen to get breakfast started early and was downstairs now laying the table for his kids and me. I relaxed under the water. He always made such an effort, I marvelled, with warm porridge, fresh fruit and local honey, not to mention wonderful artisan bread and . . .

Suddenly, I heard a voice that made my whole body freeze up, despite the warmth of the shower. I strained to listen. It was . . . but, but . . . it *couldn't* be!

Below me, I had heard Stuart's voice cutting angrily through the sunny day.

Now I quickly turned off the shower and hopped out, throwing a towel around my body. It was definitely him! Stuart's voice was shouting obscenities and getting louder and louder. *What the hell is he doing here?* There was no need for any contact between us. I'd seen him briefly in the office since I'd been back, and we were all making the best efforts to be civil and adult about the whole situation.

Suddenly, I was consumed with fear for Bryce's two children, and I marched out of the room and onto the landing where their bedrooms were. To my horror, I was met by the sight of Stuart running up the stairs with Bryce following closely on his heels. I had only a moment to notice that Bryce was bleeding from his right cheek.

'You can't go up there!' Bryce was shouting desperately. 'My children are up there!'

'Where is she?' Stuart ranted, now pushing open doors. 'Where the fuck is she? Where's Dawn? I'm fucking taking her home.'

'THAT'S MY DAUGHTER'S ROOM!' Bryce yelled. 'DO NOT go in there!'

'Stuart!' Now I called to my husband from across the landing. 'Stuart, go downstairs. We're all going to go downstairs.'

I spoke in a low, firm voice to try and calm this potentially incendiary situation. How had he found us? He must have followed me here: it was the only thing I could think of. *Up to his old tricks again . . .* I could see he was dressed all in black with black gloves on and his face was almost crimson with rage. He obviously meant business and my blood chilled in my veins.

'Right, *you*!' Stuart was jittery, agitated and I recognized the mood immediately – he was so angry, he was unhinged and at that moment I feared for my life. 'Right, get your stuff, get your fucking stuff. You're coming home now.'

He whipped his head back to where he saw Bryce was coming up behind him: 'Stay away, Bryce, if you know what's good for you!'

Now the kids – Nathan and his older sister Charlotte – had come out of their rooms, still in their pyjamas, and were staring at all of us in turn, but especially at this stranger in black who was swearing and snarling like a pit bull.

'Kids, come down here!' Bryce called to them and they scurried down the stairs to their father. I slowly followed after them, and eventually I noted that Stuart also came downstairs to the open-plan kitchen-living area. I stepped lightly in bare feet, my eyes moving swiftly to take in the scene: the hammer on the floor, the upended kitchen table and the porridge spattered all over the kitchen tiles, studded by the remains of the broken crockery.

Once we were all downstairs I asked Bryce to take the kids to their rooms. I had no idea what Stuart would do next but I didn't want to draw these innocent children in any further.

'I'm not going anywhere,' Bryce said, breathing hard. He seemed not to notice there was an alarming amount of blood now pouring from his cheek. So I asked Nathan if he could get a cloth for his father's face.

'SHUT UP! Just shut up, all of you,' Stuart cut in. 'Right. Dawn, get your fucking stuff. You're coming home with me.'

'No, I'm not coming home with you, Stuart,' I said, slow and firm. 'I've left you. I'm with Bryce now.'

'BRYCE!' Stuart barked, his eyes still locked on mine. 'Tell her she's going home, if you know what's good for you.'

'I'm not saying anything,' said Bryce steadily. 'She has to make the decision for herself on where she wants to be.'

For a while there was silence as we watched Stuart to see what he would do next. His eyes were darting from corner to corner and I felt my whole body tense as I tried to think ahead of him. My eyes kept returning to the hammer – I was closer and quicker than him. *If he tries to grab it*, I thought, *I'll get there first and I'll hit him with it using all my strength.* At that moment, I was quite prepared to kill him if I had to. If he left me no choice, I would bring that hammer down on him so hard he wouldn't be able to get back up again.

'You fucking LIED to me!' he finally erupted. 'This is all your fault. One minute everything's fine and the next you've fucking left me!'

He's the one who's lying, I thought. *Lying to himself. Things had not been fine between us for a very, very long time – if ever.*

'I think you need to leave now, Stuart,' I said. Then I repeated slowly: 'I am not coming with you. I am no longer your possession. Please leave this house.'

I just wanted to end this without any further bloodshed. I could see the danger was passing. Once I had stood up to him and refused to go home with him, once I had proved I wasn't scared of him anymore, he was done.

Still, he was full of bluster: 'Just don't think of calling the fucking police for this because you'll be sorry. You'll be fucking sorry if you call the police.'

'Okay,' I said. 'We're not going to call the police, Stuart – just please leave now.'

He turned away and the four of us exchanged relieved looks, but then, just as he was walking towards the front door, he patted himself down. 'Wait!' He suddenly stopped, stock still.

What now? I braced myself against an attack – *what's he looking for in his pockets? A knife, a gun?*

'I've lost my car keys,' he sighed. 'They must have fallen out of my pocket.'

Oh Jesus!

'Okay, kids,' said Bryce slowly. 'Let's all look for Stuart's car keys, shall we?'

It was almost comical the way the five of us spent the next ten minutes crawling around on our hands and knees for his keys, until eventually Charlotte found them halfway up the stairs.

Once Stuart finally left, I got Bryce cleaned up. While we were in the bathroom and out of earshot from the kids, he filled me in on what had happened.

While Bryce was in the kitchen making porridge, Stuart had smashed one of the glass panels next to the front door and let himself in. He'd stood there for a moment, hammer in his hand, assessing the situation, and then he'd walked deliberately towards Bryce, swinging the hammer, smashing photos and pictures as he went. He pushed over the breakfast table, sending dishes flying. And then Stuart threw himself on Bryce, punching him several times before biting down hard on his cheek. As he said the words, I realized I could see the indentation of Stuart's teeth marks on Bryce's torn and bleeding skin.

'Where is she?' he'd demanded. 'I'm taking her home. Dawn is mine. She was always mine and she always will be.'

He'd jumped off Bryce to look for me – and that's when

I'd come out onto the landing and found them both pounding up the stairs.

'We should call the police,' I said as I dabbed at Bryce's cheek with disinfectant. 'After we've taken the kids to school, we should call the police.'

'What about Callum? This is his father.'

'I don't care. We can't have this, not with your kids around.'

'Let's think about it,' said Bryce. 'I just don't know if it's for the best.'

But Bryce, as wonderful as he was, just didn't understand the way Stuart worked. I knew that unless we reported him now, he would keep coming back for more until something terrible happened. I decided to phone the authorities as soon as I got to the office.

I went with Bryce to the hospital first, and then drove on to work. All the way there, I kicked myself for believing that the list Stuart had offered me at the start of this split was going to magically free me from him. Of course he would never let me go so easily! I felt like a fool.

In the three months since I had told Hannah to accept his terms, Stuart had barely communicated with me. I had wondered what the hold-up was, given we were allegedly both in agreement to divorce – and now, this!

When I finally managed to get into the office that morning, however, I was horrified to see that Stuart was already there. He followed me into my private office so that Hannah couldn't overhear us. I could feel the threat in every sinew of his body.

'So, have you been to the police?' he said quietly.

'No.' *I've been too busy taking my partner to the hospital to get him stitched up*, I thought angrily, but I didn't let my feelings show; I sensed that would not be wise.

344

'That's sensible,' he said thoughtfully. He was totally calm now, the opposite of the madman who had broken into Bryce's home and attacked him earlier that morning. In a way, it was even more chilling.

'Because you wouldn't win,' he went on. 'I'm a sick man, don't you know?' He gave me a crafty smile. 'I've been on antidepressants since you left and I tried to kill myself so if I crack, I mean, if I suddenly go insane and, say, *kill you both*, well, you should have seen it coming because of what you did. I think a court will be able to see that it was temporary insanity because of what you did.

'Don't you?'

I just nodded but, inside, I had turned cold with dread. He was actually threatening to kill us both. And not in the heat of a temper tantrum – this was cool and calculating and with absolute knowledge of what he was doing. As he always was, he was in control.

Hands shaking, I spoke politely to him, a politeness crafted through so many years of learning how not to set him off. I told him that Bryce and I had discussed it and agreed not to go to the police for the sake of Callum.

'Very sensible,' he said again. He turned to leave but at the last minute swung to face me again, his eyes hard. 'Don't even *think* about changing your mind.'

Finally, he left.

That's when I called Bryce – and told him we had no choice now: we *had* to contact the authorities.

From that moment, everything changed. The police came to the house and took forensic samples for analysis, they interviewed all of us and Stuart was arrested and charged with breaking and entering and assault. He pleaded not guilty, of course, which meant the case would go to trial.

What happened next was a real eye-opener. For the first time since I'd left him, Stuart and I were now in open dispute and, to my horror, I found that people I had assumed were my friends or at the very least neutral lined up on his side. One was Mike Turner, our family lawyer – the attorney who had come to help me in the police station when I was only fifteen and Stuart was to be charged with having sex with me underage. Perhaps it shouldn't have been a surprise when he told me he was now going to act for Stuart in the criminal case, but in truth it was a real blow because I had thought we had become good friends over the years and I'd hoped he wouldn't take sides. But this was a criminal matter, Mike said, and that was his area. He couldn't turn Stuart away after all the years of history they shared, he said.

I'd committed the ultimate sin by grassing Stuart to the police and now Mike would use his talents to keep his client out of prison, which meant we were up against a formidable opponent.

Then, one night, my mother called. She had always disapproved of my leaving Stuart, believing that a marriage was for life – even if you happened to be married to a violent psychopath – and now she pleaded his case.

'Is it really necessary to take this to court?' she asked sweetly, as if I was the aggressor and he the innocent victim.

'He could plead guilty,' I said. 'And save us all a load of hassle.'

'I mean, the poor man hasn't been himself since you left and I should know, he's round here every single day . . .'

'Really?' I was shocked. *Why would Stuart be going to visit my mother every day?*

'Yes! The man is lonely. I mean, he's very helpful to me, bringing in the shopping, driving me round to my appointments and mending things round the flat. But I can see it's very distressing for him – all of this – and he knows he shouldn't have come to see you and confront Bryce in that way but, my dear, he was just trying to save his marriage!'

'Mum!' I exploded. I couldn't bear the way they had twisted the story until it no longer bore any relation to reality. 'He bit a fucking hole in Bryce's face. That's not trying to save a marriage. That's assault!'

'So you want him locked up? You want Callum's father in prison?'

'I want justice!' I seethed. 'Callum is his own man now, he's not a child. And I don't want him to think any man can get away with something like this . . .'

'I'm just asking you to think about it a bit more,' she went on smoothly. *He's obviously put her up to this*, I fumed. *Oh, now he's sunk really low, trying to get at me through my mother!*

I didn't want to talk about it anymore so I changed the subject. For a little while we caught up on family news and then, just as we were about to finish up, she added blithely: 'Oh, by the way, John's been through a rough patch recently and needs a bit of support so he's coming to stay with me for a while. Just so you know.'

The way she said it, it was all so smug, like it was a *fait accompli*. I couldn't stand it any longer. That man in *my property*?

'How long are you planning on having him, Mum?'

'Oh, I don't know, just until he can get on his feet again . . .'

What? An open-ended invitation? No way.

Quietly, I said: 'That's not happening, Mum.'

'Why should it bother you? After all, you don't even live in the city right now.'

'That man is a fucking paedophile and he made my life hell. If he's coming up to Glasgow, he can stay somewhere else. Not in my property.'

'Well, that's not acceptable to me,' Mum answered primly. 'If this is my flat then I should be able to have anyone round that I want.'

'You *can* have anyone you want to stay, anyone in the whole world, apart from *him*! Not *him*!'

There was a brief silence and then, in a low voice, she said: 'If you can't let me have my own children in my own home then perhaps I should leave.'

This was Mum's forte: a touch of emotional blackmail to make me feel guilty so I insisted she stayed. But not this time. I was tired of her games. She was always on everybody else's side but mine.

'That's a fucking great idea!' I exclaimed. 'I think you *should* go. I want you out within the month.'

Then, before she had a chance to reply, I put down the phone. I was livid with rage. Nobody could hurt me like that woman! Mum had lived rent-free for twelve years and now she wanted my paedophile brother to stay? Forget it. First Stuart; then John. Why did she insist on putting these men's needs before mine? I just didn't understand it. It didn't take long – within the month Mum had found a new apartment to rent and had moved out.

As it turned out, Mum's pleas on Stuart's behalf were all for nothing. In April 2009 my husband was found guilty of breaking and entering and common assault. His weasel words were no match for the forensic evidence and four honest testimonies.

But it was a hollow victory. To my astonishment, he brought a huge retinue to court, including Mike, his cousin Adam (they were clearly back on good terms), my mother and Aunt Jenny. Of all the people who lined up to support him and give evidence as character witnesses, it was my mother's betrayal that hurt the worst. *How can she support him against me?* I wondered. *Even if she didn't want to be on* my *side, she didn't have to take* his*!*

I saw her with my own eyes, walking into court with him, sitting on his benches, offering sympathetic smiles and the occasional shoulder squeeze. She didn't even look at me. That cut me very deeply.

In May, the court returned for sentencing. Stuart's defence team submitted a psychological report from their expert witness, who claimed that Stuart had suffered a depressive episode that had pushed him over the edge. Then, during the pleas of mitigation, his loyal troops marched through the witness box, parroting the same old sob story over and over again: how I had left him a broken man; how he'd been a pillar of the community, a property developer who had put a huge amount into the city, but was now unwell. They all said the attack was completely out of character. A normally peaceful man, he had never done anything like this before in his life, they all swore.

If only they knew what went on behind closed doors, I thought in disgust, thinking of the times he'd punched me and hurt me, all the violent threats he had made against me, day after day. But it was a successful ploy – he got off with community service.

During the court case, I found out that Stuart's cousin Adam was now advising him on the divorce case. This meant my ex had gone cap in hand back to the cousin who had callously betrayed him. And of course Adam, being the complete arsehole that he is, convinced Stuart that he was giving away too much to me, even though the proposed split was fair – and even gave Stuart more than I got.

The letters from his lawyers became increasingly aggressive and uncompromising. Now he was divorcing me on the grounds of adultery – and he wanted half of everything. So he wanted a list of all my matrimonial assets, including all the dresses, shoes and jewellery I'd ever bought. He wanted them valued. He wanted back the ring he had given me on my sixteenth birthday. He wanted half of everything we had bought as a couple and the value of any presents he had bought me over the years. (I actually laughed when I read that one. Being the stingy git that he was, he'd bought me nothing!)

The original split he had offered was no longer on the table. And it was worse than simply wanting half of everything. Now he said he wanted to keep all of Mayfair Holdings, claiming it was never in the matrimonial pot – despite the fact that it was in my name and it was the very company I'd been working so hard to build up over the past few years. He wanted 60 per cent of Silverbridge too. Plus he wanted to split our two houses and the art collection as well.

It was a proposal that would leave me with around 10 per cent of what we owned jointly as a couple; 10 per cent of what I had given blood, sweat and tears to build up over the years.

So this was now a real war – and I needed a damn good lawyer to fight my divorce case.

But that was easier said than done. My first lawyer, whom Bryce had kindly found for me, was very nice but charged me thousands of pounds just for getting to grips with the whole Panamanian affair. In the end, I got fed up of her exorbitant fees just for playing 'catch up' and moved onto another firm which specialized in complex financial cases.

For the next month, I kept my head down, just trying to keep the business afloat while Stuart's lawyer's letters attacked me from every angle. I was still going to work every day, while Stuart continued to sit on his arse at home, as he had always done. But he wasn't entirely lazy; another plan was afoot. I learned from Callum that my art collection at home was gradually disappearing from the house.

Thankfully, my son and I were now back on speaking terms again; about the only bright spot at that time. He could see how much happier I was without his father and though he didn't want to take sides in the divorce, he supported my bid for freedom. I appreciated just what a mature and wonderful young man he had become. Our relationship was now rock solid and over the following months he met Bryce a few times too. He confided in me that he liked Bryce and was sorry he had been so rude about him at first.

'It's okay,' I told him. 'I knew you were just angry. Look, hopefully all this will be over soon. But whatever happens, you're still my son and I love you, no matter what.'

I always tried to look on the bright side. After all, how much worse could things get?

I was about to find out.

Early one the morning I drove to the office after a training session at the gym. Hannah had just taken her annual leave, so I was now running the office on my own for the next two weeks – and that meant trying to stay on top of 130 properties. No small task! And now that I was holding the fort, I was at the front desk instead of my own office, which was always a nuisance. At least Stuart had stopped coming to the office after the court case, so I wasn't worried about seeing him anymore.

At 8.30 a.m., I unlocked the door, slung my copy of the *Scotsman* onto my desk, pulled open the shutters and opened the window. Next I plonked myself down in my seat and turned around to the wall behind me, to check the chart that listed all our properties.

But only a blank wall faced me. *The chart! Where's the chart?* It was gone. Confused, I thought it must have fallen off the wall and dropped behind the cabinet. *How annoying! I'm going to have to try and move all the furniture later to rescue it.* It was far too important to leave there, as it held all the details for the current tenants in our properties and kept track of when the rents were due.

My eyes now slid across the back wall. With alarm, I noticed that the filing cabinets were gone too. The cabinets that held all our important documents – contracts, invoices, tenancy agreements, sales slips, everything. They were gone. *What the hell is going on around here?*

With a creeping sense of horror, I now ran round the desk to look for the key safe. The key safe, which held every single key for all our properties in Mayfair Holdings, was kept underneath Hannah's side of the desk. I felt the breath rush out of me. *Gone!*

Oh no, oh no, oh no . . . What's happened? In desperation, I returned to my desk and switched on my computer. I saw the email straight away.

> *Dear Dawn,*
>
> *I'm so so sorry for what has happened. I didn't want to take sides but I had to put my own family first. I hope you can understand and forgive me. You have Bryce now, and I know he can look after you and that he will make you very happy. You deserve to be.*
>
> *Love, Hannah x*

I collapsed in tears. I couldn't believe it. She had betrayed me! The one person I considered closer than family, who I had relied upon and trusted with my life, had gone over to Stuart's side – and she had taken Mayfair Holdings with her. She had to put her own family first, she wrote, which meant she thought Stuart could keep her in a job. Why? Why didn't she have faith in me? I'd never let her down before; I was always the money-maker. I couldn't believe that she too had bought into the idea of Stuart as the puppet-master, the one who held all the power. I called Bryce in such a state, he couldn't even hear me through the sobbing.

'Just calm down,' he said sternly. 'I'm on my way.'

It didn't take him long and when he arrived he found me curled up on the floor.

'They've taken everything,' I said as he walked in.

'What? They can't do that!' he said.

'Look at her computer! Go on – look at it!' I had discovered the template of the letter Hannah had written to all the tenants, which was still up on her desktop. It instructed them to send all future rents to a new office address for Mayfair Holdings.

'But you still have Silverbridge . . .' Bryce started.

'Silverbridge is tiny. Peanuts!' I said. 'It doesn't bring in any money. Over the years we did all the deals through Mayfair because it had the biggest assets. Silverbridge only holds a handful of properties and we don't collect rents on them.'

I read Hannah's email again in a state of bewilderment. *Why has she done this?* I knew she had been very distressed by the fallout from the divorce, but I never dreamed for a minute that she would betray me.

'I thought we were friends . . .' The tears now started again. 'We were like sisters . . .'

'Come on.' Bryce picked me up off the floor. 'I'm taking you home.'

'He must have told her a pack of lies,' I went on, letting Bryce take me by the elbow. 'He must have promised her a better job, better money. I don't know! Oh, how could she do this to me?'

For the rest of the day, I was a mess, unable to believe the scale of Hannah's betrayal. She must have been working with Stuart for the past month at least to plan something like this. *Why? What have I done to her that was so bad? Did she hate me? If she didn't hate me, why not just walk away? Why take everything from me? What made her go over to his side?* The questions went round and round in my head, over and over again.

I went through all the things I could have done differently. *I should have been more supportive of her when I left Stuart,* I thought, *I should have been more grateful.* But would it have made any difference?

Now I questioned everything we had said and done in the past few years – and even further back. My mind went over conversations we'd had decades before. *How long has she been working with him?* I wondered. *How long has she been on his side?* My whole world was shaken; I didn't believe in anything anymore.

And I now found myself in an impossible financial situation. The mortgages for the Portuguese villa and the office were all in my name, meaning I personally owed £4,000 a month. And yet, because Stuart was now collecting all the rents, I had no income. So I was snookered. If I didn't think of something quickly, I was going to go bankrupt within a few months.

This wasn't a war anymore; it was an assassination. Stuart and his team wanted to kill me financially – and I knew that Adam Kelly was the man with the gun. After all, I had exposed his scheme years before and driven a wedge between the cousins. Now it was payback time – and he wanted me out of the picture altogether.

I couldn't even afford my divorce lawyers anymore, so Bryce stepped in to help me out with cash flow, but he was struggling too with a divorce of his own. How much longer before we both went under?

I couldn't think straight; that was the cousins' plan, of course. I was exactly where they wanted me to be. I had seen the way this family had behaved in the past to former business associates and ex-wives. First they took the things they believed would hurt you most, immobilizing you, and then, when you were at your weakest, they forced you to take whatever pathetic deal they had on the table. I had seen it too many times before not to recognize the pattern.

But what good did the knowledge do me? I was helpless. Stuart held all the cards: my family, my friends and now my business too.

In those first few days, I simply crumbled, engulfed by the enormity of my problems. The betrayals had been overwhelming and I had never felt more alone in my life. The banks were closing in, the money was gone . . . Only one thought remained.

What the hell am I going to do now?

Chapter 26

A Change of Luck

'What? Not another writ?' I ripped open the envelope which the courier had just handed to me. Immediately, I recognized the heavy ivory stationery from Stuart's lawyer's office and my heart started to race. It was the third in the last fortnight. I couldn't cope anymore; I couldn't *afford* it anymore. Already my lawyer's bill was up to £5,000 this week alone. I had to pay it by Friday or they would stop acting for me.

My eyes scanned the letter. This time it was a demand for £3,524, half of the amount due on Stuart's credit card bill. Stuart was fighting me on everything, and since all our debt had to be split too, this was another painful way to bleed me dry of all my resources.

'Oh, for fuck's sake!' I erupted as I slung the letter onto the desk. My whole head throbbed and, instinctively, I reached into my handbag for my packet of co-codamol. Quickly, I popped four out of the silver foil and knocked them back in one go, followed by a large glug of cold black coffee. My heart was racing and I was breathing heavily but I knew it would only take twenty minutes for the drugs to kick in.

Just calm down, I told myself as I paced up and down the

office, fighting for every breath. It felt like someone had tied a rope around my chest and was pulling hard, squeezing all the air out of me. I just couldn't get enough air into my body and if I didn't breathe hard, I felt like I would suffocate. It was panic, pure panic, but I knew the drugs would help. *Come on . . . come on . . .*

This had started the month before. After a particularly gruesome day, I had discovered that the strong painkillers helped me to weather the worst of my emotional storms. At first I had just taken two at a time – but it wasn't long before I needed more.

Now, I flopped down in my chair and tried to think calming thoughts. In a little over fifteen minutes the familiar warm, soothing feeling came over me, bringing my heart rate down and allowing me to breathe normally again. Something clicked in my brain and now I experienced a lovely floating feeling; the painkillers were working their magic on me. I knew it was wrong, taking drugs to fight my panic attacks, but right now, it was the only thing that worked. And now that I had returned to Planet Earth, I picked up the letter and reread it. *Time to phone the lawyer*, I thought grimly.

I ploughed through the rest of the morning, mostly on the phone to the bank, trying to explain why the mortgages had not been paid that month. It made no difference to them, of course, that I had lost control of the company and Stuart was refusing to pay. My name was on the mortgage deeds so I was responsible.

At 1 p.m. an email pinged into my inbox from Melvin, my accountant: 'I have good news. Can I come and see you later?'

I replied straight away: 'Of course! Good news is always welcome. Swing by any time.'

An hour later the intercom buzzed and when Melvin walked in, he was grinning like the Cheshire Cat. Instinctively, I smiled back. It was so lovely to see him in his smart, three-piece tweed suit, looking like he had just come from a shooting party in the country. Not that he was from the upper classes. No, Melvin was an ordinary boy from the projects with a sharp brain and an even sharper eye. He just liked to look posh so that people never underestimated him and he certainly carried it off, with his charm and easy manner. Nothing was too much trouble for Melvin and he had even managed to take the divorce in his stride. He'd told both Stuart and me early on that he wouldn't take sides.

'Dawn,' he announced as he walked in. 'I've got something for you and I think it's going to change your life.'

Now *that* sounded very good.

'I don't like what Stuart's done to you,' he started. 'I really don't. It's just not fair, trying to steal from you in this way. But I think I have the solution.' And, with a flourish, he pulled out a piece of paper from his briefcase and held it above his head.

'This! This piece of paper is going to solve your problems.'

'I'm all ears,' I replied. *God knows I need something – anything!*

Now Melvin sat down opposite me and put the paper down on the desk. He leaned forward conspiratorially and said: 'Dawn, do you remember when Stuart and Adam fell out and I advised you to set up a new company to hold Mayfair Holdings' assets?'

'Erm. Sort of . . .' I wracked my brains.

'Hexagon Properties it was called, do you remember?'

'Oh yes, Hexagon!'

359

'Do you recall that we held a board meeting and the transfer documents were signed by yourself and Stuart in front of an independent solicitor? They transferred all the shares from Mayfair to Hexagon, but you didn't want to pursue it for whatever reason, and the company was struck off.'

'Okay . . .'

'I have the original share transfer document signed and stamped by the Treasury which proves that that transfer happened. And, funnily enough, you are the sole director and shareholder of Hexagon. So now we can apply to have the company reinstated. If we do that, you, Hexagon, will own Mayfair and you will be able to put yourself on the board and sack Stuart and Adam as the current directors.'

I felt the smile spreading across my face: 'Really?'

'You'll be in complete control of the company again.'

It almost sounded too good to be true. Could I really hope to get the company back so easily?

'Oh Melvin, you are a genius! When can it be done?'

Melvin said he would get started straight away but it could take up to two weeks for the whole process to be completed. In the meantime, I was to tell no one our plan so that the other side couldn't scupper it. I couldn't wait but, at the same time, I hardly dared hope that it would work. After all, so much had gone wrong recently and I was terrified that this was just another useless roll of the dice.

So I was stunned when, exactly two weeks later, Melvin called me up to say it was complete.

'That's it, Dawn. You own Hexagon, which owns Mayfair. The company is yours. The rest is up to you.'

Melvin gave me the codes for my login to the Companies House website and, half an hour later, I was staring at a screen which had the names of the directors of Mayfair Holdings. Now I appointed myself as director and I lined up my husband and his cousin for 'removal'. It gave me great pleasure to punch the return button over each name, the sound of the key firing like a bullet from a gun. First my husband – *bang!* – gone. Then the cousin – *bang!* – gone. Smiling, I printed off confirmations of their removal and read each, line by line, just to make sure they were fired. Mission accomplished.

The next day I sent the documents to the bank which held the company accounts; they checked and confirmed they were all legal and correct and they contacted Stuart and Adam themselves. *Yes!* All the assets from Mayfair were now transferred over to me, giving me instant cash to pay the mortgages. I also now had the funds to fight my divorce case.

But it wasn't all good news. Once I had hold of the company accounts, I discovered the cousins had already sold six properties in the company and pocketed the money. They had turfed out the tenants of several more flats, presumably ready to sell them quick and cheap. Worse, they had failed to keep up payments on the company loan, plunging Mayfair into special lending.

I knew what they were up to – they were trying to liquidate the company before the divorce so they could take the money and run. *Typical!* Stuart was going to sell everything for cash. It was the same old story; they would rape the business, claim it was worthless and piss off with the cash. The thing was, I knew my husband well and I had anticipated this course of action; so, through my very expensive lawyers, I had supposedly put a cap on the properties which *prevented* them from being sold without a court order. It was called an interdict – a fancy name for a stop order – and it was bulletproof, or so they had told me. Yet now I could clearly see six bullet holes in my company.

How the hell did we lose six properties with my very expensive interdict in place? I was straight on the phone to my lawyer – and I could not believe what she had to say. Sheepishly, she admitted that the conveyancing for the sales had actually been done by their own firm, on the floor upstairs! Of course I sacked her on the spot.

Now I needed a new lawyer, my third in this bloody battle for my freedom. It wasn't easy. I had already been to the top firms in my area and nobody wanted to deal with my divorce. It was too tricky, too dirty. Finally, I was given the name of a solicitor, a lone wolf by the name of Tim Haddon.

Well, if Tim was a wolf, he certainly didn't look the part. He was a thin, frail man with thick-rimmed glasses and a brown cardigan with suede elbow patches. Surrounded by books and papers, he was less like a wolf and more like an owlish academic and I wondered if he was made of the right stuff for this fight. So when we had our first meeting, I didn't sugar coat it. I told him about the kind of people we were up against. I explained that this was a family with a lot of money stashed away in suitcases, people who always played dirty and would go to any lengths to try and destroy me. I told Tim about all the nasty and vindictive things I had witnessed over the years, about Stuart's conviction for attacking Bryce, about the way they had tried to take my companies away from me twice already – and I warned him that this was just the start.

'So I'll understand,' I concluded, 'if you don't want to act for me.'

To my surprise, an impish little smile broke out across his face.

'Of course I'll act for you!' He even grinned. 'It sounds like fun. I'm looking forward to the challenge!'

I don't know why but, immediately, I knew this man would be as good as his word. He explained that he had worked for many of the big companies in his time but always preferred to be his own boss. Straight away, he instructed a QC as he said we were going to need counsel to work with. Within two weeks we had our QC, a fearless firebrand from Newcastle called Deirdre, who was highly respected in the courts. Now I had both money and might in my corner, but the battle was only just beginning.

My first job was to secure Mayfair. Adam and Stuart's raping of the company – selling our properties but pocketing the cash, rather than reinvesting – had left a huge hole in the company accounts, but that wasn't the only problem. Right now, the rents didn't cover the company loans; an all-too-familiar story thanks to the recession. Everywhere I looked I saw previously rock-solid businesses going to the wall. The banks weren't lending anymore so if you needed money, you had to find it yourself or fold. I only had a short timeframe to get my finances in order or Mayfair and I would also go the same way.

So, first, I rented out the house in Portugal to cover the mortgage. Then I got a court order to get Stuart removed from our Glasgow house. He wasn't paying rent, so he had no right to be there. This would be another uphill battle but, after seven months, he was finally evicted and I managed to rent that out too. But still the rents from the properties weren't enough to cover the bank loan to the company and I needed cash. Fast.

'I can put you in touch with some men,' Melvin said when I told him I needed £50,000 to cover my outgoings. 'But these are serious criminals, Dawn. You don't mess them around. If you don't pay them back, they will come after you.'

'Okay,' I said. Desperation made me fearless. I wasn't thinking in terms of months anymore, I just had to survive from one week to the next. Besides, I had a meeting set up with the bank in a few days' time and I was hoping that that would help ease the pressure. In the meantime, I had bills to pay and absolutely no means of paying them. So now I borrowed £50k cash from a criminal gang.

The transaction took place at an empty industrial estate where I met a middle-aged man in a leather jacket who handed me a Tesco's carrier bag. He gave me one month exactly to return the money.

'Are you crazy?' Bryce was shocked when I told him about my dodgy deal that night at home and showed him the bag full of rolled-up £50 notes. 'You could get yourself killed!'

'I won't let him win, Bryce,' I snapped back. 'I won't let that bastard drag me under. I know this is a risky strategy but, trust me, I'm going to make it work.'

'So what happens if you can't pay him back in a month?' Bryce looked worried.

'I'll pay him back.'

'But what if you can't?'

'Please, Bryce, just have a little faith in me. I've got a plan. You've just got to trust me.'

The following Monday, I walked into the bank for a pre-arranged meeting about the company loan. They had asked who would be present and I'd lied, saying it would just be me. So the receptionist was surprised when I turned up with Melvin, Tim and my QC, Deirdre, in tow. Already, I had them on the back foot and that's just where I needed them for this crucial fight.

Like many small businesses, we had been sold something called a structured collar loan in the heyday of bank lending, before the recession hit in 2008. They were recommended to us as the best products on the market and, admittedly, they sounded like a pretty good deal at the time. If interest rates went up from, say, 2 per cent to 7 per cent, we still only paid interest on 2 per cent. So the loan repayments were capped for a certain length of time, or given a 'collar' to prevent them going up, hence the name 'collar' loans. However, if interest rates went down, we would have to pay a 10 per cent premium on the loan.

'But when would that happen?' the bank had argued. 'Never!'

Many of us in business at that time had been convinced that interest rates would never drop. Then the world economy went belly up and the Bank of England cut interest rates to 0.5 per cent. All of a sudden, loads of businesses were made bankrupt by loans that had used to cost £2,000 a month but now cost them £12,000 a month. It had happened to us, too, except now the Financial Services Authority had stepped in and said it was reviewing the mis-selling of these products and, in the meantime, our payments were returned to what they had been before, which was a huge relief.

But it wasn't enough to put me back on top. Yet Melvin and I had worked out that Mayfair Holdings was owed £500k from the mis-selling. If I could claw back some of what we were owed, I might just be able to rescue the company. That's what I was hoping to achieve from today's meeting. It was make-or-break time.

I was nervous and I could hear the sound of my own heart thudding in my ears so now, as we waited for our meeting, I slipped my hand into my bag and popped open two pills. I was on about twelve pills a day, including tramadol, which had the same effect as the co-codamol. Nobody knew, not even Bryce.

A minute later, Sadie Peach, the business development manager, appeared, flanked by two assistants, each carrying a boxful of files. We exchanged polite hellos and handshakes, then took our seats opposite each other at a large conference table, like two rugby teams squaring up for a match.

My QC didn't waste any time: 'Ms Peach, we've calculated that in the mis-selling of the structured collar loan you currently owe my client £500,000. My client wants her money back and she wants it quickly. She has a business to run and she cannot afford to wait for the result of the FSA investigation. And because we don't trust your bank we decided to look at another loan you made to Silverbridge dating back to 2001. Did you know that it says the interest on the loan is 4.6 per cent but you've been charging her 5.3 per cent for the last eleven years, so you owe her £18,000, which we want by close of business today. Plus interest, of course.'

There was a momentary silence and then Sadie whispered something inaudible to her assistants on either side. Each nodded in turn, then she looked up at us all and smiled condescendingly.

'I'm afraid we can't do that,' she started. 'Until the results of the nationwide . . .'

'Yes, you can!' Deirdre barked at her. 'You can because my client has large legal and tax bills to settle and if she goes bust because you owe her half a million, we will sue the bank for the amount the company was worth at the time of liquidation as well as compensation.'

Sadie, who I had known for many years, turned a strange shade of mottled grey.

'Just give me a minute,' she said quietly as she got up. Then she hurried out of the room. Her two advisors quickly followed after her and at that moment I wondered what would happen next. Everything hung on this meeting. If I didn't get the money, Mayfair and I were going to go under.

It took another fifteen minutes before Sadie reappeared.

'Okay, I think we can go a long way to accommodating your requests,' she said. 'Of the structured collar loan, we can repay up to £100,000 by close of business today, but the rest will have to wait until after the full compensatory investigation. We've also looked into that Silverbridge loan. We've calculated the compensation is worth £25,000, including the interest. Again, we can get that to you by the end of the day. Would that be enough to stabilize your client's business?'

Deirdre looked at me. 'Is £125,000 enough for now?'

I took a long time to think about it. Then I looked at Sadie sternly and said: 'Only just. I suppose it will have to do until the rest of the compensation is settled.'

'Yes, my client thinks that is acceptable for now.' Deirdre was equally severe but I could tell that everyone was palpably relieved to have come to an agreement. I left the accountants and lawyers to settle up the details while I went outside to make a call.

Once I had rounded the corner, I let out a tiny squeal of delight.

'We've done it!' I breathed down the phone to Bryce. 'We've got enough money to keep the company afloat.'

367

'And pay back the £50,000?' Bryce asked.

'Yup, and pay them back too! Deirdre was amazing. We've got £125,000 going into the company account by the close of business today!'

'Congratulations! Dawn, I'm so proud of you.'

'Thanks Bryce. I'm proud of me too!'

And I really was. For the first time in ages, I felt strong. Now I had enough money to pay off my dodgy debt as well as refurbish the empty properties on my books in order to let them out. That would bring in some extra income to keep the company ticking over.

I had won another battle; a crucial battle. Wresting back control of Mayfair and securing the company were both vitally important in giving me the means to keep fighting Stuart as he tried to steal everything I'd built from under my nose. And with each victory, I became a little stronger.

That night, I threw away my whole stash of co-codamol and tramadol. I wasn't going to let this bloody divorce destroy me from the inside. I *knew* I could do this without the drugs. The fact was, I had been to the very bottom and now, with a little bit of fair play and good luck, the tide was turning.

I was getting stronger and stronger every day. Stuart had done his very best to destroy me – but I was still standing.

And, now, I wanted revenge. Now, I wanted to make him pay.

Chapter 27

Going Nuclear

'How can she say that?' I whispered, tears trickling down my cheeks. I swiped them away with the heel of my hand. I couldn't believe what I was reading – every single word was like a stab to my heart.

I had just received the latest case documents from my solicitor, signed affidavits that Stuart's side had logged with the court. Though it had now been two and a half years since I'd asked my husband for a divorce, I felt no closer to gaining my independence than when I'd got on that plane to Cyprus. So far, this long and bitter affair had seen us back and forth to court every few weeks for various hearings. I could cope with Stuart and his lies, but this was a different sort of attack from my own family and it made my blood run cold. Now I read through the formal statements of my mother and her sister Jenny in stunned silence.

They said, in sworn affidavits, that I had seduced Stuart as a sexually promiscuous teen and then duped him into marriage by falling pregnant. Stuart hadn't stood a chance, apparently. The poor man didn't know what he was dealing with. According to them, I was a fifteen-year-old femme fatale who had set out to destroy Stuart's marriage, ruin his relationship with his son and drive a wedge between him and his cousin. Stuart had been a successful businessman and I was just a silly teenager. In conclusion, both statements said I had brought nothing to the marriage and my settlement should reflect this. These were legal documents, documents that would be used against me in my divorce.

By the time I had finished reading, my jaw was nearly on the floor. I could hardly begin to process the scale of this betrayal. This was going further than I had ever imagined in my very worst nightmares.

And there was even worse to come. For in my mother's statement, drawing on shameful secrets that I had confessed to her in complete confidence, she claimed I had been sexually active since the age of twelve and that I had therefore set out to seduce this man and destroy his marriage.

I flung the statements at Bryce, too disgusted to read any more.

'Sexually active at twelve?' I exploded, pain making my voice ragged. 'Lying bitch! I was raped by my own brother at twelve years old. I see she conveniently forgot to mention that it was him. And it was fucking rape! It wasn't consensual!'

'Calm down!' Bryce was now used to watching me fly off the handle. But I had every right to be angry. My mother and her sister were using the abuse I'd suffered as a child as a weapon against me in my own divorce. It was reprehensible.

'That's it,' I spat out fiercely. 'I've had enough of watching my reputation being dragged through the mud for something that was not my fault. That poor excuse of a mother failed to protect me as a child, then she persuaded me not to go to the police as an adult, and now she is actively using that abuse to hurt me again. I've got to do something. I've got to set the record straight.'

'Think about this,' Bryce said solemnly. He knew what I was planning. We had discussed this many times before; it was what we jokingly referred to as the 'nuclear option' because, once it was done, it could not be undone. Was it finally time to go nuclear?

'It's all I've got left.' My mind was made up. 'I don't need to protect him anymore, I don't need to protect anyone but myself. And this is the only way . . .'

Despite my strong words, that night I lay awake for hours, mulling over my situation, asking myself if this was a battle I was prepared to lose; if it was one I had the strength to fight to the very end.

But this isn't about fighting anymore, I realized with a jolt. *This is about telling stories. A court case is about so much more than facts and fighting.*

For the past two years, I had been constantly on the defensive because the stories the other side had told about me made such a compelling narrative. Stuart was the victim, the spurned older husband, while I was the young, adulterous temptress and a gold digger to boot. The backstory that Mum told about me being a 'sexually active' pre-teen fitted perfectly with all of that. No, I would always be fighting a rearguard action if I let *them* tell *my* story.

When it came to judging this divorce and deciding who was telling the truth, it wasn't just about who had the best evidence, it was also about who made the most sense. And at this moment, even I could see that, on paper, with the way their side had twisted the facts to suit their narrative, Stuart and my mother's story made the most sense.

I only had one way to change the story now – and that was to tell the truth. I had to go on the offensive.

It would mean being honest – the most honest I had ever been in my whole life. It would mean dropping all the safety mechanisms I had built up over the years to try to keep myself safe; the safety mechanisms I had used, over and over, to stop myself from thinking too hard about what I had been through. For the first time, I would be shining a light into the darkest places in my memory, and I knew that light could well hurt me as well as the monsters who lurked there.

But I had nothing to be frightened of now. I had to do it. I *wanted* to do it. I had stayed silent far too long.

So, at 8.30 a.m. the following morning, I walked into my local police station. My palms were sweating, my hands shook . . . but I was more determined than I had ever been in my life.

The young man with the goatee on the front desk signalled for me to wait a moment while he took a call about a missing mobile phone. It was a banal, run-of-the-mill exchange and I waited patiently, allowing myself to bask in the surrealness of the moment. I was on the very brink of exposing the darkest secret of my life and this guy was trying to describe the cover of a Samsung Galaxy! Finally, when he had finished, he asked how he could help.

'I would like to make a report about sexual abuse,' I said levelly.

'Right, is that someone you know, something you witnessed or is it about yourself?'

'Sexual abuse against myself.'

'And when did this happen?'

'In 1974 and 1984.'

And, with that, he rolled his eyes. He actually rolled his eyes! I couldn't believe it, but I didn't say a word. Instead I just stood there, holding myself perfectly upright and unblinking, as he said: 'Okay, if you hang on a minute, I'll get someone to come and talk to you.'

Then he closed down the little shutter in front of his window and made a call. A few minutes later, a policewoman opened the door from the main station into the waiting area and, smiling, said: 'Hello, please do come through.'

She led me through to a small interview room and offered me a cup of tea. Then, when she had got herself settled down with a cuppa and a large A4 pad, she asked me to tell her about the abuse.

'You say it started in 1974,' she prompted. 'Can you tell me about that?'

'Yes, it was my brother,' I said, frankly. It was odd: now the moment had come, it wasn't hard to tell the truth. I found I could do so in an almost matter-of-fact way. Perhaps my mind was still protecting me, preventing me from engaging with the facts emotionally, but whatever the reason, I was calm, considered and concise in my statements. They *had* to take me seriously, so I was solemn and straight in how I spoke. 'He started abusing me when he was fifteen and I was five and it went on for about two years. Then it happened one last time when I was twelve.

'The 1984 abuse, that wasn't my brother.' I paused for a moment, on the brink of something huge. My resolve never wavered for a second. I was now a woman who understood the wrongdoings of older men who chased and abused young girls. I had been a pawn in Stuart's sick games and I understood now that what he did to me all those years ago was criminal. I thought about that time in the car in London in front of Wolfie, Pete and the Vauxhall van man. I thought about the cowed, scared and weak young girl who had suffered such an appalling humiliation and knew I had to finally speak for her. After all these years of silence, I had to stand up for her.

'I was abused by a man called Stuart Kelly at fifteen. And the fact is, I got trapped by pregnancy and we ended up in a long-term relationship, but there's no avoiding the fact he was with me when I was fifteen – so now I want to report him.'

'I see . . .' The woman made a few notes in her pad, then said: 'Well, let's take this one step at a time, shall we? When was the first occasion your brother sexually abused you?'

It took six hours to tell her everything about John and Stuart, during which time she asked me very explicit questions about what they had done to me. I had never spoken in such detail to anyone before and I can't deny that it was harder than I had imagined. For years I had tried to keep it all locked up, shut away so it couldn't hurt me anymore, but now it all had to come out. She asked me what sexual positions we had done, where my brother had ejaculated, where we had been at the time, how long it had lasted and even how I could remember the details.

This was harder than I imagined it would be. All those awful details that I had locked away for so long were now wrenched out of me, and I squirmed uncomfortably at the words that came out of my mouth, shocking myself at the thought of those squalid encounters. How could I have believed that he loved me? I felt so stupid and ashamed telling a stranger all of this, but I tried to keep hold of my emotions, sipping occasionally from a plastic cup of water when I felt my voice beginning to crack. Still, despite my embarrassment and shame, I was determined to tell my story, determined to tell the truth as I should have done years before.

The policewoman, Joan, was a plump, grey-haired woman in her mid-fifties and had a motherly, matronly air about her. She spoke softly and kindly offered me several cups of tea throughout the interview. Nevertheless, there was something odd in her manner, as if she didn't quite believe me. The questions she asked, it was like she thought I was making it all up.

'Who else knew about your brother's abuse?' Joan asked.

'My mother, aunt and my sister,' I told her and gave her their full names.

'And what about the abuse by Stuart?'

'Everyone! His ex-wife, the police, the school, my family . . . There must be records from the time. I was arrested and taken in handcuffs to the police station for having underage sex. Of course I didn't confirm it at the time but then, what did I know? He *told* me to keep quiet; he told me he'd go to prison if I said anything and I thought I loved him, I wanted to protect him. God, I was only fifteen! I thought I knew it all, but I didn't know a bloody thing.'

'He knew about the abuse by your brother?'

'Of course,' I said, through gritted teeth. 'I trusted him, I told him my most shameful secret and he said that what my brother had done was awful, really terrible, but that sex itself wasn't a bad thing and if it was with someone you loved then it was a very beautiful thing. And that's how he made me believe that it would be different with him, that because he loved me, it was all okay.'

'In other words, he groomed you,' Joan added.

'What do you mean?'

'It's the classic technique of an abuser: grooming. It's when someone builds an emotional connection with a minor to gain their trust for their own sexual gain, like your husband Stuart. A sexual predator engages his victim, gains the minor's trust, breaks down their defences, and manipulates them into performing or permitting the desired sex act. That's what Stuart did with you, he groomed you. He told you he was your friend, your only friend, and he made you think you could trust him. Knowing you had been sexually abused from a young age made you an easy target for him to start grooming for his own sexual gratification. First, because it meant you knew what sex was. Second, because he knew you could keep a secret.'

I sat back and let this information sink in. I was groomed; it was a momentous insight to me. Until this time, I had thought all my choices had been my own, that the decisions I had made as a teenager were based on my own thoughts, desires and interests. It had never occurred to me that because of the abuse I had suffered as a young child, Stuart was able to manipulate me for his own ends. Now it was all falling into place and, for the first time, I felt able to connect the jagged pieces of my life.

'So you're saying that if it hadn't been for John, I might never have fallen for Stuart?'

'Hmm ... it's possible, I suppose, but unlikely. Can I ask you something, Miss McConnell, have you ever had counselling?'

'No, not yet at least,' I said. 'I'm too angry for that. Right now I want to see justice done and I don't think any amount of counselling is going to cure me of all this anger inside.'

'Why now, though?' she probed gently. 'I mean, what prompted you to come here today?'

What to tell her? That I wanted revenge on them both? That I was sick of being portrayed as a teenage temptress? That I wanted my husband to stop trying to screw me in the divorce? It was all true – all of it – and now there was a new reason.

'Closure,' I said finally. 'I want closure.'

'Alright,' said Joan. She closed her notebook firmly; she had filled two of them with her notes on my interview. 'We'll start looking into it and I'll be in touch as soon as I have some news.'

Staggering out into the sunshine that day, I felt utterly drained and exhausted – all my words used up, all my energy gone. I had dragged up the most excruciating encounters from my past to a complete stranger and God, it was hard. And yet . . . and yet . . . here I was! Still alive. Still standing. The world hadn't collapsed. Somewhere inside I felt a shining sense of euphoria. I had begun to shape my own destiny, to take control of my future. I knew I was on the road to healing. No more shame, no more hiding. I had started to let it go.

It was two whole weeks before Joan called, asking if she could come to the house to update me on her enquiries. When she walked in the door, I tried to read her face for clues but she had obviously perfected her 'poker face' over many years in the job. However, once I showed her through to the lounge, she quickly got down to business.

'I want to deal with the claims against your husband Stuart Kelly first. Look, Miss McConnell, we've tried to find reports from 1986 and I'm afraid there aren't any. No records. None at all. I'm really sorry. Nothing in the police files or from the school. And I'm sorry to say but because you married him, it doesn't add any strength to your case.'

'What's that supposed to mean?' I responded angrily. 'That it didn't happen? That I'm just making it all up? Or do you think that I was just a teenage slut too and that I deserved everything I got?'

'Certainly not. Look, Miss McConnell, *I believe you*. I really do. I believe every word but we are going to find it very difficult to prove.'

'What did Stuart say?'

'We haven't spoken to him.'

'Why not?'

'Right now, we haven't got enough corroborating evidence to bring him in for questioning. He'll just deny it and then we'll have nothing. So what I'd like to do instead is to speak to you about the allegations against your brother. These are more serious because he was your brother and because of the age that the abuse began.'

'Okay . . .'

'So we interviewed your mother about the disclosure you made to her as a child and again when you were twenty-two. And . . .' Here, unusually, Joan paused to take a deep breath. She met my eye apologetically as she continued. 'She denied it all.'

I couldn't believe my ears. 'You're kidding!'

'No, I'm not. We told her what you'd said and she replied: "Is *that* what Dawn said?" And then she shook her head with this sort of pitying expression on her face and said it was all lies. She said that you were . . .' Joan suddenly whipped out a small notepad from her breast pocket and started flicking

through it until she came to the page she was after. 'Ah yes
. . . here it is! She said, and I quote, that you were "a very
damaged individual", a "pathological liar" and that you had
been "very vindictive all your life". She told us not to believe
a word you say.'

I was reeling. I could just picture it – I could just picture
my mother sitting there, calm and charming, shaking her
head sadly, eyebrows arching in disbelief. I wanted to kill her
right then. Judas! How could she deny the truth like this? The
shock was crushing, a physical pain deep in my chest. My
mouth went dry, and I felt my body start to shake. Questions
swirled around and around in my head. *Why? How? The police
. . . did they think I was a liar?* I couldn't speak. I was too
scared to speak, as I knew I would cry. I had to remain strong
and took deep breaths through my nose, telling myself to pull
myself together. The scale of her betrayal was truly breathtak-
ing. But I wouldn't let it break me. Maybe that would come
later. For now, my anger and the truth rose up around me to
protect me.

'But you're not giving up just like that, are you?' I implored.
'You're going to speak to John, aren't you? And what about
my sister Susy? She knows all about it too.'

'John is out of the country but we have issued a warrant for
his arrest so the moment he returns he'll be brought here for
questioning. In the meantime, your mother said she didn't
have any contact details for Susy. She says she hasn't spoken
to her in years.'

'What rubbish!' I actually laughed. The audacity of my
mother was something else. 'They're in touch every week. My
mother is the liar, officer. I'll just go and get Susy's number
for you so you can speak to her. I've not been in touch with

her for a couple of years – there's been a lot going on here – but I still have her address and home number in London.'

As I handed her Susy's details, I started to think of other possible ways we could shore up the charges against Stuart. I wasn't giving up that easily, not now that Joan had helped me to see how cruelly he had manipulated me – how I had been groomed as an underage and vulnerable girl.

'What about his ex-wife? Stuart's ex?' I said, keenly. 'I mean, she was the one who found out first. She hired a private detective and tracked us down. Maybe you could contact him . . . ?'

'Miss McConnell, please!' Joan spoke firmly. 'I know you're angry and upset but there are only so many police resources we can put into this. I will get in touch with your sister, but even if she supports everything you say about your brother, we still can't do anything until he returns to the country.

'As for the allegations about Mr Kelly, well, I can't see this going to court.'

At least she was truthful.

When she left, I felt vaguely depressed. It sounded like the case against Stuart was hopeless. After twenty years of marriage to the man, the police weren't interested in pursuing him for abusing me when I was fifteen. He was going to get away with that particular crime.

But I still had hope that, with John, there seemed to be a real chance of finally achieving justice. And, in a way, that would have to serve for both of my abusers. After all, as Joan had said all along, Stuart might never have successfully groomed me if it hadn't been for John. A few months later, in December 2010 John flew back into London, only to be arrested at the airport and driven straight up to Glasgow for questioning.

And who was waiting for him when he got here? Why, my mother and Mike Turner of course! Life had truly come full circle now: the man who had kept Stuart out of prison all those years ago for abusing me was working the exact same trick for my brother.

He briefed John well. Say nothing, nothing at all. And so, during the six hours of police interview, my brother replied 'no comment' to every single question.

Joan told me the bad news over the phone: 'We can't hold him,' she said apologetically. 'It's your word against his and your own mother says you're making it up. I've been trying to track down your sister but she's no longer at that address you gave me.'

'Oh Christ! No! No, no no!' I was desperate and furious at the same time. But, most of all, I felt helpless, so bloody helpless.

I felt like I was five years old again.

'I'm sorry, Dawn, we had to let him go.'

As soon as I slammed down the phone, I burst into tears. *How has he got away with it AGAIN?* But I didn't want to give up. Not now – I had come so far and I was determined that the truth would win out. So, as my brother once again fled the country, I hired my own private detective and I finally managed to track my sister down in Margate, Kent.

'I had no idea you'd left London,' I said, when I rang her in distress.

'I sent a "We're moving" card to your old address . . . but I suppose you didn't get it?' Susy hadn't realized I wasn't at my old marital home anymore, as we hadn't kept in touch while I'd been fighting fires on all sides through my divorce.

'No, sorry. I've been through the mill a bit recently.'

So I filled her in on my divorce and all the difficulties I'd faced with Stuart. Then I told her about how I had finally screwed up the courage to report our brother to the police – only for our mother to perjure herself and deny it ever happened.

'How could she deny it?' Susy was breathless with shock. 'I just don't understand. She *knows* he did it. She *knows* it!'

'Don't ask me, Susy. That woman hates me for some reason and of course her poisonous sister is backing up every word she says. So now you're my only hope. Will you give a statement to the police?'

'Of course! Look, I've got to stay here this weekend for the kids but I can fly up early next week. Tell the policewoman you've been dealing with that I want an appointment on Monday. Tell her that!'

Now, finally, I had someone on my side. True to her word, Susy came up to Glasgow the following week and gave an eight-hour interview to the police, confirming everything I'd said was true. That night, she came to stay with me and met Bryce for the first time.

Hugging my sister made me want to cry. Susy hadn't changed much over the years: she still had the same mischievous look in her eye, though her face was now framed by dark, pixie-cropped hair, and she still had that bubbly, infectious laugh I recalled from childhood. She told me all about her two daughters in Kent and her stellar career as a graphic designer. I was so proud of her, and not just because of all she'd achieved; she seemed like a thoroughly decent person. Over chicken stew and a couple of bottles of red wine, we caught up on our lives. It felt wonderful to reconnect with my real sister again and I asked her why she never came back to Scotland to live.

'It was Mum.' She shrugged, but I could tell her feelings about it ran deep. 'She was a nightmare when we were growing up. She hated Dad and she used me to prop up her marriage, coming into my room every night, pouring out her heart. I mean, what mother in their right mind tells a seven-year-old that she's not having sex with her husband? I was conscripted as a soldier in her war and, frankly, I hated it. I had to escape as soon as I could. And then, of course, free from her bitter clutches, I couldn't bear to come back. I'm sorry I wasn't in touch more. I suppose your life was so entwined with Mum's, it was easier not to contact you. I'm sorry for that. I wish I'd known what you were going through.'

There was a little pause, and then she added: 'I called her, you know.'

'Who? Mum?' I asked.

'Yeah, after we spoke. I had to find out why she lied.'

'And what did she say?'

'She said – really haughtily – she said: "I will not protect that child."'

'Me? She meant me?'

'She meant you. So I said: "Mum, you lied to the police. That's serious." You know what she said? She said: "Susy, this conversation is now over." And we haven't spoken since.'

I blew out my cheeks.

'I can't forgive her, you know,' Susy added. 'Not for covering up for him like that. John should face justice. He needs to face the truth, for his own sake as much as for anyone else's.'

Chapter 28

My Day in Court

On a balmy day in August 2011, I walked up the steps of the High Court in Glasgow, wearing my favourite red Dolce & Gabbana dress and a pair of sleek black Louboutin heels. Bryce had offered to come with me today, but I didn't want him here. Bryce was part of my future, not my past, and I knew it was up to me now finally to put an end to my marriage.

Once inside the darkened corridors, I found our appointed courtroom and pushed open the heavy oak doors. There, on one side of the room, were Deirdre and Tim and their assistants, arranging and rearranging folders, files and paperwork on a desk, readying themselves for the big fight ahead. We'd been preparing for this day for years now and, having worked together so closely for so long, we were a strong and solid team.

Deirdre moved briskly and efficiently round the desk, checking the files, as she spoke quietly to me: 'Look, all you need to do is confirm your name and address. After that, just leave it up to me. We know our strategy. We know what we want.'

I nodded. I trusted Deirdre 100 per cent and I knew she

would try to get me the best deal possible. Because that was really what all this came down to now: splitting the marital assets. Stuart had fought low and dirty for years now, trying to push my back up against the wall, but despite all his efforts I was here today, stronger than ever and ready to fight for my fair share of the wealth I had helped build over the course of our marriage.

Although we had been pencilled in for a six-day court hearing, with over thirty witnesses lined up on both sides, I knew that nobody wanted this to go on any longer than was strictly necessary. After all, the sheriff disapproved of protracted divorce cases; a waste of court time, that's how the officials saw it, and I couldn't disagree. *What are we really here to do? Sling mud at each other?* That was pointless. No, we were here to split the assets and now that I had wrested back control of Mayfair, Stuart could no longer claim the Panamanian company was out of the matrimonial pot. It was there, along with the villa in Portugal, the Glasgow house, the art and Silverbridge. Jointly we were worth a little under £5 million, but how was this going to be split? Only time would tell.

I quickly glanced over to the other side of the room – Adam Kelly was there, as were my mother, Aunt Jenny and a handful of lawyers. *No Stuart*, I noted, a little perplexed. But I gave nothing away as I slid myself into a chair and arranged my files in front of me. Really, I didn't need any notes, for I knew it all like the back of my hand. Now I closed my eyes and focused on my breathing: in for ten, hold for ten and out for ten, just like I had learned in yoga recently. It had been Bryce's idea and it helped in moments like this when I needed to control my nerves. Better than popping pills, anyway. *You're ready for this*, I told myself. *More than ready.*

Ten minutes later, the sheriff took his seat in court and the clerk called my name. I stood up, confirmed my name and address and then sat down again.

'Stuart Kelly!' the court clerk read out. Curious, we all looked to the other bench, where Adam now stood up.

'My name is Adam Kelly, resident of . . .'

'Who are you?' The sheriff, a large, bearded man, leaned forward, fixing Adam with a look of disgust, like he was something unpleasant he'd just found on his shoe.

'My name is Adam Kelly, your honour. As his cousin and advisor, I have power of attorney for Stuart Kelly . . .'

'Why are you here, Mr Kelly?' the sheriff boomed. He had moved from disgusted to furious, very quickly. 'She wasn't married to you, she was married to Stuart Kelly.'

'But . . .'

'Get out of my court! I don't want you. I want your cousin here by 12 noon at the latest. The latest!'

Then the sheriff left. For a second I just looked at Deirdre and Tim and then we all started to giggle. The hearing hadn't even started yet and already the other side had pissed off the sheriff. Now Adam exchanged urgent whispers with the lawyers and then he strode out of court, clearly in search of my absent husband.

'Look, while he's cleared off, let me talk to the other side,' said Deirdre. 'The sheriff wants us to cut a deal as quickly as possible. Let's see what they're after . . .'

So Deirdre approached the other team. She was so strong, so secure in herself and I admired her hugely. The lawyers spent a long time talking in what appeared from my side of the court to be a very amicable discussion. *Well, that's why we need lawyers,* I thought to myself. *They take all the emotion out of the equation.* I couldn't imagine me and Stuart being able to talk calmly at this moment.

'Come with me.' Tim now led me to a waiting room. On our way out of the court, we passed Stuart on his way in, looking hassled. He wore a crumpled grey suit and his worry lines were deeper than when I'd last seen him, making him appear a lot older than his years. *Good,* I thought. *Let him worry for a change.*

We were in the waiting room for ten minutes before Deirdre returned.

'Stuart wants the houses in Glasgow, Portugal and £1 million cash,' she said starkly.

'No,' I replied. 'He can have Mayfair. It's worth £2 million.'

Deirdre duly went out and returned five minutes later.

'He doesn't want Mayfair.'

'He doesn't?' I was a little taken aback. I thought that was what he had wanted all along. It was the more valuable company, after all. 'Why do you think he doesn't want Mayfair?'

Suddenly, before she even answered, it clicked with me – he thought the company was going to the wall because of the properties he'd sold and the way he'd failed to keep up with the loan repayments! The last thing he knew, Mayfair was in special lending. He had no idea I'd turned it around.

'Dawn, do you want Silverbridge?' Deirdre now asked. 'I mean, if you're not particularly bothered, why don't we offer him Silverbridge?'

I wasn't bothered which one I gave him, I just wanted a fair split, that was all. I wanted what I had earned over the years, what I had put my heart and soul into building up.

'But he'll never take Silverbridge,' I said. It was only worth

£500,000 and, in the grand scheme of things, the properties in the company's portfolio weren't that impressive.

'Why don't you offer him Silverbridge and the house in Glasgow?' Deirdre suggested. I shrugged. *Why not?* It was worth a try.

Two minutes later, she came back.

'He'll take Silverbridge and half a million in cash. You sell and split the Glasgow house. What do you think?'

'What do I think? I think we're getting closer but we're not quite there . . . Just give me a minute. I need to think properly.'

Now I kicked off my high heels and started to pace the room. I knew if I worked this deal properly, I could make sure Stuart got what he really deserved. He wanted cash. Of course he did! He always wanted 'easy' money. But I didn't have the cash to give him and I wasn't about to start dismantling the companies in order to pay him off. Cash . . . He wanted that more than anything – and I knew he would do all he could to get it. Cash was my husband's biggest love . . . and his biggest weakness too. He had spent years putting me to work in cash businesses so that he could come in every day and plunder them for notes. Cash was Stuart's first love. If only I could make that work for me . . . There had to be a way . . . There had to be a . . .

YES.

And then it came to me. I knew what we had to do.

'Okay, listen to me, Deirdre. I can't get him cash but Silverbridge is worth about £500,000 now. Okay?'

'Okay . . .'

'So we split the house in Glasgow and I'll give him Silverbridge in six months' time. And in those six months, I'll double the value of the company. I'll make it worth a million.

The cash he wants will be in the company. And if I fail, if I don't make the company worth a million, I'll give him a million in cash.'

'What? How are you going to do that?' Deirdre asked.

'Don't worry about it.' I brushed aside her concern. 'Just make them the offer.'

'Are you sure about this, Dawn?'

'Trust me, I've never been more sure of anything in my life . . .'

Now Deirdre banged out of the room and I was left biting my nails, hoping the other side would agree to my strange terms. It suited me that Deirdre was worried – that would play well with the other side, make them think they had me on the run. I listened to the clock on the wall as the seconds ticked slowly by . . . *Tick tock, tick tock, tick tock . . .*

Tim was slouched low in his chair, hands held together as if in prayer, his lips resting on his fingers when he spoke: 'Of course, the devil will be in the detail.'

'Or the lack of it . . .' I added.

'Yes. Big on concept, small on detail, right?'

Now I knew that Tim was on my wavelength. I grinned at him. He had supported me all the way and he could see the way my mind was working. *Tick tock, tick tock . . .* Just as I was about to give up hope, Deirdre flung open the door: 'He went for it!'

'Yes!' I actually jumped for joy. It was an amazing moment. Tim also rose out of his chair and we hugged each other.

'Fantastic news!' he said.

'Glasgow house to be sold and split,' Deirdre was reading from her notes. 'He keeps the art collection, you get Portugal and Mayfair.'

I actually laughed at that. Stuart hated art – he just wanted to keep the paintings because he thought I wanted them. He was still trying to get to me, to rile me, and yet he didn't know that I couldn't give a stuff about the art. I didn't want anything from my old life, in fact. He could have it.

'Okay, Tim, let's make this happen.' I instructed him to start drawing up the deal. Meanwhile, Deirdre took me aside.

'So how does this work for you, Dawn?'

'It's a terrible deal for him,' I whispered. 'He'll take the company if it's worth £1 million. That's all we've agreed. We haven't said *how* I'm going to make it worth that much.'

I knew my husband. I knew his greed would be his downfall in the end. The deal was drawn up on just two sheets of paper and everyone, including Stuart and his cousin, signed it. Happily, I'm sure, relishing the prospect that I would fail in my ambition to give him a company worth £1 million and would therefore have to sell everything to give him cash. He didn't see the pitfalls, he didn't see the danger signs – all he saw were the pound signs and the promise of £1 million cash blinded him to the truth.

'Just one more thing,' I said, hesitating before I signed the settlement deal. 'I want to be divorced today. I want to walk away a free woman.'

'Hmm . . . I'll see what I can do,' said Deirdre. And, incredibly, she came back half an hour later and said the sheriff had agreed to grant me my decree absolute today.

'The sheriff was pleased you managed to work out an agreement,' she said with a smile. 'You'll be divorced by the end of the day.'

And, with that, I signed my name: Dawn McConnell.

*

I can't even begin to describe the feeling of exaltation I experienced on leaving court that day. I was beyond happy, I was released, reborn. I was a new woman. For the first time in twenty-seven years I was free from the man who had controlled and mentally abused me most of my life. Under his despotic rule, I had grown up in fear, I had suffered in silence, I had borne the brunt of his brutal, violent ways and I had cowered with shame. But no more. He had told me I could never leave him and for so long – too long – I had believed him. He had told me he owned me and for so many years I'd thought that was true. But I had fought back and, now, I was stronger than him.

As I skipped down the court steps, I smiled quietly to myself: for *I* owned *him*. He just didn't know it yet.

I called Bryce.

'It's over,' I said with the most enormous smile. 'You can start planning the wedding.'

It didn't take me six months to make Silverbridge worth £1 million; it didn't even take three. When Stuart later discovered the mistakes his lawyers had made, my ex-husband was dismayed to find that it wasn't stated anywhere on the settlement deal exactly how I was to make the company worth £1 million. That was my gamble and Tim's genius. The wording was left so vague: nowhere did it state that I had to make it up with cash. But not one person on their hotshot team of lawyers had thought to question the wording on the deal.

And, once it was signed, there was no going back.

So, I simply took some of the worst performing properties in Mayfair Holdings and transferred them over to Silverbridge. These were properties in bad areas which would be costly to refurbish, hard to rent and difficult to sell when the time came. I bought another three decrepit flats in an even more deprived area and stuck those in there too. Finally, there was just £50,000 left to make the company worth £1 million. But instead of putting in cash, I reduced the company loan by £50,000. So there it was – a company worth £1 million and a load of headaches for Stuart. I walked away with Mayfair, readies from the sale of the Glasgow house, plus our beautiful Portuguese villa.

I had won. In the final fight, I had got the better of Stuart and his crooked cousin, and I had won the war.

And it felt every bit as good as I'd imagined.

Epilogue

In September 2012 Bryce and I married in a beautiful, simple ceremony at a church in the hills above the Algarve. Bryce had done all the planning, all I had to do was pick a dress and turn up. It was a magical day – my son gave me away, my sister Susy and all her family came, as did all the close friends I had come to love and depend on in the past few years. Melvin and his wife were there, as were Tim, Deirdre and her wife and even my bank manager Sadie, who was by now a great pal. We had the sunshine all day long as we feasted on the balcony of our hotel. Later, after the sun went down, the band struck up and we danced the night away.

It was a fairy-tale wedding and one I could never have imagined for myself just a few years before. This was the start of my new life and I was so pleased to have the people I loved by my side. My son, who was now strongly in my camp having seen the pain and suffering I had endured at the hands of his father during our bitter divorce, had grown into a fine young man. It was a pity he no longer saw my mother, his grandmother, but after the case Stuart and my mother grew ever closer and when they started taking holidays together, sharing a double room, Callum said they had crossed a line. His grandmother and his dad? He couldn't stomach it.

He occasionally sees his father now but says he is not an easy man to be around. Bitter and self-pitying, Stuart lives in a small flat lent to him by his cousin and collects housing benefit and social security. Not that he is deserving of it, of course – the man has contributed nothing to society, so what gives him the right to take from it? After so much acrimony and so many attempts to destroy me, he has wasted all his money on divorce lawyers. His half of the proceeds from the sale of our house was just enough to cover his legal bills. So he no longer drives a flashy sports car, drinks the best wines or goes on luxury holidays. But he only has himself to blame. I would have happily split our assets fairly on day one and parted amicably – but Stuart wouldn't do it. He tried to bring me down and he failed. He took me on and he lost.

He has so far refused to take control of Silverbridge, claiming I duped him, but the sheriff has thrown out his appeals. So now he is stuck in a tiny flat, penniless and helpless. He has clung desperately to my mother these past few years. She still has her pension and a handful of properties that give her a decent income. I bet it is a surprise to her to find that she is the richer of the two of them. I wonder, now, if she was also groomed by him in some way, whether he made her extravagant promises he had no intention of keeping. I don't know. We haven't spoken since that day I told her to leave the flat. They are welcome to each other, as far as I am concerned. I honestly can't think of two people more suited to each other than my mother and Stuart Kelly.

In the years since the divorce, I have rebuilt my relationship with my sister and started new ones with her husband

and delightful children. Susy and I have been surprised to discover joy and meaning in our shared history, and finally we each feel able to talk openly about the crazy family we both survived. There are times we laugh like we are never going to stop – and I think that is something only the two of us can experience together. Reconnecting with Susy has made me feel whole in some ways; I am more accepting of myself, of the person I was as a child, and I feel it's okay to like myself again. Knowing how much she was hurt by the same family makes me really believe that it wasn't my fault. After all, we were both just kids. Susy can't forgive our mother for lying to the police and they don't speak anymore. I will never take my sister's love or loyalty for granted.

Meanwhile, my brother has disappeared to India and I doubt he will ever return. He is a fugitive from justice, a man running from himself and his past. I hope one day he will have the courage to come home and face the truth. It makes me sad, thinking about him, that whatever path he chose in life, he did not seek the help that he so desperately needed. I hope that he finds something to heal his wounds before it is too late. And before anyone else gets hurt.

Now, as well as running my property company, I have started an online retail business with Bryce. It's fun and I love the challenge of getting to grips with a new industry. Funnily enough, we've been doing quite well and last year we opened three new offices on the continent. Bryce and I really enjoy working together and I'm so proud to call him my husband. Every day I wake up feeling blessed to have found such a wonderful, caring man to share the rest of my life with. I owe him everything.

I look back on what I have been through and as hard as it

may be for me to rationalize my life, I know that somehow I have managed to survive when it seemed all the odds were stacked against me. Why? I think that being a positive person has helped. The glass is always half full in my view, and if it isn't, you can always fill it up! Though I have been laid low, I have always tried to keep a little perspective about life. After all, there are always people I can think of with far worse problems than mine. Knowing that I am lucky and that I have my health and much more besides, this sees me through to the next day.

The other thing that helped was the sense of being different. I know it may sound strange, but I never felt like the other girls I knew as a child, girls who grew up dreaming of becoming air hostesses, nurses or teachers. These were the 'expected' children, the ones who came from good households that expected them to turn out a certain way. Their parents were lawyers, doctors or professionals and they would be 'expected' to follow in their parents' chosen career until they all ended up the same way. I didn't want to end up the same way as my parents. Money was all my parents seemed to care about. It was made to seem a very important part of my life from a very young age. Not happiness, contentment or fulfillment – no, it was money. Never once did Mum or Dad sit us down as I did with Callum and say: 'I just want you to be happy.'

My parents of course had my life mapped out for me, and I was an 'expected' child, as were my siblings. However, from an early age I decided I would not accept the map they had laid out. I knew that I would be successful and my determination to achieve and have everything I wanted is what pushed me through every part of my journey. I took all my bad experiences as just another bump on the journey. I always got up, brushed myself down and started again. Everything that has happened to me has sculpted me for the next journey in my life and given me the tools for my next battle. We all have lessons to learn that are not always in the classroom.

Yes, there have been some terrible betrayals in my life but I'm not so blind that I can't see the mistakes I made along the way. I take full responsibility for many of my wrong assumptions. Was Hannah really my friend? No, I don't think so. I was her employer and it was my mistake to believe I was anything more. I've learnt that you can't buy people with money and, if you can, you don't want them in your life because they'll never be truly loyal. I wish Hannah and her family well. We all have our crosses to bear and I wonder if her actions have weighed heavily on her heart. I hope not. I forgave her years ago.

The fact is, I found good people to help me on my journey and to them I shall be forever grateful. Melvin, Tim, Deirdre and others – they changed the course of my life for the better, going beyond the call of duty to assist me in my time of need. Conversely, my enemies have also given me a lot. I believe I wouldn't be the woman I am today without them. They made me stronger than I ever believed myself to be. Fighting their dirty war made me look inside myself and realize who I really am and what I believe in.

Of my past, I cannot deny that the abuse still disturbs me to this day. I have never had counselling for what I suffered as a child but then, after my experiences with the police, I have never wanted to pour my soul out to another stranger. Writing this book has been a great aid in healing some of those wounds but I must admit that they will never go away completely.

I am changed by my experiences, as surely we all are. I am less trusting of people than I was before and I believe almost nothing until I see it for myself. I am also stronger than before, impatient with incompetence and intolerant of bullshit. Those who know me in business might say I'm a hard woman, but then, I don't consider that a bad thing in business! For too long I lived with humiliation and shame, blaming myself for the bad things others did to me. Today, I won't stand for that.

I think I've got my priorities straight these days – but I'm always looking for ways to make myself a better person. Callum comes first now; something I didn't always appreciate when I was younger. I am a better parent to him now than when he was a child growing up. For this, I have apologized to him and I am humbled that he has forgiven me. Now, if we ever fight, I'm always the one to break the silence. He comes first, not me. That was something I had to learn for myself, something I was never taught as a child. What counts is being there, come what may. Who cares what others think? What the neighbours will say? What it looks like on the outside? The most important thing is to live an honest, authentic life and to show love to those you love the most. After all, this life is all we have. Let's try to live it the best way possible.

I am still an angry person, maybe more than ever, but I refuse to push that anger down. Because my anger is real and it helps me. It helps me to act in the right way, to do the right thing and to stand up for myself when I need to. In my previous life, I didn't have the luxury of anger. I was repressed and my emotions suppressed. I was too scared to be angry because I was told over and over that if I walked out of the door, I would never get back in. Now, I believe that everyone has the right to decide where they want to be, what they want to do and with whom. And I exercise that right every single day. I am the mistress of my own life and my anger helps me to ensure that I'll never take that for granted.

So here we are ... at the end of the book, though this is far from the end of the story. After all, at forty-seven I have so much more to see, do and experience and I can't wait to jump out of bed every day and get going. I started writing this book the day after I completed the divorce settlement and turned over the company. That to me was the end of the road. I knew nobody else could tell this story. Nobody in the world knew what I had been through or could explain the twists and turns in my life. And somewhere along the way, I learnt that it was important not to let others tell my story for me. I had to speak up, whatever the consequences.

I had to show other women that it was possible not just to escape a bullying, dominating husband, but to get the better of them. History, after all, is written by the victors and today *I* am the victor.

Winston Churchill once said: 'If you're going through hell, keep going.' That's what I did. I kept going, no matter how bad things seemed, no matter how big the mountain I had to climb, and today I don't have a single regret about breaking my silence. I own this story. I own my life, as every woman should.

Today, if you met me in the street, you'd never guess how it all started. In my immaculately tailored suits and my salon-styled hair, you wouldn't imagine for one minute that I was an abused girl and wife, that I made my fortune from pulling pints, changing beds and taking out bins. I was written off as the dropout: a teen mum and a failure. Nobody thought I could make something of my life, and yet I defied all their expectations. The only person who ever believed in me was my father. I still hear his voice today:

'Dawn, you'll be alright. You're a fighter, like me. A warrior, a proud Scottish warrior.'

I think about my father often, and I smile when I do. Yes, I am a warrior, just like him.

The journey continues, the battles go on . . . but I have strength now. I know who I am and relish the fight. Beware my enemies, I know who you are too and I'm ready to take you on . . . any time!

Advice and Help

A word about coercive control:

If you have experienced anything similar to Dawn or know someone affected by the same issues, there is help and advice out there: please see our list below. The law on domestic abuse has changed and now includes 'coercive control', just like Dawn experienced with Stuart. 'Coercive control' is when one partner tries to control another through threats, intimidation, isolation and restrictions, denying their partner freedom and stripping them of their rights and sense of self. This can involve unreasonable demands, degradation, stalking, harassment, surveillance, bullying, taking away access to money, and controlling access to other people and means of transport. It is like being a hostage in an unreal world created by the abuser, and it carries up to a five-year jail term. There is more awareness than ever that 'coercive control' is a real and deadly form of domestic abuse, leading to long-term physical and psychological abuse. It is also a crime.

Childline: For confidential advice on a wide range of issues, you can talk to a counsellor online, send an email or post on message boards.

Call 0800 1111 or visit www.childline.org.uk

NSPCC: The National Society for the Prevention of Cruelty to Children runs a helpline for adults and if you're worried about a child, even if you're unsure, you can contact their professional counsellors 24/7 for help, advice and support.
Call 0808 800 5000 or email help@nspcc.org.uk
Further information and advice is available at
www.nspcc.org.uk

Woman's Aid: Woman's Aid provides life-saving services and helps to provide refuge for women and children suffering domestic abuse.
You can call their national, 24-hour freephone helpline on 0808 2000 247 or visit their website for guidance and support: www.womansaid.org.uk

Refuge: For help and advice, and to find out the warning signs of abuse and control, visit www.refuge.org.uk

The Samaritans: Available 24 hours a day to provide confidential emotional support for those who are experiencing feelings of distress, despair or suicidal thoughts.
Call 0845 7909 090 or visit www.samaritans.org.uk

Rape Crisis: Specialist services for women and girls who have been raped and/or experienced any other form of sexual violence at any time.
For England and Wales, visit www.rapecrisis.org.uk
For Scotland, call 08088 01 03 02 or visit
www.rapecrisisscotland.org.uk

Shelter: call 0808 800 4444 or visit www.shelter.org.uk

Victim support: call 0808 168 9111 or visit
www.victimsupport.org.uk

Crimestoppers: call 0800 555 111 or visit
www.crimestoppers-uk.org

extracts reading groups
books competitions books new events
discounts extracts extracts discounts reading groups
competitions extracts reading groups extracts
books new discounts
events books events
extracts books reading groups
new titles reading groups
interviews events new
reading groups events extracts extracts books
books discounts new books
extracts new books events events interviews new books
events new interviews new extracts
discounts extracts discounts
www.panmacmillan.com books
extracts events reading groups
competitions books extracts new